Coding as a Playground

Coding as a Playground, Second Edition focuses on how young children (aged 7 and under) can engage in computational thinking and be taught to become computer programmers, a process that can increase both their cognitive and social-emotional skills. Learn how coding can engage children as producers—and not merely consumers—of technology in a playful way. You will come away from this groundbreaking work with an understanding of how coding promotes developmentally appropriate experiences such as problem-solving, imagination, cognitive challenges, social interactions, motor skills development, emotional exploration, and making different choices. Featuring all-new case studies, vignettes, and projects, as well as an expanded focus on teaching coding as a new literacy, this second edition helps you to learn how to integrate coding into different curricular areas to promote literacy, math, science, engineering, and the arts through a project-based approach and a positive attitude to learning.

Marina Umaschi Bers is Professor in the Eliot-Pearson Department of Child Study and Human Development with a secondary appointment in the Department of Computer Science at Tufts University, U.S.A. She heads the Developmental Technologies (DevTech) research group where she studies innovative ways to promote positive childhood development through new learning technologies. Marina co-developed the ScratchJr programming language in collaboration with the MIT Media Lab and the PICO company. She is also the creator of KIBO, a robotics platform for children aged 4 to 7 that can be programmed with wooden blocks (no screen needed), which allows young builders to learn programming and engineering while integrating arts and crafts.

Other Eye On Education Books
Available From Routledge
(www.routledge.com/k-12)

Culturally Responsive Self-Care Practices for Early Childhood Educators
Julie Nicholson, Priya Shimpi Driscoll, Julie Kurtz, Doménica Márquez,
and LaWanda Wesley

**Implementing Project Based Learning in Early Childhood:
Overcoming Misconceptions and Reaching Success**
Sara Lev, Amanda Clark, and Erin Starkey

**Advocacy for Early Childhood Educators: Speaking Up for
Your Students, Your Colleagues, and Yourself**
Colleen Schmit

**Grit, Resilience, and Motivation in Early Childhood:
Practical Takeaways for Teachers**
Lisa B. Fiore

A Teacher's Guide to Philosophy for Children
Keith J. Topping, Steven Trickey, and Paul Cleghorn

**Exploring Key Issues in Early Childhood and Technology:
Evolving Perspectives and Innovative Approaches**
Chip Donohue

Coding as a Playground

Programming and Computational Thinking in the Early Childhood Classroom

Second Edition

Marina Umaschi Bers

Routledge
Taylor & Francis Group

NEW YORK AND LONDON

Second edition published 2021
by Routledge
52 Vanderbilt Avenue, New York, NY 10017

and by Routledge
2 Park Square, Milton Park, Abingdon, Oxon, OX14 4RN

Routledge is an imprint of the Taylor & Francis Group, an informa business

© 2021 Taylor & Francis

First edition published by Routledge 2017

Library of Congress Cataloging-in-Publication Data
A catalog record has been requested for this book

ISBN: 9780367900960 (hbk)
ISBN: 9780367900502 (pbk)
ISBN: 9781003022602 (ebk)

Typeset in Optima
by Swales & Willis, Exeter, Devon, UK

Contents

Meet the Author   vii

Acknowledgments   ix

Introduction   1

PART I: CODING AS PLAYGROUND   15

1. **In the Beginning There Was Language**   17

2. **Tools for Expression**   24

3. **Playing with Code**   35

PART II: CODING AS LITERACY   45

4. **Natural and Artificial Languages**   47

5. **Coding Stages**   62

6. **A Pedagogical Approach**   72

PART III: COMPUTATIONAL THINKING   85

7. **Thinking about Computational Thinking**   87

8. **Powerful Ideas in the Early Coding Curriculum**   103

9. **The Coding Process**   117

10. **Personal Growth through Coding**   130

PART IV: NEW LANGUAGES FOR YOUNG CHILDREN   149

11. ScratchJr   151

12. KIBO   174

13. Design Principles: Programming Languages for Young Children   207

14. Teaching Strategies: Coding in the Early Curriculum   217

Conclusion   227

Meet the Author

Marina Umaschi Bers was born in Argentina and moved to the U.S. in 1994 for graduate school. She received a Master's degree in Educational Media from Boston University and an M.S. and a Ph.D. from the MIT Media Lab, where she worked with Seymour Papert. Today, she is a professor and chair at the Eliot-Pearson Department of Child Study and Human Development and the Department of Computer Science at Tufts University, and she heads the interdisciplinary DevTech research group. Her research involves the design and study of innovative learning technologies to promote positive youth development.

Dr. Bers was awarded the prestigious 2005 Presidential Early Career Award for Scientists and Engineers (PECASE), a National Science Foundation (NSF) CAREER Award, and the American Educational Research Association's Jan Hawkins Award. Over the past 25 years, she has conceived, designed, and evaluated diverse educational technologies ranging from robotics to virtual worlds. When she had her own three children, Tali, Alan, and Nico, she decided to focus her research on technological environments for young children, aged from 4 to 7 years old. Dr. Bers has received multiple grants that have allowed her to develop and research such technologies, resulting in ScratchJr, a free programming app, and KIBO, a robotics kit that can be programmed with wooden blocks, sold by KinderLab Robotics, Inc. (a company she co-founded in 2013 and for which she received the 2015 Women to Watch award by the *Boston Business Journal*).

Dr. Bers' philosophy and theoretical approach for developing these technologies, as well as her pedagogical approach, curriculum, and assessment methods, can be found in her books *Blocks to Robots: Learning With Technology in the Early Childhood Classroom* (2008, Teachers College Press), *Designing Digital Experiences for Positive Youth*

Development: From Playpen to Playground (2012, Oxford University Press), *The Official ScratchJr Book* (2015, No Starch Press), and, most recently, the first edition of this book *Coding as Playground: Programming and Computational Thinking in the Early Childhood Classroom* (Routledge, 2018). Dr. Bers loves teaching and, in 2016, she received the Outstanding Faculty Contribution to Graduate Student Studies award at Tufts University. In addition, she teaches seminars on learning technologies for educators and does extensive consulting for schools, museums, after-school settings, toy and media companies, and nonprofits.

More on Dr. Bers: sites.tufts.edu/mbers01/.

Acknowledgments

"Much have I learned from my teachers, more from my colleagues, but most from my students" (Talmud, Ta'anit 7b). This book is the result of many years of conversations and explorations, collaborations, and observations. My journey into coding began in the mid-1970s, back in my homeland of Buenos Aires, Argentina. I was only 8 years old when my parents signed me up for a computer programming class to learn LOGO. Little did I know that decades later Seymour Papert, the father of LOGO, was going to become my mentor. Throughout my doctoral work at the MIT Media Lab, Seymour guided me to find good questions to ask and pushed me to pursue my dreams and ambitions. Mitch Resnick, a young professor at the time, provided me with the needed steady support. Years later, it is an honor and a privilege to collaborate with him on projects such as ScratchJr and to discuss ideas over breakfast, eating his homemade bread. Sherry Turkle, my doctoral thesis reader and always-present inspiration, still reminds me about the importance of bringing humanity back to technology.

While at MIT, I mostly conducted research with programming languages and educational robotics with elementary and high school children. However, when I had my own children and became a young assistant professor at Tufts University, I quickly realized the need for bringing ideas from computer science to the early years. My colleagues at the Eliot-Pearson Department of Child Study and Human Development became my teachers. In particular, Debbie LeeKennan, who was then the director of the Eliot-Pearson Children's School, Becky New, then director of the Early Childhood Education Program, David Elkind, David Henry Feldman, and Richard Lerner. Chris Rogers, professor of Mechanical Engineering and founder of the Center for Engineering Education and Outreach at Tufts, became a "partner in crime," always ready to go on a walk to discuss co-teaching a course, to design educational toys, maker spaces, 3D printing, or simply to provide wise advice.

I was always fascinated with the similarities between written and programming languages, and with the potential of coding to become a literacy that can truly impact the way we think and bring about educational and societal change. For writing this book, I went back to readings I had done on the topic of literacy and orality when I was doing my undergraduate studies and working as a teaching assistant with Anibal Ford and Alejandro Piscitelli at the Universidad de Buenos Aires. This time, I read those old books and articles with a different lens. I felt that the circle was closing. I started my academic life looking at the role of language and stories, communication and expression. Now, 25 years later, I came back to those seminal ideas.

Since the first edition of *Coding as a Playground* was released, coding has become even more widespread and popular in U.S. education and throughout the world. However, the approaches for how to bring coding to early childhood in a developmentally appropriate way have not always spread hand in hand with the policy growth. This book proposes two main metaphors that are important for introducing coding in early childhood: Coding as Playground and Coding as Literacy.

The second edition of the book will address both of these metaphors by focusing on the positive impact of a playful, developmentally appropriate approach to teaching coding in early childhood and will provide more examples of curricular activities, vignettes, and projects, as well as new case studies of children, teachers, and parents creating their own programming projects with ScratchJr and KIBO. These two widely popular programming environments for young children, designed by the author, have grown in impact all over the world since the publication of this book's first edition. KIBO, for example, is now used in over 60 countries while ScratchJr has 13 million users.

Over the years, I have been privileged to have an amazing interdisciplinary group of undergraduate and graduate students, as well as research staff, working on my DevTech research group at Tufts University. Dr. Amanda Strawhacker, Riva Dhamala, Madhu Govind, Emily Relkin, Angie Kalthoff, Dr. Ziva Hassenfeld, Megan Bennie, Apittha Unahalekhaka, and Kaitlyn Leidl have directly contributed to some of the research and vignettes on ScratchJr presented in this book. In the first edition of this book, Dr. Amanda Sullivan served as my right hand and contributed with literature reviews and vignettes, and conducted a thorough editing of this book. I am indebted to her, not only for her intellectual contributions to the research, but for her kindness and good spirits. In this second edition, Dr. Amanda Strawhacker served this role. Amanda brought her detailed-oriented eye and her organizational skills to the project to make sure that the research was updated and that the book presented a unifying voice in telling stories. She also brought her smile and her readiness to help. This book, which tells the story of the research happening at my DevTech research group, would not have been possible without these two incredible Amandas, two women whom I was lucky to mentor and to witness their growth into becoming amazing researchers and human beings.

When KIBO became ready to leave my DevTech research lab at Tufts University and become a product, Mitch Rosenberg and I initiated the life-transforming adventure of co-founding KinderLab Robotics to commercialize KIBO and to take it worldwide. I thank him for believing in my ideas and for putting his heart and soul into this journey. I also thank the wonderful team at KinderLab Robotics and its board members, for making it possible for KIBO to reach thousands of homes and schools all over the world.

I want to thank my husband, Pato O'Donnell, for so much love, caring, and companionship. In the lake, we found happiness. Wholeness came to my life. My three children, Tali, Alan, and Nico, are my life teachers and my harshest critics when designing programming environments. They were part of every iteration of KIBO and ScratchJr, played with early prototypes, and gave me feedback. As they grew older, they travelled with me all over the world and helped me to present demos and teach workshops. At dinner parties, they are the best at giving demos. Gracias, chicos, por todo! My mother, Lydia, had the early vision to introduce me to computer programming and is a constant fan and supporter. I couldn't work and be the mother that I am without her help. My dad passed away too young, but there are sparks of him in everything I do.

I thank the National Science Foundation (NSF) and the Scratch Foundation for supporting my work, and also the people who read early drafts of this book and gave me valuable feedback: Dr. Amanda Sullivan, Dr. Amanda Strawhacker, Paula Bontá, Cynthia Solomon, Adeline Yeo, Claudia Mihm, Clara Hill, Madhu Govind, Emily Relkin, Angie Kalthoff, Dr. Ziva Hassenfeld, and Megan Bennie, Apittha Unahalekhaka, Kaitlyn Leidl, Alan Bers, Tze Hui Low, Valeria Larrart, and Riva Dhamala. Finally, I want to thank the thousands of children and early childhood educators, principals, and administrators, all over the world, who have been part of my research over so many years. I have learned from them what no book can teach us.

Introduction

Liana, 5 years old, is sitting with an iPad in her kindergarten class. She is focused. Every so often, she wiggles. She suddenly screams, to no one in particular, "Look at my cat! Look at my cat!" Liana is excited to show her animation. She has programmed the ScratchJr kitten to appear and disappear on the screen ten different times. She has put together a long sequence of graphical programming blocks, purple blocks to be more specific, called Looks blocks. Liana cannot read yet, but she knows that these programming blocks can make her ScratchJr kitten show and hide. She is in control of the kitten's behaviors. She can decide how many times it will appear and disappear on the screen by choosing the blocks to put together in a sequence. As a 5-year-old, Liana, like most children her age, wants to make the longest possible sequence, so she puts together a script with ten blocks, until she runs out of space in the programming area.

When Liana's kindergarten teacher hears her excitement, she walks over to see Liana's project. Liana is proud to show "my movie," as she calls it. "I made it. Look at my cat. It appears and disappears, it appears and disappears, it appears and disappears. Many times. Look!" She clicks on the "Green flag" on the ScratchJr interface and the animation starts. At that point, Liana's teacher asks her, "How many times does the kitten show and hide?" "Ten times," replies Liana. "I ran out of room. I wanted more times." The teacher shows her a long orange programming block, called "Repeat." This block allows for other blocks to be inserted inside its "loop." It then runs the blocks inside the loop as many times as the programmer decides. Liana notices that this block looks slightly different than the purple ones and it is orange. It belongs to a different category, called Control flow blocks.

After some trial and error, in which Liana plays with inserting different combinations of the purple show and hide blocks inside the "Repeat" block, she figures it out. She can put just one of each purple block inside the "Repeat" block, and set the number of repetition times to the highest she can think of. She chooses the number 99 and clicks the "Green flag" to see the animation. The kitten starts appearing and disappearing. After a few seconds, she gets bored of watching. So, she goes back to her code and changes the number of repetitions to 20 (see Figure 0.1).

During this experience, Liana engaged with some of the most powerful ideas of computer sciences that are accessible for a young child. She also developed computational thinking. She learned that a programming language has a syntax in which symbols represent actions. She understood that her choices had an impact on what was happening on the screen. She was able to create a sequence of programming blocks to represent a complex behavior (e.g., appearing and disappearing). She used logic in a systematic way to correctly order the blocks in a sequence. She practiced and applied the concept of patterns, which she had learned earlier in the year during math time in class. She learned new blocks that allowed her to achieve her goals. She discovered the concept of loops and parameters. At the same time, she engaged in problem-solving and also exercised her tenacity at

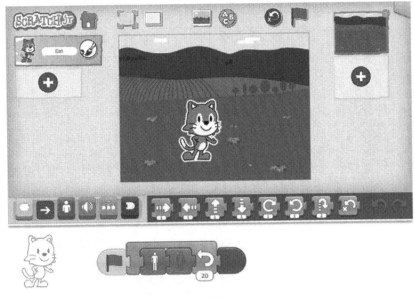

Figure 0.1 The ScratchJr interface with Liana's "Disappearing Kitten" program. In this photo, the kitten is programmed with a repeat loop to appear and disappear 20 times.

tackling something she truly cared about (i.e., having a very long kitten movie). Finally, Liana was able to create a project from her own original idea and turn it into a final product, a project she chose and to which she was personally attached. She was proud to share it with others and happy to revise it when the final outcome did not meet her expectations (i.e., it ended up being so long that it was boring to watch). She also engaged with mathematical ideas of estimation and number sense (i.e., 99 is way longer than 20).

To code, Liana used ScratchJr, a programming language specifically designed for young children that runs on tablets as well as desktops, and that can be downloaded for free. ScratchJr was designed and developed by my DevTech research group at Tufts University in collaboration with Mitch Resnick's Lifelong Kindergarten group at the MIT Media Lab and Paula Bontá and Brian Silverman from the Playful Invention Company (PICO) company in Canada. To date, over 13 million young children all over the world are using ScratchJr to create their own projects.

Liana's teacher integrated ScratchJr into a learning environment in which children had the freedom to make a project they cared about. Liana was excited and passionate. She was not going to give up until her cat did exactly what she wanted. She worked hard and she rejoiced in that process. She enjoyed learning and was fully engaged in it. For her, developing computational thinking involved more than problem-solving; it meant gaining the concepts, skills, and habits of mind to express herself through coding.

This book explores the role of coding for young children. Most specifically, it focuses on the developmental milestones and learning experiences that children can attain by becoming programmers and by thinking like computer scientists. Coding engages children as producers, and not merely consumers, of technology. Children such as Liana can create their own movies or animations, interactive games or stories. Coding is not only a cognitive activity that involves problem-solving and mastering programming concepts and skills, but it is also an expressive medium that engages emotional and social domains. Liana stuck to her project and debugged it because she truly cared about it. She felt proud and in control. Her "cat movie" allowed her to show an aspect of who she is. Liana loves animated movies and she was thrilled to make her own.

Just like any natural language—English, Spanish, or Japanese—that allows us to express our needs and desires, our discoveries and frustrations, our dreams and everyday doings, programming languages such as

ScratchJr provide a tool for expression. We need to learn their syntax and grammars and, over time, the more we engage with them, the more fluent we become. We know when we have truly learned a new language because we are able to use it for different purposes: to write a love poem, to make a shopping list for the supermarket, to compose an academic essay, to order a pizza, or to discuss political events at a social gathering. A language helps us to think and communicate in new ways. Furthermore, the night that we dream in that new language, we know that we have mastered it.

Coding with Objects

Programming languages have different interfaces that support different ways of expression. Coding can happen on the screen, as in Liana's case with ScratchJr, or it can happen through objects in the world. For example, the KIBO robot, also developed in my DevTech research lab (DevTech, 2020) at Tufts University, and now commercialized by KinderLab Robotics, allows young children to code without screens of any kind. The programming language is composed of wooden blocks with pegs and holes that can be inserted into each other forming a tangible sequence of commands. Each block represents an instruction for KIBO: forward, shake, wait for clap, light on, beep, etc.

Let's look at Maya and Natan's experience with KIBO. They are also in kindergarten. They are working on a joint KIBO robotics project. Maya is choosing the blocks to make KIBO dance the Hokey Pokey. She starts with the green "Begin" block and concludes with the red "End" block. She needs to figure out the blocks in between. She forgot the KIBO Hokey Pokey song that the teacher taught them, so she is at loss about which blocks to choose. Natan, her teammate, reminds her of the song:

> You put your robot in
> You put your robot out
> You put your robot in
> And you shake it all about
> You do the Hokey Pokey
> and you turn yourself around
> That's what it's all about!

Maya sings along and, as the song progresses, she chooses the blocks and starts putting them together in a sequence. Begin; "You put your robot in," forward; "You put your robot out," backward; "You put your robot in," forward; "And you shake it all about," shake. She suddenly stops and says, "Natan, I can't find the 'Do the Hokey Pokey' block!" "There is no block for that, silly," responds Natan. "We need to make it up. Let's have KIBO turn on the blue and red light instead. That will be our 'Hokey Pokey' block." Maya agrees, adds those two blocks to the sequence and also adds "shake," "spin," and "beep" to represent the "what it's all about" part of the song. Maya and Natan look at their program while singing the song to make sure that they have put together all the needed blocks. Then they turn on KIBO to test things out. The red light of KIBO's scanner (the "mouth," as Maya calls it) is flashing, meaning that the robot is ready to scan each of the barcodes printed on the wooden programming blocks (see Figure 0.2).

Natan takes his turn and scans the blocks one by one. He goes too fast and skips the "Red light" block. Maya points that out, and he restarts

Figure 0.2 The KIBO robot scanning a version of the Hokey Pokey Program: begin, forward, backward, forward, shake, spin, end.

the scanning. The children are excited to see their robot dance the Hokey Pokey. "When I count to three, you start singing," says Maya to Natan. They know the drill. They have practiced it during technology circle time in class. Natan sings and both KIBO and Maya dance the Hokey Pokey. It goes too fast. KIBO dances too fast. "Can you sing faster?" asks Maya. Natan tries one more time, but it still doesn't work. "We have a problem," he says, "I can't sing fast enough to keep up with KIBO." Maya has an idea. For each action in the song she puts two blocks, so KIBO's motions will last longer. For example, for the "you put your robot in" part, instead of just one "Forward" block, she puts two forwards, and so on for each of the commands. Natan tries singing again, and this time KIBO dances at the right pace.

Both children start clapping, shaking their bodies, and jumping up and down. Without knowing it, just like Liana with her ScratchJr animation, they engaged with many powerful ideas of computer science, such as sequencing, algorithmic thinking, and debugging, or problem-solving. They also explored math concepts they are learning in kindergarten, such as estimation, prediction, and counting. Furthermore, they engaged in collaboration. Marisa, their kindergarten teacher, explains,

> Children already have too much screen time at home. When they are at school I want them learning new concepts and skills in STEM, but just as importantly, I want them learning to socialize and collaborate with others. I want them looking at each other, and not at the screen. KIBO is just perfect for that.

During technology circle time, Marisa asks every group of children to give a demo of their dancing KIBOs. Everyone else is invited to stand up and dance alongside. There is laughter and clapping. There is physical activity, socialization, language development, problem-solving, and creative play. It is fun. It feels like a playground, not a coding class. In previous work, I coined the metaphor "playground vs. playpen" (Bers, 2012) to discuss the role that new technologies can have in young children's lives. Coding can become a playground, an environment to be creative, to express ourselves, to explore alone and with others, to learn new skills, and to problem solve. All of this, while having fun.

High-Tech Playgrounds

Playgrounds are open-ended. Playpens are limited. Playgrounds invite fantasy play, imagination, and creativity. The "playground vs. playpen" metaphor provides a way to understand the kind of developmentally appropriate experiences that new technologies, such as programming languages, can promote: problem-solving, imagination, cognitive challenges, social interactions, motor skills development, emotional exploration, and making different choices. In contrast to the open-ended playground, playpens convey lack of freedom to experiment, lack of autonomy for exploration, lack of creative opportunities, and lack of risk-taking. Although playpens are safer, playgrounds provide infinite possibilities for growth and learning.

This book focuses on the activity of coding as a playground. Coding can happen by using different programming languages, just as expressing ourselves can happen through different natural languages such as Spanish, English, or Mandarin. Liana used ScratchJr to make an animated movie of her kitten appearing and disappearing. Maya and Natan used KIBO's wooden blocks to make the robot dance the Hokey Pokey. They all became programmers, producers, makers of their own projects. Throughout the book, we will learn more about both ScratchJr and KIBO. We will also explore the potential of powerful ideas of computer science for early childhood education. In this book I am proposing a playful approach: a playground approach, and not a playpen approach. In this journey, we will also dive into the role of computational thinking and its relationship to coding.

Coding in Early Childhood

There is a new push for coding. President Obama became the first U.S. president to write a line of code during a very publicized event. His administration launched the Computer Science for All initiative, to bring programming into every single educational level (Smith, 2016). Since then, research and policy changes over recent years have also brought a new-found focus to coding (A Framework for K12 Computer Science Education, 2016; Barron et al., 2011; International Society for Technology in Education [ISTE], 2007; NAEYC and Fred Rogers Center for Early Learning and

Children's Media, 2012; Sesame Workshop, 2009; U.S. Department of Education, 2010).

At the time of writing, 33 U.S. states have K-12 computer science standards in place and an additional five have them in progress. This means that over three-quarters (76 percent) of all U.S. states have or will have standards in place, while 24 percent still have no standards nor a plan to put them in place at this time (State of Computer Science Education, 2019). Many countries in Europe alone integrate coding into the curriculum at the national, regional, or local level, including: Austria, Belgium, Bulgaria, the Czech Republic, Denmark, Estonia, Finland, France, Hungary, Ireland, Israel, Lithuania, Malta, Poland, Portugal, Slovakia, Spain, Turkey, and the U.K. (Balanskat & Engelhardt, 2015; European Schoolnet, 2014; Livingstone, 2012; Uzunboylu, Kınık, & Kanbul, 2017). Outside of Europe, countries such as Australia, Singapore, and Argentina have also established clear policies and frameworks for introducing technology and computer programming in K-12 education (Australian Curriculum Assessment and Reporting Authority, 2015; Digital News Asia, 2015; Jara, Hepp, & Rodriguez, 2018; Siu & Lam, 2003).

According to Code.org, which encourages schools nationwide to adopt programming curricula and promote broad participation in computer science, over 720 million elementary, middle, and high school students across 196 countries completed the "Hour of Code" tutorials between 2013 and 2018 (Code.org, 2019a). In January 2015, the Hour of Code reached 100 million "hours served," making the Hour of Code the largest education campaign in history (Computer Science Education Week, 2016). That number jumped to over 910 million hours served in 2019 (Code.org, 2019b). Furthermore, tools, such as the online Scratch programming community, aimed at creative coders aged 8 and older, have collectively shared 50,350,184 coding projects as of February 2019 (scratch.mit.edu/).

The push for incorporating coding in education starting in kindergarten, responds to the growing needs of the economy. Each month, there are an estimated 500,000 openings for computing jobs nationwide, and a lack of adequately trained people to fill these positions (Code.org, 2020). According to the Bureau of Labor Statistics, computer-related occupations are projected to yield over 1 million job openings from 2014 to 2024 (Fayer, Lacey, & Watson, 2017). In less than ten years from now, it is estimated that the United States will need 1.7 million more engineers and computing professionals (Corbett & Hill, 2015). The workforce needs coders. Thus, initiatives are on the rise. However, if coding is to be included in early years schooling, it needs more reasons than to fulfill the needs of the future economy. This book will explore them. Learning to code is more than job preparation. It is about learning to think in systematic ways and learning to use language, a programming language, to express our ideas. It can be taught in playful developmentally appropriate ways and can promote socialization and create creative problem-solving.

This book does not advocate for coding in early childhood as a way to fulfill the workforce's demands. This book proposes that coding is a new literacy for the twenty-first century. As a literacy, coding enables new ways of thinking and new ways of communicating and expressing ideas. Furthermore, literacy ensures participation in decision-making processes and civic institutions. From an historical perspective, and currently in the developing world, those who can't read and write are left out of power structures. Their civic voices are not heard. Will this be the case for those who can't code? For those who can't think in computational ways?

We start teaching kids to read and write in early childhood. However, we don't expect every child to grow into a professional writer. I believe textual literacy is both an important skill and an intellectual tool for everyone. So it is with coding. I do not advocate for all children to grow into software engineers and programmers, but I want them to have computational literacy so that they can become producers, and not only consumers, of digital artifacts.

While, to date, most nationwide coding initiatives target older children, there are new endeavors focusing on early childhood education. For example, in April 2016, the White House launched a STEM (science, technology, engineering, and math) initiative for early education (White House, 2016) by convening researchers, policy makers, industry, and educators. As part of this group, I was invited to discuss the role of coding and computational thinking (White House Symposium on Early STEM, see: www.youtube.com/watch?v=iUvEks2tutw&feature=youtu.be&t=36m). Countries such as the United Kingdom have adapted their curriculum to include coding, beginning in early childhood. In Asia, Singapore is currently launching nationwide projects to bring programming through a PlayMaker initiative that brings KIBO robotics, amongst other technologies, into early childhood classrooms (Digital News Asia, 2015; Sullivan & Bers, 2017). Chapter 12 will describe this initiative.

Only recently, has there been emphasis on integrating computing into the early years due to the development of new programming interfaces, such as ScratchJr and KIBO, and a growing body of research that suggests that children who are exposed to STEM curriculum and computer programming at an early age demonstrate fewer gender-based stereotypes regarding STEM careers (Metz, 2007; Steele, 1997) and fewer obstacles entering technical fields (Madill et al., 2007; Markert, 1996).

Research shows that, both from an economic and a developmental standpoint, educational interventions that begin in early childhood are associated with lower costs and more durable effects than interventions that start later on (e.g., Cunha & Heckman, 2007; Heckman & Masterov, 2004). Two National Research Council reports—*Eager to Learn* (2001) and *From Neurons to Neighborhoods* (2000)—document the significance of early experiences for later school achievement. For example, literacy research shows that the foundation for reading success is formed long before a child reaches first grade and that children who fail and do not improve by the end of first grade are at high risk of failure in other academics throughout school (Learning First Alliance, 1998; McIntosh, Horner, Chard, Boland, & Good, 2006). Will the same be true for coding?

I understand the cognitive and economic benefits that underlie the push for introducing coding in early childhood education, and I am happy to see computer programming becoming popular again. However, in this book I build a different case for coding. Not only is it important for children to start programming at a young age to prepare them for the booming computing workforce, but, most importantly, coding provides a systematic way of thinking and a language for expression and communication. While coding, children learn to become better problem solvers, mathematicians, engineers, storytellers, inventors, and collaborators. These individual and interpersonal skills are introduced and refined through the process of sequencing a simple program: a kitten appearing and disappearing on a screen, or robots dancing the Hokey Pokey alongside a kindergarten class.

Coding engages and reinforces computational thinking. At the same time, computational thinking engages and reinforces coding. In this context, coding is the action of putting together sequences of instructions and debugging or problem-solving when things do not work as expected. In the process (note that coding is a verb, not a noun, so it implies unfolding over time), children encounter powerful ideas from computer science and thus engage in computational thinking. Is coding the only way to engage in this kind of thinking? Definitely not. As we will see later in this book, there are approaches to do so through low-tech games, singing, and dancing. However, in this book, I advocate that coding should be part of every young child's computational thinking experience. Furthermore, I also advocate for a playground approach to coding, as opposed to a playpen experience.

After this introduction, the book has four parts: Part I: Coding as Playground; Part II: Coding as Literacy; Part III: Computational Thinking; and Part IV: New Languages for Young Children. Throughout the book I present vignettes of children and teachers, as well as results from different studies, theoretical frameworks, technology designs, and curriculum recommendations. I will challenge the reader to think about the many ways that coding can engage young children in some of the same developmental milestones as the playground experience. New initiatives for introducing coding and computational thinking in early childhood education are growing. New standards and frameworks are being developed alongside new programming languages and interfaces. It is our responsibility to make sure that the emphasis on play and creativity, social interaction and emotional growth, are not left out when computer programming enters kindergarten.

References

A Framework for K12 Computer Science Education. (2016). *A Framework for K12 Computer Science Education*. N.p. Web. Retrieved July 13, 2016, from https://k12cs.org/about/

Australian Curriculum Assessment and Reporting Authority. (2015). *Digital technologies: Sequence*. Retrieved from www.acara.edu.au/_resources/Digital_Technologies_-_Sequence_of_content.pdf

Balanskat, A., & Engelhardt, K. (2015). *Computing our future: Computer programming and coding. Priorities, school curricula and initiatives across Europe*. Brussels: European Schoolnet.

Barron, B., Cayton-Hodges, G., Bofferding, L., Copple, C., Darling-Hammond, L., & Levine, M. (2011). *Take a giant step: A blueprint for teaching children in a digital age*. New York, NY: The Joan Ganz Cooney Center at Sesame Workshop.

Bers, M. U. (2012). *Designing digital experiences for positive youth development: From playpen to playground.* Cary, NC: Oxford University Press.

Code.org. (2019a). *Code.org 2018 Annual Report.* Retrieved from code.org/files/annual-report-2018.pdf

Code.org. (2019b). *Hour of Code.* Retrieved from hourofcode.com/us

Code.org. (2020). *Promote computer science.* Retrieved from https://code.org/promote

Computer Science Education Week. (2016). Retrieved from https://csedweek.org/

Corbett, C., & Hill, C. (2015). *Solving the equation: The variables for women's success in engineering and computing.* 1111 Sixteenth Street NW, Washington, DC 20036: American Association of University Women.

Cunha, F., & Heckman, J. (2007). The technology of skill formation. *American Economic Review, 97*(2), 31–47.

DevTech Research Group. (2020). *DevTech Research Group.* Retrieved from ase.tufts.edu/devtech/

Digital News Asia. (2015). *IDA launches S$1.5m pilot to roll out tech toys for preschoolers.*

European Schoolnet. (2014). *Computing our future: Computer programming and coding.* Belgium: European Commission.

Fayer, S., Lacey, A., & Watson, A. (2017). STEM occupations: Past, present, and future. *Spotlight on Statistics,* 1–35.

Heckman, J. J., & Masterov, D. V. (2004). The productivity argument for investing in young children. Technical Report Working Paper No. 5, Committee on Economic Development.

ISTE (International Society for Technology in Education). (2007). *NETS for students 2007 profiles.* Washington, DC: ISTE. Retrieved from www.iste.org/standards/netsforstudents/netsforstudents2007profiles.aspx#PK2

Jara, I., Hepp, P., & Rodriguez, J. (2018). Policies and practices for teaching computer science in Latin America. *Microsoft.*

Learning First Alliance. (1998). Every child reading: An action plan of the Learning First Alliance. *American Educator, 22*(1–2), 52–63.

Livingstone, I. (2012). Teach children how to write computer programs. *The Guardian*. Guardian News and Media. Retrieved from www.theguardian. com/commentisfree/2012/jan/11/teachchildrencomputerprogrammes

Madill, H., Campbell, R. G., Cullen, D. M., Armour, M. A., Einsiedel, A. A., Ciccocioppo, A. L., & Coffin, W. L. (2007). Developing career commitment in STEM-related fields: Myth versus reality. In R. J. Burke, M. C. Mattis, & E. Elgar (Eds.), *Women and minorities in science, technology, engineering and mathematics: Upping the numbers* (pp. 210–244). Northhampton, MA: Edward Elgar Publishing.

Markert, L. R. (1996). Gender related to success in science and technology. *The Journal of Technology Studies, 22*(2), 21–29.

McIntosh, K., Horner, R. H., Chard, D. J., Boland, J. B., & Good, R. H., III. (2006). The use of reading and behavior screening measures to predict nonresponse to schoolwide positive behavior support: A longitudinal analysis. *School Psychology Review, 35*(2), 275.

Metz, S. S. (2007). Attracting the engineering of 2020 today. In R. Burke & M. Mattis (Eds.), *Women and minorities in science, technology, engineering and mathematics: Upping the numbers* (pp. 184–209). Northampton, MA: Edward Elgar Publishing.

National Association for the Education of Young Children (NAEYC) & Fred Rogers Center. (2012). *Technology and interactive media as tools in early childhood programs serving children from birth through age 8.* Retrieved from www.naeyc.org/files/naeyc/file/positions/PS_technology_WEB2.pdf

National Research Council. (2000). *From neurons to neighborhoods: The science of early childhood development.* Washington, DC: National Academies Press.

National Research Council. (2001). *Eager to learn: Educating our preschoolers.* Washington, DC: National Academies Press.

Sesame Workshop. (2009). *Sesame workshop and the PNC Foundation join White House effort on STEM education.* Retrieved from www.sesameworkshop.org/newsandevents/pressreleases/stemeducation_11212009

Siu, K., & Lam, M. (2003). Technology education in Hong Kong: International implications for implementing the "Eight Cs" in the early childhood curriculum. *Early Childhood Education Journal, 31*(2), 143–150.

Smith, M. (2016). Computer science for all. *The White House blog*. Retrieved from www.whitehouse.gov/blog/2016/01/30/computerscienceall

2019 State of Computer Science Education. (2019). Retrieved from https://advocacy.code.org/

Steele, C. M. (1997). A threat in the air: How stereotypes shape intellectual identity and performance. *American Psychologist, 52,* 613–629.

Sullivan, A., & Bers, M. U. (2017). Dancing robots integrating art, music, and robotics in Singapore's early childhood centers. *International Journal of Technology & Design Education*. Online First. doi:10.1007/s10798-017-9397-0.

U.S. Department of Education, Office of Educational Technology. (2010). *Transforming American education: Learning powered by technology.* Washington, DC. Retrieved from www.ed.gov/technology/netp2010

Uzunboylu, H., Kınık, E., & Kanbul, S. (2017). An analysis of countries which have integrated coding into their curricula and the content analysis of academic studies on coding training in Turkey. *TEM Journal, 6*(4), 783.

White House. (2016). *Fact sheet: Advancing active STEM education for our youngest learners.* Retrieved from www.whitehouse.gov/thepressoffice/2016/04/21/factsheetadvancingactivestemeducation-ouryoungestlearners

PART

I

Coding as Playground

In the Beginning
There Was Language

In 1969, a young woman named Cynthia Solomon and MIT professor Seymour Papert went to the Muzzey Jr. High School in Lexington, MA, a Boston suburb, to teach students how to program. At the time, "programming" was a strange word and very few people knew what it meant. Although the students were learning programming, there was no computer to be found in the classroom. The computer was a few miles away at the Bolt, Beranek and Newman (BBN) research lab, and the classroom had teletypes, which resembled big typing machines. The information was sent over to a big computer, a PDP-1, one of the first modern commercial computers, back at BBN. This was a dedicated LOGO time-shared system. Users saved and retrieved their work sitting at teletype terminals. Although expensive and huge, the PDP-1 had computing power equivalent to a 1996 pocket organizer and a little less memory, and it used punched paper tape as its primary storage medium. In its basic form, the PDP-1 sold for $120,000 (roughly equivalent to $950,000 today) (Hafner & Lyon, 1996).

Despite all of this, children were invited to use it, to become programmers. Solomon (in a personal e-mail) describes how the children "made up hilarious sentence generators and became proficient users of their own math quizzes." This was the beginning of the first programming language for children, LOGO. Led by Seymour Papert at MIT and Wally Feurzeig and Dan Bobrow at BBN, over time, many people contributed and developed different prototypes of this child-friendly version of the LISP programming language. The home for this work was the MIT Artificial Intelligence (AI) Lab, then co-directed by Seymour Papert and Marvin Minsky. Thus, it is not surprising that LISP is considered by some to be the favored programming language for AI. By 1969, the LOGO group at MIT had been formed, with Papert as its director. As new versions of LOGO were developed, researchers would go to schools to teach and observe what happened in the classroom. Inspired by the Piagetian tradition of using clinical observations of children to learn about cognition, they documented their observations in several dozen LOGO memos later published by MIT (MIT LOGO Memos, 1971–1981; Piaget, 1964).

"By the 1970–71 school year we had a floor turtle and a display turtle," recalls Solomon in her wiki (Solomon, 2010). While the floor turtle had to be attached to a terminal and children shared it, the display turtle was designed to let users at four different terminals alternately take control of the turtle. By then, LOGO, the first programming language specifically designed for children, included a way to write stories, a way to draw with a programmable object (i.e., the turtle), a way to have the programmable object explore the environment, and a way to make and play music. As early as 1970, the first programming language for children provided tools for creative expression, and not only for problem-solving.

Because Seymour Papert was trained as a mathematician, he could see the potential for LOGO to help children to understand mathematical ideas by playing with them. He also realized the value of the two different interfaces: the screen-based turtle and the floor-based turtle. The floor turtle would, decades later, evolve into the LEGO® MINDSTORMS® robotics concept through a partnership between the LEGO company and MIT. The onscreen turtle became available through different venues, both commercially and free (i.e., Terrapin Logo, Turtle Logo, Kinderlogo). Geometry and LOGO were a natural match. The children could program the turtle to do anything that they wanted. Instructions were given to the turtle to move about in space, and the turtle dragged a pen to draw a trail. Such drawings gave birth to turtle geometry (see Figure 1.1). The turtle could draw squares, rectangles, and circles of all sizes, inviting children to explore the concept of angles. Through coding, mathematics became playful and expressive. Back in those early days, Seymour and his colleagues already wanted children to learn how to code so that they could become creators.

"Forward 60, right 90." How many times does this procedure need to be repeated to draw a square? And how should it be adapted to draw a rectangle? While exploring these questions, children would solve multiple problems. However, LOGO engaged children in creating beautiful shapes, not calculating angles. They needed math to make a project of their choice. They learned to see math as a useful, creative tool.

Figure 1.1 This example of "turtle geometry" was created using Terrapin Logo using the following code: repeat 44 [fd 77 lt 17 repeat 17 [fd 66 rt 49]]. This nested code loop translates as, "Repeat 44 times the following: [forward 77, repeat 17 times the following: [forward 66 right turn 49]]."

The story of LOGO is also the story of how, for those early researchers devoted to bringing the power of computation to education, programming was associated with children's ability to make something they cared about. They provided tools that offered multiple paths for expression: drawing, story-telling, games, and music. Programming was at the service of expression. Back then, researchers would have flinched at the idea of only associating coding with STEM (science, technology, engineering, and math). Those disciplines provide important skill sets and knowledge, but programming takes the young coder beyond: it provides a tool for personal, communicative expression.

Constructionism

Back in the late '90s, when I was a doctoral student working with Seymour Papert at the MIT Media Lab, the joke was that Seymour did not come in the LOGO box. What we meant was that although we were bringing LOGO and its full expressive potential to schools, many teachers tended to use LOGO in traditional, instructionist ways. Creativity and personal expression were left out. Our internal joke hid our wish to have Seymour come inside the LOGO box, so that when we needed to convince teachers to let their students freely explore and to create a project of their choice, he would come out and help us with his charming personality.

We spent hours sharing his theory, philosophy, and pedagogical approach with as many teachers as we could find. Seymour did not come in the LOGO box, but Constructionism, the framework he developed, came in a book, *Mindstorms: Children, Computers and Powerful Ideas* (Papert, 1980). This wonderful book summarizes Papert's approach to how children can become better learners and thinkers through coding. LOGO was carefully designed so that young children could create their own personally meaningful projects. However, a top-down curriculum and an instructionist pedagogy could turn LOGO into a completely different tool in classrooms where teachers did not understand the principles of Constructionism. Although LOGO was designed as a playground, it could easily become a playpen. Seymour's choice of this word, Constructionism, to name his pedagogical and philosophical approach is a play on Piaget's Constructivism (Ackermann, 2001; Papert & Harel, 1991). Seymour had worked with Jean Piaget in Switzerland and, amongst many things, he learned the importance of learning by doing.

While Piaget's theory explains how knowledge is constructed in our heads through a process of accommodation and assimilation, Papert pays particular attention to the role of computationally rich constructions in the world, as a support for those in the head. Papert's Constructionism asserts that computers are powerful educational technologies when used as tools for creating projects that people truly care about. Programming is a vehicle for creation, either on a screen or in the physical world, as shown by the early work on LOGO with both turtle interfaces. Papert's Constructionism believes that independent learning and discovery happen best when children can make, create, program, and design their own "objects to think with" in a playful manner (Bers, 2008). Computational objects can help us to think about powerful computational ideas, such as sequencing, abstraction, and modularity, but they also provide an opportunity to communicate our own voices. Coding, then, becomes both a vehicle for new forms of thinking and expression of the resulting thoughts. Chapters 7 and 8 will look at this and explore the powerful ideas of computer science that coding reveals.

Constructionism is my intellectual home. It is from there that I write this book. I apply what is useful to early childhood education and I extend it with my own theoretical framework, which I call Positive Technological Development (PTD). Chapter 10 will expand on this.

Seymour Papert refused to give a definition of Constructionism. In 1991, he wrote, "It would be particularly oxymoronic to convey the idea of constructionism through a definition since, after all, constructionism boils down to demanding that everything be understood by being constructed" (Papert & Harel, 1991). Respecting his wish, in my past writings I have always avoided providing a definition (e.g., Bers, 2017); however, I have presented four basic principles of Constructionism that have served early childhood education well (Bers, 2008):

1. Learning by designing personally meaningful projects to share in the community;

2. Using concrete objects to build and explore the world;

3. Identifying powerful ideas from the domain of study;

4. Engaging in self-reflection as part of the learning process.

These principles are consistent with the general agreement in early childhood education about the efficacy of "learning by doing" and engaging in "project-based learning" (Diffily & Sassman, 2002; Krajcik & Blumenfeld, 2006). Constructionism extends these approaches to also engage children in "learning by designing" and "learning by programming." From a Constructionist perspective, there is a continuum of learning opportunities that spans from blocks to robots (Bers, 2008). For example, while wooden blocks can help children explore size and shape, robots allow exploration of digital concepts, such as sensors. Nowadays, these are found in most "smart objects" around us, from water dispensers to elevator doors. The early childhood curriculum is supposed to focus on children's experiences in the world, and smart objects like these are a growing presence in our world.

When children are provided tools to learn about these "smart objects" by making them, fixing them, or playing with them through educational robotics, they not only become producers of their own projects, but they also explore disciplinary realms of knowledge, such as coding and engineering, as well as the nature of knowledge itself. They "think about thinking." They become epistemologists, just like Piaget who was deeply interested in the nature of knowledge, and just like Papert, who named his research group at the MIT Media Lab "Epistemology and Learning."

In Memoriam

Seymour Papert was a South African mathematician who worked with Jean Piaget in Geneva and then moved to Boston and became the co-director of the AI Lab at MIT. He was one of the founding pioneers of the MIT Media Lab. After he died in July 2016, Gary Stager wrote a beautiful obituary for *Nature:* "Few academics of Papert's stature have spent as much time as he did working in real schools. He delighted in the theories, ingenuity and playfulness of children. Tinkering or programming with them was the cause of many missed meetings" (Stager, 2016). I recall those missed meetings with frustration. I was an eager student trying to make sense of many questions.

Seymour loved questions but he did not have enough hours in the day to explore them all. By the time I met him, Seymour was already a prominent figure and embarked on frequent trips. So, escorting him to the airport was a wonderful and rare opportunity to have his undivided attention. He was always travelling, so such meetings became frequent. I remember discussing my questions in the back of a taxi or an airport coffee shop while he was waiting for his next plane. I also remember having to interrupt a thought-provoking discussion because his flight was leaving.

Seymour was a man of ideas. I believe he fell in love with computer programming because of its potential to bring about new ideas, both at the personal and societal level. Ideas can change the world, and Seymour wanted to change the world. However, in order to make abstract ideas concrete, we need a way to express them. Seymour understood that programming languages can serve as tools for expression. The next chapter will explore this concept.

References

Ackermann, E. (2001). Piaget's Constructivism, Papert's Constructionism: What's the difference? *Future of Learning Group Publication, 5*(3), 438.

Bers, M. U. (2008). *Blocks to robots: Learning with technology in the early childhood classroom.* New York, NY: Teachers College Press.

Bers, M. U. (2017). The Seymour test: Powerful ideas in early childhood education. *International Journal of Child-Computer Interaction*. doi:10.1016/j.ijcci.2017.06.004.

Diffily, D., & Sassman, C. (2002). *Project based learning with young children*. Westport, CT: Heinemann, Greenwood Publishing Group, Inc.

Hafner, K., & Lyon, M. (1996). *Where wizards stay up late: The origins of the Internet* (1st Touchstone ed.). New York, NY: Simon and Schuster.

Krajcik, J. S., & Blumenfeld, P. (2006). Project based learning. In R. K. Sawyer (Ed.), *Cambridge handbook of the learning sciences* (pp. 317–333). New York, NY: Cambridge University Press.

MIT LOGO Memos. (1971–1981). *Memo collection*. Retrieved from www.sonoma.edu/users/l/luvisi/logo/logo.memos.html

Papert, S (1980) *Mindstorms: Children, Computers and Powerful Ideas*, NY: Basic Books.

Papert, S., & Harel, I. (1991). Situating constructionism. *Constructionism, 36*(2), 1–11.

Piaget, J. (1964). Cognitive development in children: Piaget, development and learning. *Journal of Research in Science Teaching, 2*, 176–186.

Solomon, C. (2010). *Logo, Papert and Constructionist learning*. Retrieved November 15, 2016, from http://logothings.wikispaces.com/

Stager, G. S. (2016). Seymour Papert (1928–2016). *Nature, 537*(7620), 308.

2   **Tools for Expression**

Naomi is a first grade student and is working hard on her classroom project: Tell a story about your school break. Her teacher allowed the children to use any kind of medium to tell their stories. Other children are using illustrations, dioramas, and recorded audio. Naomi chose to tell her story using ScratchJr. Over the school break, her family welcomed a new baby at home and she is excited to share what happened with her classmates. She has already programmed the first page of the story, showing her grandmother walking with her to the hospital. She drew both of the characters herself, and even took a picture of her face to make sure her "Naomi" character looked realistic. As she starts her second page, she frowns. "Melanie" she calls, turning to her table partner, "I want to make the baby hide until I walk into the room. How do I do it?" Melanie, who has also used ScratchJr for class projects, points to the pink blocks and Naomi reads each icon until she finds the one she wants—a block with an invisible outline of a person, which makes a character "hide." She tells her friend, "Thanks! Now this is just like how it was. Baby Jonas was hiding when I came in the room until my mommy showed him to me!" She keeps working with the hide and show blocks to make the baby hide at just the right time. Before she shares her project with her class, she adds a "Turn page" block to her first page, so that the story flows seamlessly from one event to the next.

In this vignette, Naomi is using ScratchJr to express herself by "writing" code. Naomi also knows how to write in English. However, this story is not in English. This is a story written in a different language: a programming language. Like natural languages, programming languages, such as ScratchJr, provide a symbol system and a way to organize it (i.e., a grammar) that can serve to express ideas. While using natural languages allows us to communicate directly with other humans or "smart interfaces," programming languages serve to communicate with a computer, which will interpret our instructions and provide an output for our expression. The choice of programming language will enhance or hinder our possibilities of expression, and some languages might be better suited for certain tasks and not others. At the same time, our own fluency with the chosen language will play an important role. I can write in four different languages. However, I choose the language based on the communicative function I am seeking to accomplish. I was born and raised in Argentina, so Spanish is my mother tongue and the one I feel most comfortable with above all. And, of course, I can write in English; I learned it as a second language before moving to the U.S. for graduate school and it is my language of choice for writing about work. I can also write in French and Hebrew. I learned those languages as a child, living in both the Ivory Coast and Israel, but I am not a very fluent writer, since I stopped developing and using those skills. However, despite the language of choice, over the years I have developed textual literacy independent of any written language. I can use the writing system in any of those four languages, to translate spoken language into symbols that others can read. I understand the concept of symbolic representation and the basic tenets of literacy. Each language has its own syntax and grammar, but since I understand the fundamental principles of writing, I can apply those when writing in a new language. My ability to write in a fluent way has influenced my way of thinking. I can think in linear and sequential ways. And, most importantly, I can apply that knowledge when telling my own stories.

I can produce different textual artifacts. I can write a love letter, a grant proposal, or a thank-you note. I will probably choose Spanish for the first task and English for the second and third tasks. Each language has unique qualities that I believe facilitate my purpose to communicate with others or with myself: my husband is also from Argentina and thus Spanish is our shared language; the funding agency I submit grants to is American; and my everyday life happens predominantly in English, so most of my thank-you notes are in that language. These are all creative endeavors in which I become a producer of new content. The natural language I am using supports my creative task, but it can also be used in noncreative ways. As a child, when learning to spell, I was asked to copy the same word 100 times. My teacher claimed that it was a necessary step to build the required skills. If she had read Bruner, she probably would have realized that it is possible to use language and learn about language at the same time, and she might have chosen a more expressive activity to build and reinforce skills (Bruner, 1983). The intention of the user of the language determines how much creativity is displayed. The natural language is a vehicle, a medium for expression.

Programming languages are also tools for expression. I can do boring or creative things with them. I can choose ScratchJr, LOGO, or Java. I used to code with LISP when I was a graduate student, but I have forgotten it because I have not used it in many years. Each of these programming languages also has its own syntax and grammar, and some are better for certain tasks. If I want to make an animation, I will do it with ScratchJr. If I want to program a recommendation system, such as the ones Netflix or Amazon have, I will use Java. If I want to make a beautiful drawing with geometrical shapes, I will use LOGO. Over the years, I have gained a certain degree of computational literacy. I am not an expert programmer; I could not make a living working as a software engineer, but I know enough to call myself fluent in some of these languages. I can use them for expression and communication.

Languages are nouns, not verbs. They do not convey actions. Writing and programming are verbs: there is a subject that performs an action. There is intentionality and choice. Like natural written languages, programming languages have syntax and grammar, they are a reliable form of information storage and transfer, and they invite the process of decoding, encoding, reading, and writing. Like natural written languages, they are artificial and need to be taught. In this learning process, one develops new ways of thinking.

The process of writing and the process of coding both lead to the creation of a final product that can be shared with others. The parallels between writing and coding are powerful: both involve comprehension and generation; both welcome different levels of fluency, from beginner to expert; both involve the use of tools and the use of language; both can fulfill the need for expression and communication. Literacy, both textual and computational, emerges from knowing how to use the language. Once we know how to use the language, we can apply our knowledge in different ways. One can create many projects and quickly learn new languages. This is only achieved over time and after many struggles; it doesn't come easily. But it can be a lot of fun.

Tools for Young Children

Young children, with their own developmental needs and abilities, need programming languages specifically designed for them. Part IV of this book will expand on this. These must be simple languages that still support multiple combinations, have syntax and a grammar, and offer multiple ways to solve a problem. They must be playgrounds, not playpens. They need to provide opportunities for creating a computational artifact that can be shared with others and support a growing range of computational literacy skills, from beginner to expert. A child who is fluent in a particular programming language is more likely to learn a second one with ease. This child has probably mastered some aspects of computational thinking and can transfer that mastery to different situations.

In the last few years, several programming language and robotic systems specifically designed for young children have come to market. I have personally been involved with two of them: ScratchJr and KIBO. Chapters 11 and 12 describe them both in depth and, throughout the book, several vignettes depict children's experiences with them in a variety of early childhood settings. For now, the following vignettes describe young children's experiences while learning and playing with other existing tools and their encounters with the powerful ideas of computer science and computational thinking.

Exploring Control Structures with Daisy

Sean has been working with Daisy the Dinosaur in his first grade classroom for a couple of weeks when his mother decides to download the app on her iPad. She wants him to practice programming at home. Daisy the Dinosaur is a free iOS app that allows children to explore programming by making a green and pink dinosaur named Daisy move around onscreen (Hopscotch Inc., 2016). Daisy can be programmed through two modes: a structured challenge mode and a free play mode. Like ScratchJr, the app has simple but playful graphics that are appealing to young children. It has limited instructions so that children can jump into coding right away. Children explore foundational coding by programming Daisy to complete simple actions such as move, spin, jump, and roll. Advanced coding can be explored using Daisy's "when" and "repeat" commands. One of the key differences between Daisy the Dinosaur and ScratchJr is that ScratchJr's programming blocks are graphical and require no reading. Daisy the Dinosaur, on the other hand, requires reading simple words such as "turn" and "shrink" in each programming block.

At first, Sean's mom sets the app to "Challenge Mode." She wants to know how much he can do. Sean has explored most of these challenges at school and cruises through them quickly to show his mom that he is ready for the "Free Play" mode. This allows him to program Daisy to do whatever he wants. He makes Daisy spin, walk around, grow, and shrink onscreen. Because the app requires some reading, especially when it comes to the programming blocks, his mom sits with him to refresh his memory on the word meanings. Eventually, his mother leaves him alone.

Around 15 minutes later, to his mother's delight, Sean says he's programmed a magic trick for her to see. "I'm the magician and I can make my dinosaur Daisy turn into a super gigantic dragon!" he explains. "How can you do that?" his mom asks. "With just the touch of my finger and the magic word: Abracadabra!" Sean taps Daisy and she grows very large. "See?" he says proudly, showing off his code. "I just learned this new block called 'When,' and Daisy only grows when I tap her. We didn't learn this one at school." Sean's mom is impressed by his imagination and his ability to naturally master a new concept just by having free time to play and explore on his own.

Sean has encountered control structures. He is learning that he can control when or if something happens to Daisy based on the state of his iPad. This is a very powerful concept in computer science. He shows his mom how he can start a program by touching Daisy or even by shaking the iPad. Sean cannot wait to tell his friends at school all about the new blocks he learned!

Sequencing with a Bee

Suzy is a 5-year-old kindergartener who loves mazes. Each day during choice time she draws mazes out on paper for her friends to solve or explores activity books that have mazes in them. On Tuesday morning, Suzy's teacher, Mrs. McKinnon, reveals a big surprise to the kids at circle time: the class will be getting a new robot friend named Bee-Bot! Bee-Bot is a robot that resembles a yellow and black bumblebee (www.beebot.us). Bee-Bot has directional keys on its back that are used to enter up to 40 commands which send Bee-Bot forward, back, left, and right. Pressing the green Go button starts Bee-Bot on its way. Mrs. McKinnon gives the class a demo of Bee-Bot. She tells them that during choice time, she will bring students one at a time to help program Bee-Bot to move along the path on a colorful floor map.

Later that day during choice time, Suzy is happily scribbling away at a maze when Mrs. McKinnon calls her down to play with Bee-Bot. Reluctantly, Suzy leaves her drawing to join her teacher on the floor. Mrs. McKinnon shows Suzy the different buttons on Bee-Bot's back: Forward, Backward, Turn Right, and Turn Left. To program Bee-Bot to move along the map, she shows Suzy how to press the keys in the right order. Next, she sends the program to Bee-Bot by pressing the Go button. She tells Suzy to give it a try.

"See, this is a map of a school," Mrs. McKinnon explains, showing Suzy a large square map on the floor illustrating different places like the music room, cafeteria, and library. "Why don't you try to program Bee-Bot to go to the music room?" Suzy presses the Forward button a few times and then presses Go. She watches Bee-Bot move straight along the map. "Oh no!" exclaims Suzy. "Why did Bee-Bot drive to the gym?" Mrs. McKinnon explains that Suzy should look at the map and then program the robot to follow the path. "Imagine that this map is a maze and Bee-Bot needs to get to the music room to beat the maze," says Mrs. McKinnon. "Does Bee-Bot need to turn? When? Think about the order and sequence of instructions."

Suddenly, the process of programming makes sense to Suzy. She needs to tell Bee-Bot, by pressing the buttons on its back, to take a series of ordered steps to get to the music room. She starts by sending one instruction at a time to Bee-Bot instead of a long, complete program. She can't remember all the needed steps and Bee-Bot, unlike KIBO, doesn't provide a way for children to see the program that they are sending to their robots. With her teacher's help, Suzy tries out a few different strategies for problem-solving, such as breaking down the large task into simpler, manageable units by just programming Bee-Bot to take one or two steps at a time. Eventually, she gets Bee-Bot to the music room. "Bee-Bot made it!" Suzy squeals with delight. Her joy of solving mazes has come to life with this colorful robot and she spends her choice time navigating along the different floor maps that come with Bee-Bot. The next day, when

Mrs. McKinnon invites her to play with Bee-Bot again, Suzy refuses: "I already did all the mazes." So, Mrs. McKinnon encourages her to design her own Bee-Bot floor maze for herself and her classmates to solve.

A Drawing Turtle

Cindy is a kindergartener who is just beginning to spell and write basic words. She hasn't had much experience using a computer or keyboard but is excited that she will be visiting the computer lab with her class today. She loves to play games in computer class. At the computer lab, her teacher, Ms. Santos, explains that today they will be learning how to program. "A program is a list of instructions that makes something happen onscreen," she says. Ms. Santos shows them how to program using Kinderlogo (www. terrapinlogo.com). This version of LOGO allows young children to explore programming freely by moving a little graphical "turtle" around the computer screen using letter commands instead of full words. Unlike more complex languages, including other versions of LOGO, Kinderlogo makes it easy for young children who are "prereaders," like Cindy. Instead of spelling and typing out long commands such as "forward," "right," "left," etc., the turtle can move with simple keystrokes. For example, Ms. Santos shows the children that they can press the F key to make the turtle go forward, R to make it turn to the right, and L to make it turn to the left. As the turtle moves around on the screen, it draws a line as if a pen were attached to it. The kids are delighted to see how the turtle can be programmed to draw shapes!

Ms. Santos asks the children to program their own turtles to draw their favorite shapes onscreen. Cindy remembers that pressing the "F" key makes the turtle go forward and pressing "R" makes the turtle turn right, but she has very little experience using a keyboard and has trouble finding the letter keys. She has many problems to solve in order to program her turtle: remembering the correspondence between each key on the keyboard and the actions for the turtle, figuring out the right order to press the keys to create a shape, all while navigating a keyboard of letters when she is still learning the alphabet and how to type. This process proves frustrating for Cindy, who is having trouble finding any key except "F" on the keyboard.

Ms. Santos sees that Cindy is struggling. She sits with her to better understand her frustration. She quickly realizes that Cindy understands the concept of programming and the steps she needs to take, but she has a hard time with the keyboard. She helps Cindy out by putting colorful stickers on the F, L, and R keys so that she can find them easily. Now, Cindy can focus on sequencing her program in the correct order to create a shape. Cindy wants to draw her favorite shape, a square. First, she draws a straight line and then iteratively adds new ones. She also tries out the different turn commands until she gets it right. She has to stop often to make changes and fix things that do not work. Twice she even decides to start over and make a whole new square. By the end of computer class, she has a square onscreen. "Look! Ms. Santos! Look! I programmed my turtle to draw a square!" Cindy beams with pride as Ms. Santos helps her save a screenshot of her program and the square so that she can print them and take them home. As she hands Cindy the printouts, Ms. Santos reminds her how hard she worked in class today and tells her to make sure she shows her parents the printout of her code, too, not just the final square she made. Cindy nods and says she already has a plan for the next time she gets to use Kinderlogo. "Next time, I'm going to try to program the turtle to draw my whole name." Ms. Santos smiles and challenges her to find the different shapes hidden in the letters of her name.

Coding Life

Calvin is a 6-year-old attending a summer camp, where he is participating in a research project conducted by doctoral student researcher Amanda Strawhacker from my DevTech research group at Tufts University. This project investigates how to introduce children to the field of bioengineering, which uses genetics as a kind of programming language to design certain aspects of living things (Loparev et al., 2017; Strawhacker, Sullivan, Verish, Bers, & Shaer, 2018; Strawhacker, Verish, Shaer, & Bers, 2020). Just like other research projects in my lab, this one also uses a simple tangible programming language to allow children to write and debug their code (Strawhacker, Verish, Shaer, & Bers, 2020). This tool, called CRISPEE, allows children to build, test, and change "gene programs" for glowing bioluminescent animals, like fireflies (Verish, Strawhacker, Bers, & Shaer, 2018). With CRISPEE, children make gene codes to change the color of LED lights on toy versions of their animals (see Figure 2.1).

Figure 2.1 The tangible CRISPEE kit allows children to explore coding with genes to create colorful bioluminescent animals, in this case a firefly shown in a faceplate attached to CRISPEE. Children use the wooden blocks (bottom of image) to turn light colors on with solid bricks or off with X-marked bricks. They can see their glowing programmed light on the CRISPEE itself and in an interactive plush toy.

Calvin is using CRISPEE to code a firefly to glow his favorite color, blue. He has a picture book lying on the table next to him about bioluminescent animals, open to a page about the blue crystal jellyfish. "Amanda!" he calls out to the researcher, "I'm going to invent the crystal firefly!" He selects the wooden "Gene" block that means "shine a blue light," then two more blocks that turn blue light off and green light off. He puts his code into the CRISPEE and pushes the buttons to test his program. Calvin frowns and says "CRISPEE is confused by my program," as he points to the wooden firefly on the CRISPEE that is not glowing. Amanda asks him to explain his program.

> I want it to make lots of blue so I can make a firefly that looks like the crystal jellyfish, like in the book we read. So I used blue-on and blue-off and—Oh wait, I know! I told it to turn blue on and turn blue off. It can't do both things at once!

Amanda watches as Calvin replaces his blue "Off" block with a red "Off block." He tests his program and pumps his fist in the air when his firefly glows blue. Calvin spends the rest of the morning showing his friends how he made a blue firefly, and drawing a picture of his "crystal firefly" to put inside his CRISPEE design journal.

Sean, Suzy, Cindy, and Calvin found ways to express themselves, and make their abstract ideas concrete, by using different programming languages and creating different projects. In the process, they also engaged in computational thinking and explored different powerful ideas of computational thinking. These ideas will be further explored in Chapter 8. However, despite the differences in programming languages used, projects created, and powerful ideas explored, they all shared something: they had fun in the creative process. They engaged with coding in a playful way. The next chapter will explore the role of play when coding in early childhood.

References

Bruner, J. (1983). *Child's talk: Learning to use language.* New York, NY: W. W. Norton & Company.

Hopscotch Inc. (2016) Daisy the Dinosaur (version 2.2.0) [Mobile application software]. Retrieved from https://apps.apple.com/us/app/daisy-the-dinosaur/id490514278

Loparev, A., Sullivan, A., Verish, C., Westendorf, L., Davis, J., Flemings, M., Bers, M. U., & Shaer, O. (2017, June). BacToMars: Creative engagement with bio-design for children. In *Proceedings of the 2017 Conference on Interaction Design and Children* (pp. 623–628).

Strawhacker, A., Sullivan, A., Verish, C., Bers, M. U., & Shaer, O. (2018). Enhancing children's interest and knowledge in bioengineering through an interactive videogame. *Journal of Information Technology Education: Innovations in Practice, 17,* 55–81. doi:10.28945/3976.

Strawhacker, A., Verish, C., Shaer, O., & Bers, M. U. (2020). Young Children's Learning of Bioengineering with CRISPEE: A Developmentally Appropriate Tangible User Interface. *Journal of Science Education and Technology.* 1–21.

Verish, C., Strawhacker, A., Bers, M., & Shaer, O. (2018, March). CRISPEE: A tangible gene editing platform for early childhood. In *Proceedings of the Twelfth International Conference on Tangible, Embedded, and Embodied Interaction* (pp. 101–107).

3 Playing with Code

Coding can become playing if it is taught with a playful approach. Research in early childhood has shown how play is a wonderful way for children to learn (Fromberg, 1990; Fromberg & Gullo, 1992; Garvey, 1977). Play has been described as a vehicle for the development of imagination and intelligence, language, social skills, and perceptual motor abilities in young children (Frost, 1992). I propose that when introducing computer science and computational thinking into early childhood education the approach must be playful. Programming languages can, and must, become playgrounds.

Although there are many academic definitions of play (e.g., Csikszentmihalyi, 1981; Scarlett, Naudeau, Ponte, & Salonius-Pasternak, 2005; Sutton-Smith, 2009), one doesn't need to be a scholar to recognize play. Play is when children are having fun, they are immersed in an activity, they are using their imagination, and they are intrinsically motivated. They do not want to stop what they're doing. Those of us who have taught young children to code with a playground approach have witnessed how they want to keep working hard on their projects, even when it is time to stop for a snack. When children play, they learn by doing.

Play enhances language development, social competence, creativity, imagination, and thinking skills (Fromberg & Gullo, 1992). Fromberg (1990) claims that play is the "ultimate integrator of human experience" (p. 223). When children play, they draw upon their past experiences, including things they have done, seen others do, read about, watched on television, or seen through other media. They integrate these experiences into their games and play scenarios, and they express and communicate their fears and feelings. As we observe them playing, we can understand them better.

Coding projects can also become integrators of experiences. Mary, a 5-year-old, uses ScratchJr to make an animation depicting the life cycle of a frog. Stephanie, a 6-year-old emergent writer, makes a game to teach younger children the letters. Xavier, a 6-year-old learning about habitats, turns KIBO into a bat that hides from the light. Claire, a 5-year-old, makes her KIBO robot turn its light on and off in a colorful pattern. In each of these examples, children bring their previous knowledge into their coding: math and science, literacy and biology, computer science and robotics.

They are also making projects that can be shared with others. Patient teachers, who observe the process of creating these projects, can learn a lot. The clues for understanding learning are not only revealed in the final computational products. Most of the learning happens throughout the experience of *doing*. The art of teaching is in recognizing this process, naming its different steps, addressing challenges encountered along the way, and providing the needed scaffolds.

When coding is taught with a playful approach, children are not afraid to make mistakes. After all, playing is just that: playing. Sometimes we win and sometimes we lose, although some forms of play do not have winners and losers. In pretend play, for example, anything goes. A box can become a castle and a stick can become a sword. Children can be superheroes and monsters. Pretend play in early childhood enhances the child's capacity for cognitive flexibility and, ultimately, creativity (Russ, 2004; Singer & Singer, 2005).

Csikszentmihalyi, an expert on creativity amongst many other things (1981), describes play as "a subset of life ... an arrangement in which one can practice behavior without dreading its consequences" (p. 14). Coding with a playground approach offers similar opportunities. It looks different from traditional computer science courses in which students need to solve a challenge under time pressure or find the correct way to answer a prompt. The approach I am proposing in this book welcomes all consequences resulting from trial and error. Everything is a learning experience.

The Theories of Play

Classic child development theorists have tackled the subject of play. Piaget observed three main stages: 1) early to late infancy: nonsymbolic practice games; 2) early childhood: make-believe and symbolic games; and 3) late childhood: games with rules (Piaget, 1962). Piaget's developmental scheme is based on changes in structure, rather than content, and reflects changes in how children develop a capacity for symbolic thought (Scarlett, Naudeau, Ponte, & Salonius-Pasternak, 2005). Programming languages for early childhood introduce the rules of grammar and syntax but support the open nature of make-believe games.

Traditional Piagetian theory holds that play, in and of itself, does not necessarily result in the formation of new cognitive structures. Piaget claimed that play was just for pleasure, and while it allowed children to practice things they had previously learned, it did not necessarily result in learning new things. In this Piagetian view, play is a "process reflective of emerging symbolic development, but contributing little to it" (Johnsen & Christie, 1986, p. 51). Other theorists, such as Vygotsky, have a different approach, theorizing that play facilitates cognitive development (Vygotsky, 1966). For Vygotsky, make-believe play could foster the development of symbolic thought and self-regulation (Berk & Meyers, 2013; Vygotsky, 1966, 1978).

I am not a scholar of play, but after decades of observing children coding with a playground approach, I can point to hundreds of instances in which children learned new things by playing with the different coding instructions embedded in programming blocks. I have seen children learn that in ScratchJr it takes 12 turning rotations to make a character flip around in a full circle, just by adding new programming blocks to see what would happen. Additionally, I have seen them tapping around the screen and discovering that they can add new pages to their programs, inadvertently learning how to use the app to tell a multipart story. In my observations, before children finish asking the question, "What does this block do?" they've already added it to their program to find out for themselves.

Sometimes children stumble upon a new command in ScratchJr and try it out on their own. This is usually the case when encountering simple concepts, such as those involved in motion. Other times, it was a teacher or a peer who introduced new ideas. It is often the most complex concepts that are learned this way. For example, in ScratchJr, a complex concept and programming block is messaging. The message-programming block allows characters to interact with each other, as one character will only perform an action when it receives a "message" sent by another character (see Figure 3.1). To help children comprehend this abstract concept, I have observed teachers use tangible analogies that children can relate to: if a

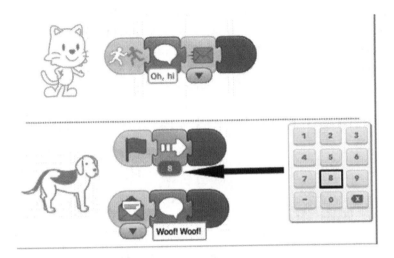

Figure 3.1 Illustration of how to use ScratchJr's message-sending blocks in order to make two characters move toward one another and have a conversation. In this example, the kitten and dog characters talk to one another. After the dog moves toward the kitten (eight steps) and bumps into him, the kitten says "hi" and sends out the orange message envelope. Next, the dog receives the orange message and replies "Woof! Woof!" The result is a perfectly timed out conversation between the two characters.

child sends a letter to a friend, what does the friend do when they receive it to find out what's inside? They open the envelope, which in turn opens their line of communication. This holds true in messaging with ScratchJr, as children can visualize themselves sending a letter to a friend as they use the blocks for creating conversations and games with their characters.

I have also seen children engaging in imaginative play and storytelling. They take on the role of animals and astronauts and used the ScratchJr Paint Editor to insert their own photos into their programs. They become both characters and directors in their own narratives. I have seen children play "dress up" with their KIBO robots and immerse themselves in an imaginary world just like they might with dolls or stuffed animals. But, unlike with dolls, they were able to program their KIBOs to respond to them with movements and sounds.

When children are provided free range to discover new things on their own, in a playful way, I have observed powerful learning outcomes. I conducted a study of over 200 K-2 students and six educators from schools across the U.S. in which we asked teachers to lead ScratchJr lessons in whatever way they preferred. Then, we asked them to administer a standardized programming assessment, called Solve-Its, to their students (Strawhacker & Bers, 2015; Strawhacker, Lee, & Bers, 2017). These assessments evaluate foundational computational thinking skills such as debugging and reverse engineering. The teachers also completed a survey to identify their unique teaching style. Our research found that the "Formal Authority" teaching style, which is characterized by a concern for correct, acceptable, and standard ways of doing things, was associated with lower scores on almost every question on the student's Solve-Its programming assessment. In contrast, the highest scoring students had teachers who exhibited a "Personal Model" style, meaning that they taught by example and placed emphasis on a hands-on and playful approach to learning (Strawhacker, Lee, & Bers, 2017).

Similarly, with my doctoral students Madhu Govind and Emily Relkin, I conducted a separate study investigating over 100 young children and their families' interactions and role dynamics as they engaged in ScratchJr and KIBO activities. This study was part of a project called Family Coding Days, in which community organizations hosted collaborative coding events for their local families using a freely available protocol devised by my DevTech research group (Govind, 2019). During these single-day workshops, families were introduced to coding technologies in an informal, multigenerational setting and were invited to collaborate on an open-ended project. Results show that Family Coding Days significantly enhanced both children's and parents' interest in coding. Families were most successful when parents acted as coaches and encouraged their children to spearhead their project ideas, allowing children to lead a playful, creative coding experience with the adults following their lead. Regardless of parents' professional background (STEM versus non-STEM) or the type of tool used (the ScratchJr app versus the tangible KIBO robotics kit), parents were able to successfully co-engage by asking questions, offering suggestions, and providing encouragement without taking the lead (Govind, 2019; Govind & Bers, 2019).

These findings are consistent with research that shows that programs with active play components may be more successful in eliciting improved executive functions or self-regulation (Shaheen, 2014). I have observed wonderful examples of digital play that promoted higher order thinking skills when children were provided with opportunities and tools to code with a playground approach. A recent policy statement released by the American Academy of Pediatrics states that

> the higher order thinking skills and executive functions essential for school success, such as task persistence, impulse control, emotion regulation, and creative, flexible thinking, are best taught through unstructured and social (not digital) play, as well as responsive parent—child interactions.
>
> (American Academy of Pediatrics, 2016)

However, what this approach misses is that any kind of play (digital or not) can foster unstructured, social, and playful interactions.

The Role of the Body

Coding environments that use screens, such as ScratchJr, offer limited possibilities for physical play. However, research suggests that learning through movement or "motor learning" is conducive to better outcomes (Dennison & Dennison, 1986). Seymour Papert, in his book *Mindstorms*, called it "syntonic learning" when referring to the Turtle Logo that allowed children to use knowledge of their own body to explore geometry (Papert, 1980).

Cognitive scientists use the term "embodied cognition" to describe how an organism's body, motion, and sensory capabilities determine how and what it thinks. For example, George Lakoff and Mark Johnson's work on metaphors shows that humans can understand basic concepts that include spatial orientations such as up, down, front, and back because they can directly experience them from their own bodies (Lakoff & Johnson, 1980).

The surge of new tangible interfaces and smart objects provide new opportunities for coding that welcome the body back into the learning experience. Furthermore, they can support gross motor skills development by engaging children in locomotor play that promotes neural and muscular coordination for healthy growth (Byers & Walker, 1995).

In a kindergarten classroom, children are lying down on the floor next to a long string of KIBO blocks (see Figure 3.2). During robotics time, spontaneously, these 5-year-olds decided to build the longest possible string of KIBO blocks. Then, one by one, they started to lay down next to the blocks to see who was taller. They counted how many blocks James was, how many

Figure 3.2 Children playing with KIBO blocks and measuring themselves.

blocks Mary was, how many blocks Shaina was, and so forth. What started as a playful game, was turned by a skilled teacher into an opportunity to explore different forms of measurements and counting. That is the beauty of play. It opens doors to different meaningful and engaging experiences.

Tools like KIBO were designed to bring the playground into coding by engaging the full range of physical play and the development of fine and gross motor skills. For example, it is customary to see children dancing with their KIBOs, marching alongside them in a robotic parade, and running through the same maze that they programmed their KIBOs to navigate. In addition, because they tend to mostly test their KIBOs on the floor (the risk of them falling off the table is too great), children are constantly getting up and down, running around to fetch different robotic parts, and stopping on the way to chat with friends.

When children are programming with others, they are engaging not only in collaboration and teamwork, but also in social play. This involves the development of social coordination skills and social scripts that are necessary for negotiating, problem-solving, sharing, and working within groups (Erickson, 1985; McElwain & Volling, 2005; Pellegrini & Smith, 1998). As we will see later in this book, the playful approach to coding makes use of social games such as Simon Says to teach children about the syntax of programming languages.

In sum, a playground approach to coding brings play into the teaching of computer science and computational thinking. If we believe that early childhood education must acknowledge the importance of play for development, then we must bring everything we know about play to the coding class. Best practices for early childhood education also apply when learning about sequencing and algorithms. Coding experiences can be more like games than challenges, or more like pretend stories than problems to solve. The playfulness of the approach can open doors to those who are marginalized from initiatives that teach programming integrated with traditional STEM subjects. For example, this hands-on, playful, and creative approach may help reach females and minorities who are traditionally underrepresented in technical fields like engineering and computer science (Wittemyer, McAllister, Faulkner, McClard, & Gill, 2014). May this be our contribution to making computer science and computational thinking more accessible to all. In early childhood, we cherish the benefits of play. Furthermore, at a time in which play is being squeezed out of the early childhood classroom, coding can bring it back.

References

American Academy of Pediatrics. (2016). Media and young minds. *Pediatrics, 138*(5). doi:10.1542/peds.2016-2591, 1–8.

Berk, L. E., & Meyers, A. B. (2013). The role of make-believe play in the development of executive function: Status of research and future directions. *American Journal of Play, 6*(1), 98.

Byers, J. A., & Walker, C. (1995). Refining the motor training hypothesis for the evolution of play. *American Naturalist, 146*(1), 25–40.

Csikszentmihalyi, M. (1981). Some paradoxes in the definition of play. In A. T. Cheska (Ed.), *Play as context* (pp. 14–26). West Point, NY: Leisure Press.

Dennison, P. E., & Dennison, G. (1986). *Brain gym: Simple activities for whole brain learning.* Glendale, CA: EduKinesthetics, Inc.

Erickson, R. J. (1985). Play contributes to the full emotional development of the child. *Education, 105*, 261–263.

Fromberg, D. P. (1990). Play issues in early childhood education. In C. Seefeldt (Ed.), *Continuing issues in early childhood education* (pp. 223–243). Columbus, OH: Merrill.

Fromberg, D. P., & Gullo, D. F. (1992). Perspectives on children. In L. R. Williams & D. P. Fromberg (Eds.), *Encyclopedia of early childhood education* (pp. 191–194). New York, NY: Garland Publishing, Inc.

Frost, J. L. (1992). *Play and playscapes.* Albany, NY: Delmar, G.

Garvey, C. (1977). *Play.* Cambridge, MA: Harvard University Press.

Govind, M. (2019). Families that code together learn together: Exploring family-oriented programming in early childhood with ScratchJr and KIBO Robotics (Master's thesis).

Govind, M., & Bers, M. U. (2019). Parents don't need to be coding experts, just willing to learn with their children. (Blog Post). Retrieved from www.edsurge.com/news/2019-12-11-parents-don-t-need-to-be-coding-experts-just-willing-to-learn-with-their-children

Johnsen, E. P., & Christie, J. F. (1986). Pretend play and logical operations. In K. Blanchard (Ed.), *The many faces of play* (pp. 50–58). Champaign, IL: Human Kinetics.

Lakoff, G., & Johnson, M. (1980). *Metaphors we live by Chicago.* Chicago: Chicago University.

McElwain, E. L., & Volling, B. L. (2005). Preschool children's interactions with friends and older siblings: Relationship specificity and joint contributions to problem behaviors. *Journal of Family Psychology, 19*, 486–496.

Papert, S. (1980). *Mindstorms: Children, computers, and powerful ideas.* New York, NY: Basic Books, Inc.

Pellegrini, A., & Smith, P. (1998). Physical activity play: The nature and function of a neglected aspect of play. *Child Development, 69*(3), 577–598.

Piaget, J. (1962). *Play, dreams, and imitation in childhood.* New York, NY: W. W. Norton & Co.

Russ, S. W. (2004). *Play in child development and psychotherapy.* Mahwah, NJ: Earlbaum.

Scarlett, W. G., Naudeau, S., Ponte, I., & Salonius-Pasternak, D. (2005). *Children's play.* Thousand Oaks, CA: Sage Publications.

Shaheen, S. (2014). How child's play impacts executive function—Related behaviors. *Applied Neuropsychology: Child, 3*(3), 182–187.

Singer, D. G., & Singer, J. L. (2005). *Imagination and play in the electronic age.* Cambridge, MA: Harvard University Press.

Strawhacker, A. L., & Bers, M. U. (2015). "I want my robot to look for food": Comparing children's programming comprehension using tangible, graphical, and hybrid user interfaces. *International Journal of Technology and Design Education, 25*(3), 293–319.

Strawhacker, A. L., Lee, M. S. C., & Bers, M. (2017). Teaching tools, teacher's rules: Exploring the impact of teaching styles on young children's programming knowledge in ScratchJr. *The International Journal of Technology and Design Education.* doi:10.1007/s10798-017-9400-9.

Sutton-Smith, B. (2009). *The ambiguity of play.* Cambridge, MA: Harvard University Press.

Vygotsky, L. (1966). Play and its role in the mental development of the child. *Soviet Psychology, 5*(3), 6–18.

Vygotsky, L. (1978). *Mind in society: The development of higher psychological processes.* Cambridge, MA: Harvard University Press.

Wittemyer, R., McAllister, B., Faulkner, S., McClard, A., & Gill, K. (2014). *MakeHers: Engaging girls and women in technology through making, creating, and inventing.* (Report No. 1). Retrieved from Intel Corporation www.intel.com/content/dam/www/public/us/en/documents/reports/makers-report-girls-women.pdf

Coding as Literacy

4 | Natural and Artificial Languages

Coding is a new literacy. That is, coding is perceived as involving a set of skills and knowledge that society highly values in our historical period. While traditional literacy is associated with reading and writing, other domains have also attained the "literacy status," such as health literacy, cultural literacy, visual literacy, and so forth (e.g., Elkins, 2009; Hirsch, Kett, & Trefil, 2002; Nutbeam, 2008). The advent of mass literacy was a world-changing event. Literacy is not only an "instrumental" tool, but also an "epistemological" tool that restructures the way we know the world. Will computational literacy become the new literacy of the twenty-first century?

The concept of literacy "is deemed to be important to the status and financial health of a nation," writes Annette Vee in her book, *Coding Literacy: How Computer Programming is Changing Writing* (Vee, 2017). Scholars in literacy studies have defined literacy as a human faculty with a symbolic and infrastructural technology that can be used for creative, communicative, and rhetorical purposes (Kramsch, 2006; Martin, 2006; Warnick, 2001). Textual literacy enables people to represent their ideas using natural languages in texts that can travel away from immediate, interpersonal contexts (to write) and to interpret texts produced by others (to read) (Brandt, 2011; Kramsch, 2006; Vee, 2013). Coding, an expressive activity associated with computational literacy, also involves the use of a symbolic system of representation, a programming language, to communicate and express ideas (Weintrop & Wilensky, 2017).

Research has explored the similarities and differences between natural and artificial languages, and interdisciplinary endeavors such as natural language processing and computational linguistics have emerged (Allamanis, Barr, Devanbu, & Sutton, 2018). While reviewing that work is beyond the scope of this book, it is important to establish that both natural and artificial languages meet three common criteria: they are meaningful, productive, and allow displacement (Norman, 2017). That is to say, both human and programming languages are symbolic representational systems, with a grammar and syntax, that can be used to convey meaning, to produce something that has never happened before, and to communicate things that are displaced in time or space (Bers, 2019a).

Since the early '60s, computer advocates have claimed that reading and writing code resembles textual literacy in many ways (e.g., Perlis, 1962; Van Dyke, 1987). Both computational and textual literacy empower individuals to think and express themselves through the use of language, a symbolic system of representation. What do we know about how we learn and use written languages?

Understanding the cognitive and neural bases that support the acquisition and use of natural and artificial languages is crucial. Not only is this an intellectual challenge, but it is also a prerequisite for developing robust educational interventions. If computer programming is a cognitive invention, like reading and writing (Wolf, 2018), how do emergent skills, such as learning a new programming language, get incorporated into already existing ones? What are the mechanisms that facilitate that process? Are they similar to the ones employed when learning how to read and write in a second language?

Understanding the cognitive bases of computer programming, and its similarities and differences with natural languages, is difficult work. However, we need more research resulting in empirical evidence. In our work with cognitive neuroscientist Ev Fedorenko and her team at MIT, we started to explore some of these questions (Fedorenko, Ivanova, Dhamala, & Bers, 2019).

It took many decades and a big financial commitment for cognitive scientists and neuroscientists to grow a research agenda to explore what mechanisms are involved when reading. What if the research agenda extended to also exploring what happens when learning how to code? As coding gains literacy status and is starting to be taught in schools in a compulsory way, why wait to realize that many children are being left behind? Research on how we learn to code is crucial for informing curricular decisions.

The field of textual literacy knows this too well, having spent time and resources on the "reading wars" over the best approaches as to teach how to read (phonics, whole language, or a balanced approach)

(Smith, 1969). While there is a rich tradition of cognitive scientists, experimental psychologists, and psycholinguists doing basic research on how the brain learns to read (Dehaene et al., 2010; Wolf, 2007) and write (Bialystok, 1991; Puranik & Lonigan, 2011) and there are well-known controversies and theoretical battles based on that research, such as the Reading Wars (Pearson, 2004) and the Linearity and Unified Hypothesis in writing (Fox & Saracho, 1990; Tolchinsky, 2003) there is a lack of research on the cognitive mechanisms involved when young children learn to code. Some research explores the differences between expert and novice programmers (Dalbey & Linn, 1985) and other studies employ tools such as functional magnetic resonance imaging (fMRI) (Fakhoury, 2018; Floyd, Santander, & Weimer, 2017; Peitek et al., 2018; Siegmund et al., 2014) to characterize mechanisms and propose a theoretical foundation to ground this novel work. In our work, we are conducting exploratory studies using fMRI to capture what happens in the brain when people are coding (Fedorenko, Ivanova, Dhamala, & Bers, 2019; Ivanova et al., 2019). Although we do not have certainties, in our pilot work we learned that the language system is involved when doing certain tasks. More studies need to follow.

Educators have long made assumptions about the relationship between programming and other cognitive skills, and these assumptions have shaped the treatment of computer science in school curricula across the world as a STEM subject (Bers, 2018; 2019b). But what if the cognitive mechanisms associated with coding were also associated with reading and writing? Would that influence our curricular grouping choices? Would that alter our guidelines and approaches for curriculum development and implementation ?

The hypothesis that learning to program may be akin to learning a (foreign) language was originally put forward by Seymour Papert, who noted a number of parallels between computer and natural languages and suggested that their acquisition and processing may draw on similar cognitive mechanisms (Papert, 1980). Within this perspective, understanding coding as a literacy is a gateway for developing educational approaches to leverage both textual and computational literacy. Chapters 5 and 6 will explore this by looking at the "Coding as Another Language" (CAL) pedagogical approach that I have developed and implemented over the years. CAL's approach and curriculum explores the parallels between programming and natural languages and their communicative and expressive functions.

Research shows that children learn to think with and through language (Vygotsky, 1978). Thus, by learning to use a programming language that involves logical sequencing, abstraction, and problem-solving, children can learn how to think in analytical ways. Wittgenstein (2009/1953) argued that the language we speak determines the thoughts that we are able to have. In other words, learning a new language can promote new patterns of thought, new conceptual frameworks, and new ways of using language (Montgomery, 1997). Wittgenstein's philosophy echoes Vygotsky's developmental perspective in terms of the relationship between language and thinking at the individual level. Furthermore, researchers such as Walter Ong, an American Jesuit priest and scholar, while studying societies that are transitioning from orality to literacy, also found a fundamental shift in their form of thought (Ong, 1982).

In his seminal work, Ong wrote:

> Without writing, the literate mind would not and could not think as it does, not only when engaged in writing but even when it is composing its thoughts in oral form [...] The fact that we do not commonly feel the influence of writing on our thoughts shows that we have interiorized the technology of writing so deeply that without tremendous effort we cannot separate it from ourselves or even recognize its presence and influence.
>
> (Ong, 1986, p. 24)

Ong describes writing as a technology that must be learned and that initiates the transformation of thinking from the world of sound to the world of sight. For example, oral cultures might not understand the concept of "looking up something." It would have no meaning because, without writing, words have no visual presence, even when the objects they represent are visual. Words are sounds, and visual metaphors can't describe them. Spoken words happen in time, not in space.

Oral cultures require mnemotechnic strategies for preserving information over time in the absence of writing. For example, they rely on proverbs, condensed wisdom, epic poetry, and characters. These oral cultures favor cyclic thought. The shaman or storyteller invites people to hear stories, which are told in cyclical, redundant ways to aid with memory. Instead, cultures of literacy favor linear, logical, historical, or evolutionary thought, which depend on writing. Ong was particularly interested in cultures in a transition phase from orality to literacy and he pointed out how early criticism of computers has similarities to early criticism of writing (Ong, 1982).

This line of work looks at literacy as an historical and social phenomenon with strong epistemological implications. The technologies of writing, which have changed over time, have impacted the way we think about the world. For example, the printing press facilitated the wide distribution of ideas, while the early scribe kept knowledge isolated and for just a few chosen readers. Furthermore, writing restructures our thinking. Fundamentally, the technologies of writing support logical sequential thinking and allow the separation of the subject from the object (i.e., of what is told from who is telling it). The object (the written text) takes a life of its own and can be analyzed, deconstructed, and interpreted. This brings about metacognition: "thinking about thinking." My mentor, Seymour Papert, used to say that "you can't think about thinking without thinking about thinking about something" (Papert, 2005). He was referring to the importance of the metacognitive level, of understanding our own way of knowing and making sense of the world. In his view, the computer, and the ability to program it, provided an opportunity for children to create "something" (i.e., a computational project) for thinking about thinking. Both the written text and the computational project provide an opportunity for metacognition, for deconstructing and interpreting our own thinking in the process of making them.

For example, a child who uses LOGO to make a game to teach young children about fractions is not only thinking about computer science and mathematics, but is also thinking about game design principles and perspective. The child needs to think about the kind of background knowledge the users will have and adapt the game accordingly; they need to think about color preferences and make interface design choices to keep users engaged. This child programmer puts herself in the shoes of the gamer and tries to understand how he or she would likely react when encountering a new challenge. We know, from long-standing research on cognitive development, that perspective taking is fundamental for thinking (Tjosvold & Johnson, 1978; Tudge & Rogoff, 1999; Tudge & Winterhoff, 1993; Walker, 1980). This child programmer was not asked to "think about thinking" in a vacuum. That task is very difficult, if not impossible. They had created something to think about: an interactive fractions game. Throughout the process of using LOGO to program the fraction game to teach others, the child developed "computational literacy" (DiSessa, 2001). However, perhaps most importantly, the child can become an epistemologist and further explore how knowledge is constructed, and how we learn what we learn (Turkle, 1984).

Textual and Computational Literacy

The computational project created by a child, as well as the text written by an author, both products of literacy, are independent from the creator and take on lives of their own. These artifacts can be shared, read, revised, and played with. They evoke an emotional response. Once out in the world, the artifact can be interpreted differently than the original intent of the author. The child who coded the game and the author of a text have no control over how their products will be received by others. The process of creation is iterative: problems are encountered and solved along the way. The child coder finds bugs in the program and fixes them. The author finds grammatical errors and leaps of thought. Revising and editing become major tasks in textual literacy, much like debugging in computational literacy.

In this process—starting with an original idea and ending with a shareable product (i.e., a computer game or a text)—the creative and the critical processes need each other. Papert quotes T. S. Eliot to make this point: "*The large part of the labor of an author in composing his work is critical labor; the labor of sifting, combining, constructing, expunging, correcting, testing; this frightful toil is as much critical as creative*" (Eliot, 1923 as cited in in Papert, 1987). The artifact detached from its creator becomes powerful in its own right. However, it can sometimes hide the process of its creation. As we will see in future chapters, when working with computational literacy we must move the process of programming to the forefront. Coding is the journey that takes us to making a final artifact. We are as interested in the journey, the learning process, as in the outcome.

In early childhood education, there is a strong tradition around documenting process. For example, the Reggio Emilia approach to education focuses on intensively documenting children's experiences, memories, thoughts, and ideas during their work, not just on the completed outcome (Katz & Chard, 1996). Documentation may include samples of a child's work at several different stages of completion, photographs showing work in progress, feedback written by the teacher, and even comments made by parents or other children. Documentation makes the hidden learning process transparent. It invites the revisiting of a created artifact to understand the path to its creation.

Similarly, the field of literacy studies aims to bring the hidden process of writing to the surface. Different sources are employed to reconstruct the journey that led the author to write the book and to unpack its structure and mechanics. The nascent field of computational literacy aims to understand the journey of encountering computational thinking in the process of coding or in creating a shareable project.

Back in 1987, Papert called for the development of a field of study, which he called "computer criticism," by analogy with literary criticism. He wrote: "The name does not imply that such writing would condemn computers any more than literary criticism condemns literature … The purpose of computer criticism is not to condemn but to understand, to explicate, to place in perspective" (Papert, 1987, pp. 22–30). Papert envisioned that this new discipline would help better illuminate the present role of computers and computer programming in society and, most specifically, in education.

While computer criticism is in its infancy compared with its sister discipline, the use of literacy as a model for understanding the role of coding is promising. Literacy, like coding, assumes the ability to produce an artifact detached from its creator. There is a producer with an intention, with a passion, with a desire to communicate something. Writing, like coding, is a medium for human expression. This perspective is mostly absent in current conversations that mainly describe coding and computational thinking as problem-solving processes. Expression requires problem-solving as well as a knowledge base; however, problem-solving is not the end goal. For example, to make an animation, I need programming skills. I solve problems I encounter along the way not because I love problem-solving (although I might), but because I want to express myself through an external artifact (an animation) that can be shared and interpreted by others.

The Power of Literacy

Computational literacy has historical, social, communicative, and civic commonalities with textual literacy. As more people learn to code and computer programming departs the exclusive domain of computer science and becomes central to other professions, the civic dimension of computational literacy comes into play. We are leaving the scribal age, when literacy was just for a few chosen ones, and entering the printing press era, when it was for the masses. Literacy has the power to bring about social change.

For example, the use of literacy campaigns that mobilize people and resources on a large scale is a long-established practice. H. S. Bhola traces literacy campaigns back to the Protestant Reformation in Europe in the early 1500s (Bhola, 1997). Often, these literacy campaigns supported social, economic, cultural, and political reform or transformation. In the 1970s, mass adult literacy campaigns were commonly initiated by governments following liberation wars with a revolutionary or decolonization agenda (Bhola, 1984).

For example, in the 1960s the Brazilian educator Paulo Freire was commissioned to head the countries' literacy campaign. Freire, most well known for his work on the pedagogy of the oppressed, believed education to be a political act that could not be divorced from pedagogy (Freire, 1996). Resnick and Siegel talk about how Freire recognized that writing is more than just a practical skill and how he led literacy campaigns in poor communities not simply to help people get jobs, but to help people learn that they can make and remake themselves (Resnick & Siegel, 2015). Freire championed the fact that education should allow socially, economically, or politically oppressed individuals to regain their sense of humanity, and literacy was his tool. He firmly believed that oppressed individuals must play a role in their own liberation. The first step was teaching reading and writing to all; literacy became a tool of liberation. Literacy provided power intellectually and politically.

In transitioning oral societies, such as Walter Ong described, power resided in those unique individuals or social groups who could read and write and who, later, had the monopoly over printed books. Those who are illiterate are disenfranchised. The phrase "coding as literacy" means not only teaching computer programming with the goal of preparing students for computer science degrees and careers (due to the shortage of programmers and software developers in the industry), but also giving them the intellectual tools to have a voice and to play a role in civic society. In today's world, those who can produce digital technologies will do better than those who can only consume them. Those who can innovate and problem-solve will create the democracies of tomorrow, ready to take on the challenges of a multicultural, multiethnic, multireligious, complex global world.

Coding is more than a technical skill; it is a way to achieve literacy in the twenty-first century, like reading and writing. It can change not only the way that we think about our own thinking, but also the way that we see ourselves in society and the way that we construct the legal and democratic mechanisms for running such a society. It can be used to bring about positive change. As we will see in future chapters, the PTD (Positive Technological Development) approach that I developed emphasizes the aim of teaching coding so that children can become contributors to society. Children can use the technology of coding to make a better and more just world. As educators, we must be aware of this when thinking about pedagogical approaches for teaching coding. If our teaching is limited to puzzle-like challenges, we deprive children of the most powerful impact of computational literacy: expression with their own voices.

The Technologies of Literacy

Inspired by Michel Foucault's philosophical construct of "technologies of the self," I propose that the technologies of literacy, both textual and computational, permit us to: 1) produce and transform artifacts; 2) use sign systems associated with meanings; 3) determine conduct of individuals; and 4) transform our own selves through thoughts (Foucault, Martin, Gutman, & Hutton, 1988). These four elements inform my construct of "coding as literacy." Literacy needs technologies. These technologies allow actions and thinking. Within this definition, technologies allow the transformation of thinking into actions: reading, writing, coding. The technologies of reading and writing vary, and different tools can be used; for example, the printing press supports the mass communication of ideas, while handwritten scrolls assign exclusivity. The pen enables creative expression, but is not great for editing our writing. The crayon is useful when learning how to make our first letter traces, but not for crafting long essays. The tools for coding also vary and there are myriad programming languages supported by different technical platforms.

How do we choose the best tools to support both textual and computational literacy? How do we design new ones that are developmentally appropriate? Early childhood researchers have spent decades understanding the best tools for supporting children's writing (Dyson, 1982; Graham,

McKeown, Kiuhara, & Harris, 2012; Graham & Perin, 2007; Graves, 1994; Taylor, 1983). Educators carefully choose the best writing tools for their young students and make recommendations to parents. In the same spirit, the nascent field of early childhood technology must make informed choices regarding developmentally appropriate programming languages and platforms for children.

It is not only the responsibility of professionals in software engineering to design the tools for computational literacy. Those of us with an understanding of learning and child development theories must work together with them. This interdisciplinary endeavor can only be possible if we learn to speak each other's languages and encounter each other's ideas. I devoted two decades of my life to this, hoping to cultivate the new generation of scholars and practitioners who can be at ease in both worlds. For example, my DevTech research group at Tufts includes students from varied disciplines, such as cognitive science, education, child development, mechanical engineering, human factors, computer science, and education, to name just a few.

In Part IV of the book, I will present two programming languages that my DevTech group has designed and developed over the years with a wonderful team of collaborators: ScratchJr and KIBO robotics. I will also propose design principles for those who are interested in being part of the conversation of what is needed, from a child development and learning perspective, when creating new languages. It is my vision that as the field matures, many different programming languages specifically designed for young children will become available. Each of them will display unique interfaces to support and promote new ways of expression. For now, the next chapter will explore what makes a programming language a unique technology for computational literacy.

References

Allamanis, M., Barr, E. T., Devanbu, P., & Sutton, C. (2018). A survey of machine learning for big code and naturalness. *ACM Computing Surveys (CSUR), 51*(4), 1–37.

Bers, M. U. (2018, April). Coding, playgrounds and literacy in early childhood education: The development of KIBO robotics and ScratchJr.

In *2018 IEEE Global Engineering Education Conference (EDUCON)* (pp. 2094–2102). IEEE.

Bers, M. U. (2019a). Coding as another language: A pedagogical approach for teaching computer science in early childhood. *Journal of Computers in Education, 6*(4), 499–528.

Bers, M. U. (2019b). Coding as another language: Why computer science in early childhood should not be STEM. In C. Donohue (Ed.), *Exploring key issues in early childhood and technology* (pp. 63–70). New York: Routledge.

Bhola, H. S. (1984). *Campaigning for literacy: Eight national experiences of the twentieth century, with a memorandum to decision makers.* Paris: UNESCO.

Bhola, H. S. (1997). What happened to the mass campaigns on their way to the twenty-first century? *NORRAG, Norrag News, 21,* August 1997, 27–29. Retrieved from http://norrag.t3dev1.crossagency.ch/en/publications/norragnews/onlineversion/thefifthinternationalconferenceonadulteducation/detail/whathappenedtothemasscampaignsontheirwaytothetwentyfirstcentury.html (Accessed 07 March 2014).

Bialystok, E. (1991). Letters, sounds, and symbols: Changes in children's understanding of written language. *Applied Psycholinguistics, 12*(1), 75–89.

Brandt, D. (2011). *Literacy as involvement: The acts of writers, readers, and texts.* Carbondale, Illinois: SIU Press.

Bright: What's new in education. Retrieved June 29, 2017, from https://brightreads.com/a-different-approach-to-coding-d679b06d83a

Dalbey, J., & Linn, M. C. (1985). The demands and requirements of computer programming: A literature review. *Journal of Educational Computing Research, 1*(3), 253–274.

Dehaene, S., Pegado, F., Braga, L. W., Ventura, P., Nunes Filho, G., Jobert, A., Dehaene-Lambertz, G., Kolinsky, R., Morais, J., & Cohen, L. (2010). How learning to read changes the cortical networks for vision and language. *Science, 330*(6009), 1359–1364.

DiSessa, A. A. (2001). *Changing minds: Computers, learning, and literacy.* Cambridge, MA: MIT Press.

Dyson, A. H. (1982). Reading, writing, and language: Young children solving the written language puzzle. *Language Arts, 59*(8), 829–839.

Elkins, J. (Ed.). (2009). *Visual literacy.* New York and Abongdon, Oxon: Routledge.

Fakhoury, S. (2018, October). Moving towards objective measures of program comprehension. In *Proceedings of the 2018 26th ACM Joint Meeting on European Software Engineering Conference and Symposium on the Foundations of Software Engineering* (pp. 936–939).

Fedorenko, E., Ivanova, A., Dhamala, R., & Bers, M. U. (2019). The language of programming: A cognitive perspective. *Trends in Cognitive Sciences, 23*(7), 525–528.

Floyd, B., Santander, T., & Weimer, W. (2017, May). Decoding the representation of code in the brain: An fMRI study of code review and expertise. In *2017 IEEE/ACM 39th International Conference on Software Engineering (ICSE)* (pp. 175–186).

Foucault, M., Martin, L. H., Gutman, H., & Hutton, P. H. (1988). *Technologies of the self: A seminar with Michel Foucault.* Amherst, MA: University of Massachusetts Press.

Fox, B. J., & Saracho, O. N. (1990). Emergent writing: Young children solving the written language puzzle. *Early Child Development and Care, 56*(1), 81–90.

Freire, P. (1996). *Pedagogy of the oppressed (revised).* New York, NY: Continuum.

Graham, S., McKeown, D., Kiuhara, S., & Harris, K. R. (2012). A meta-analysis of writing instruction for students in the elementary grades. *Journal of Educational Psychology, 104*(4), 879.

Graham, S., & Perin, D. (2007). Writing next: Effective strategies to improve writing of adolescents in middle and high schools. *A report to Carnegie Corporation of New York.* Washington, DC: Alliance for Excellent Education.

Graves, D. H. (1994). *A fresh look at writing.* 361 Hanover St., Portsmouth, NH 03801-3912: Heinemann. (ISBN0435088246, $20).

Hirsch, E. D., Kett, J. F., & Trefil, J. S. (2002). *The new dictionary of cultural literacy.* New York, NY: Houghton Mifflin Harcourt.

Ivanova, A., Srikant, S., Sueoka, Y., Kean, H., Dhamala, R., O'Reilly, U. M., Bers, M. U., & Fedorenko, E. (2019, October). The neural basis of program comprehension. *Poster session presented at the Society for Neuroscience 2019*, Chicago, IL.

Katz, L. G., & Chard, S. C. (1996). The contribution of documentation to the quality of early childhood education. *ERIC Digest*. Champaign, IL: ERIC Clearinghouse on Elementary and Early Childhood Education. ED 393 608.

Kramsch, C. (2006). From communicative competence to symbolic competence. *The Modern Language Journal, 90*(2), 249–252.

Martin, A. (2006). Literacies for the digital age: Preview of Part 1. In A. Martin and D. Madiga (Eds.), *Digital literacies for learning* (pp. 3–25). London: Facet.

Montgomery, D. E. (1997). Wittgenstein's private language argument and children's understanding of the mind. *Developmental Review, 17*(3), 291–320.

Norman, K. L. (2017). *Cyberpsychology: An introduction to human-computer interaction*. Cambridge: Cambridge University Press.

Nutbeam, D. (2008). The evolving concept of health literacy. *Social Science & Medicine, 67*(12), 2072–2078.

Ong, W. (1982). *Orality and literacy: The technologizing of the word*. London: Methuen.

Ong, W. (1986). Writing is a technology that restructures thought. In G. Baumann (Ed.), *The written word: Literacy in transition* (pp. 23–50). Oxford: Clarendon Press; New York: Oxford University Press.

Papert, S. (1980). *Mindstorms: Children, computers, and powerful ideas*. New York: Basic Books, Inc.

Papert, S. (1987). Computer criticism vs. technocentric thinking. *Educational Researcher, 16*(1), 22–30.

Papert, S. (2005). You can't think about thinking without thinking about thinking about something. *Contemporary Issues in Technology and Teacher Education, 5*(3–4), 366–367.

Pearson, P. D. (2004). The reading wars. *Educational Policy, 18*(1), 216–252.

Peitek, N., Siegmund, J., Parnin, C., Apel, S., Hofmeister, J. C., & Brechmann, A. (2018, October). Simultaneous measurement of program comprehension with fMRI and eye tracking: A case study. In *Proceedings of the 12th ACM/IEEE International Symposium on Empirical Software Engineering and Measurement* (pp. 1–10).

Perlis, A. J. (1962). The computer in the university. In M. Greenberger (Ed.), *Computers and the world of the future* (pp. 180–219). Cambridge, MA: MIT Press.

Puranik, C. S., & Lonigan, C. J. (2011). From scribbles to scrabble: Preschool children's developing knowledge of written language. *Reading and Writing, 24*(5), 567–589.

Resnick, M., & Siegel, D. (2015). A different approach to coding. *International Journal of People-Oriented Programming, 4*(1), 1–4.

Siegmund, J., Kästner, C., Apel, S., Parnin, C., Bethmann, A., Leich, T., Saake, G., & Brechmann, A. (2014, May). Understanding source code with functional magnetic resonance imaging. In *Proceedings of the 36th International Conference on Software Engineering* (pp. 378–389).

Smith, M. (1969). The reading problem. *The American Scholar*, 431–440.

Taylor, D. (1983). *Family literacy: Young children learning to read and write*. 70 Court St.. Portsmouth, NH 03801: Heinemann Educational Books Inc.

Tjosvold, D., & Johnson, D. W. (1978). Controversy within a cooperative or competitive context and cognitive perspective taking. *Contemporary Educational Psychology, 3*(4), 376–386.

Tolchinsky, L. (2003). *The cradle of culture and what children know about writing and numbers before being*. New York, NY: Psychology Press.

Tudge, J., & Rogoff, B. (1999). Peer influences on cognitive development: Piagetian and Vygotskian perspectives. *Lev Vygotsky: Critical Assessments, 3*, 32–56.

Tudge, J. R., & Winterhoff, P. A. (1993). Vygotsky, Piaget, and Bandura: Perspectives on the relations between the social world and cognitive development. *Human Development, 36*(2), 61–81.

Turkle, S. (1984). *The second self: Computers and the human spirit*. New York, NY: Simon and Schuster.

Van Dyke, C. (1987). Taking "computer literacy" literally. *Communications of the ACM, 30*(5), 366–374.

Vee, A. (2013). Understanding computer programming as a literacy. *Literacy in Composition Studies, 1*(2), 42–64.

Vee, A. (2017). *Coding literacy: How computer programming is changing writing.* Cambridge, Massachusetts: MIT Press.

Vygotsky, L. (1978). *Mind in society: The development of higher psychological processes.* Cambridge, MA: Harvard University Press.

Walker, L. J. (1980). Cognitive and perspective taking prerequisites for moral development. *Child Development, 51*(1), 131–139.

Warnick, B. (2001). *Critical literacy in a digital era: Technology, rhetoric, and the public interest.* New York and Abingdon, Oxon: Routledge.

Weintrop, D., & Wilensky, U. (2017). How block-based languages support novices. *Journal of Visual Languages and Sentient Systems, 3*, 92–100.

Wittgenstein, L. (2009). *Philosophical investigations.* Chichester West Sussex: John Wiley & Sons. (Original work published in 1953) .

Wolf, M. (2007). *Proust and the squid: The story and science of the reading brain.* New York, NY: HarperCollins.

Wolf, M. (2018). *Reader, come home: The reading brain in a digital world.* New York, NY: HarperCollins.

5 | Coding Stages

What happens in the head of a child who is coding? What happens in the head of a child who is reading and writing? How are the processes of learning these skills similar or different? What are the learning progressions from beginner to expert? To develop written language, we first need spoken language. Orality comes before literacy. Perhaps manipulating technology comes before coding? What can the field of computational literacy learn from the rich history of textual literacy to support educational interventions?

Jerome Bruner was an American psychologist and scholar who made significant contributions to cognitive psychology and educational theory. When looking at language development, Bruner offered a social interactionist perspective (Bruner, 1975, 1985). In his approach, the social and interpersonal nature of language was emphasized, in sharp contrast with Noam Chomsky's nativist account of language acquisition (Chomsky, 1976). Inspired by Lev Vygotsky (1978), the Russian theoretician of sociocultural development, Bruner proposed that social interaction plays a fundamental role in the development of cognition in general, and of language in particular. Children learn language to communicate, and, in the process, they learn the linguistic code, including its syntax and grammar. Children are "learning about" and "using" language at the same time. It is difficult to identify which comes first. Of course, children don't do it alone; they have the aid (or scaffold) of peers, adults, games, and songs. In the same spirit, in the "coding as a playground" approach I propose, children learn to code and use the code in their own projects at the same time. Fluency develops with use.

To Bruner, the desired outcomes of learning were not just the language concepts and categories, nor the mastery of problem-solving procedures invented previously by the culture through grammatical and syntactic rules, but the ability of children to invent these things for themselves and apply what they have learned to different contexts. For example, using written language to write an invitation or a book, or using coding to make an animation or a geometrical shape. The goal of teaching coding is not syntactic mastery of a programming language, but the ability to create one's own meaningful and unique project. The act of coding may facilitate computational thinking, but it doesn't always: we are all familiar with examples in which children are asked to copy code from the blackboard and memorize syntactic rules without engaging in thinking. As a literacy, coding involves doing, creating, and making, not just thinking. It involves the production of an external, shareable artifact.

In early childhood, coding assumes the understanding that there is a language that represents actions (computational instructions) and that the language can be used to create projects by combining the computational instructions in new ways. As children grow and learn more sophisticated programming languages, coding also involves playing with grammatical rules and discovering new syntax. Often, when coding "goes to school," it is in the form of challenges or logical puzzles to solve. Teachers assign the problems and students need to solve them. Such are most experiences for students who have been exposed to traditional computer science classes. While this might work well for children who are intrinsically motivated, the lack of opportunities for self-expression unfortunately turns many children off. My approach is different: the goal of coding is expression, not problem-solving. Problem-solving differs from expression. We have something to say, a project to show, an idea to explore, and we do it through making a personally meaningful project to share with others and solving problems we encounter along the way.

Programming languages that are developmentally appropriate for young children must support children's expression. Isn't the developmental task of the young child to start finding his or her own voice in the world? For example, a child can use ScratchJr to create an animated birthday card for her dad or program KIBO to dance to the beat of her favorite song. In the process, the child is learning powerful concepts and skills from computer science, and doing a lot of problem-solving. Although problem-solving is not the only goal of coding in early childhood, it is a powerful mechanism that allows children to express themselves and communicate.

Mitchel Resnick and David Siegel, when discussing the creation of the Scratch Foundation in 2013 to promote a very different approach to coding, wrote (Resnick & Siegel, 2015):

> For us, coding is not a set of technical skills but a new type of literacy and personal expression, valuable for everyone, much like learning to write. We see coding as a new way for people to organize, express, and share their ideas … In many introductory coding activities, students are asked to program the movements of a virtual character navigating through a set of obstacles toward a goal. This approach can help students learn some basic coding concepts, but it doesn't allow them to express themselves creatively—or develop a long-term engagement with coding. It's like offering a writing class that teaches only grammar and punctuation without providing students a chance to write their own stories.
>
> (Resnick & Siegel, 2015, para. 3–12)

Again, coding is connected to literacy and can be a way to express ourselves. Back in 1987, Seymour Papert promoted the idea of the computer as a medium for human expression. "If it has not yet had its Shakespeares, its Michelangelos or its Einsteins, it will," he promised (Papert, 1987, p. 23). Now, almost 20 years later, we can easily identify these Shakespeares, Michelangelos, and Einsteins. They are the creators of innovative programming languages and programmers who became successful entrepreneurs, philanthropists, and business people because they truly understood the societal power of computation.

Amy is a bright kindergartener. She is programming her KIBO to make the lion dance. She is learning about China and she wants her KIBO dressed up as a lion to make the popular lion dance. She starts by putting together a sequence of blue Motion blocks. Shake, forward, backward, shake. She repeats this sequence four times and then she has an idea. "Marina, Marina" she calls out to me. "Is there a block called 'Lion dance' that does those four steps? That way I can just use that one and repeat that block four times. That will save lot of blocks." Although Amy doesn't know it, she is asking about a computational concept called functions. Unfortunately, there is no such block for KIBO. Amy thinks for some time and, with a happy face and a sense of confidence, tells me

I will just create a new block. I will call it "lion dance" and I will make it do those four steps. I will need to find a new barcode for it. Maybe I can get one from the groceries my mom gets at the supermarket.

Although the process of inventing a new programming block for KIBO is a little bit more complicated than that, Amy, at only 5 years old, got the idea of how new "actions" and new "language"could be created.

Scholars on emergent literacy have found that children enter school with a great deal of skill and knowledge about reading and writing, although perhaps not in a formal or conventional way (e.g., Ferreiro & Teberosky, 1982; Sulzby, 1989; Sulzby & Teale, 1991; Whitehurst & Lonigan, 2001). This early knowledge lays the foundation for later literacy success, and this insight is applicable when thinking about coding. Even though there is no "orality" period, children are immersed in an interactive technologically rich world before they are even aware of what programming is, and they frequently encounter powerful ideas, such as sequencing, cause and effect, and correspondence, that are foundational for coding.

Just as children do not begin to talk by speaking in complex utterances, or decode by reading a novel (Chall, 1983), children do not begin writing in complete sentences but start by scribbling (Ferreiro & Teberosky, 1982; Puranik & Lonigan, 2011). Reading and writing are intimately related. Although research on writing has been scarce compared to that on reading, literacy researchers have identified a learning progression, or stages that can happen through instruction. The same applies to coding. Children do not start by programming complex algorithms and using nested control structures. They begin with simple sequencing (Guzdial & Morrison, 2016; Jenkins, 2002; Lockwood & Mooney, 2018) and a well-developed curriculum, such as CAL (Coding as Another Language) which will be introduced in the next chapter, can help them move through more sophisticated stages (Hassenfeld & Bers, 2019).

In my work, I have identified six coding stages based on behavioral observations and data collection from over two decades of research with young children (aged 4 to 7) who have been learning to code in different settings, using a variety of curricula, with our block-based programming languages, ScratchJr and KIBO (Bers, 2019a). The coding stages describe a child's developmental progression with coding. Sometimes, developmental progressions are seen as sequential, orderly, and cumulative. However, development is much more individualistic, directional yet not fully linear, fluid, and interconnected. After decades of observing young children coding, my DevTech research group developed a model for coding stages, which are not fixed nor fully linear, but have some hierarchy, allowing children to have varying levels of progress in different stages at the same time (see Figure 5.1). These stages help us to have a quantifiable way of measuring the shape of a child's growth in coding skills. These stages are loosely defined in order to allow adaptability across different programming languages (see Table 5.1).

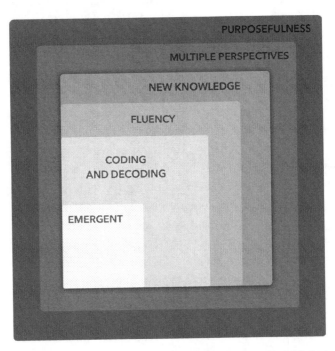

Figure 5.1 Visual representation of the six coding stages. From light to dark, the color gradient shows a typical child's directional progression with coding; with the emergent, coding and decoding, fluency, and new knowledge stages being linear due to the syntactical and grammatical knowledge being acquired. However, the multiple perspectives and purposefulness stages break this linear progression, as the progression of these stages can occur in a more fluid manner.

Table 5.1 The six coding stages that measure a child's developmental progression with coding. The stage in the left-hand column is defined in the center column, and examples of stage-appropriate child behaviors are given in the right-hand column

Coding Stage	Concepts	Indicators
1. Emergent	Child recognizes that technologies are human-engineered, understands the concept of symbolization and representation, and has familiarized themself with the interface; but is only beginning to explore the programming language (only knows the meaning of some symbols).	• Child knows how to turn the tool on and off and is able to correctly interact with the interface. • Child knows that a human programmer wrote the command or program—does not treat the tool as an autonomous entity. • Child knows that a command represents a behavior. • Child knows that a basic control structure exists.
2. Coding and Decoding	Child understands that sequencing matters and that the order in which commands are put together generates different behaviors. They have learned a limited set of symbols and grammar rules of the programming language and have begun to identify and fix grammatical errors in the code. The most growth can be seen at this stage.	• Child can correctly create simple programs with simple cause and effect commands. • Child engages in goal-oriented command exploration. • Child performs simple debugging through trial and error. • Child can identify and fix grammatical errors in the code.
3. Fluency	Child has mastered the syntax of the programming language. Child understands how to distinguish and fix logical errors in the code (i.e., a program runs, but it doesn't do what is expected).	• Child is personally motivated to create complex programs using control structures. • Child can correctly create complex programs using control structures. • Child is beginning to be strategic with how they debug. • Child can distinguish and fix logical errors in the code.

(Continued)

Table 5.1 (Continued)

Coding Stage	Concepts	Indicators
4. New Knowledge	Child understands how to combine multiple control structures and create nested programs that achieve complex sequencing.	• Child engages in more goal-oriented logical exploration with their programs. • Child is personally motivated to create nested programs to achieve complex sequencing. • Child can correctly create nested programs to achieve complex sequencing. • Child is strategic with how they debug.
5. Multiple Perspectives	Child understands how to create programs that involve complex user or tool interactions.	• Child can create programs that involve user's input. • Child can create multiple programs that interact with one another. • Child is beginning to analyze, synthesize, and translate abstract concepts into code. • Child can debug multiple control structures.
6. Purposefulness	Child understands how to analyze, synthesize, and translate abstract concepts into code. Child is coding skillfully for their needs and purpose.	• Child is personally motivated to create complex programs. • Child can analyze, synthesize, and translate abstract concepts into code. • After translating abstract concepts into code, child can correctly translate their code back into their abstract concepts. • Child is able to identify multiple ways to translate abstract concepts into code.

The characterization of coding stages proposed here focuses only on early childhood, spanning the 4 to 7 years age range (Bers, 2019a, 2019b), and has similarities with the literacy coding stages proposed by Chall (1983). Although the progression from one coding stage to the next is independent of age, the developmental level of the child informs how quickly the child can progress through the stages by being exposed to an intentional curriculum, such as CAL, which will be described in the next chapter, designed to both introduce concepts such as loops and conditionals, and also to support personal expression and creativity.

Given that young children utilize introductory programming languages, such as ScratchJr ot KIBO, it is possible to reach the more complex stages (multiple perspectives and purposefulness) with sufficient instruction and learning time, as well as to begin exploring powerful ideas from the discipline of computer science such as algorithms, modularization, representation, control structures, the design process, debugging, software, and hardware (Bers, 2008, 2019a, 2019b).

In summary, a child's pathway from the emergent to the purposefulness coding stage is not fully linear. Some children might go back and forth between stages as they learn new concepts and skills, and some might be fluent with certain powerful ideas and programming concepts, but not others. Some may master fluency in coding and decoding, but might not be able to make purposeful projects. But, throughout all stages, the curriculum invites the child to use her developing coding knowledge to create an expressive project and to share it with others. The next chapter will introduce the CAL curriculum, explicitly designed to help children transition through these stages.

References

Bers, M. U. (2008). *Blocks to robots learning with technology in the early childhood classroom.* New York, NY: Teachers College Press.

Bers, M. U. (2019a). Coding as another language: A pedagogical approach for teaching computer science in early childhood. *Journal of Computers in Education, 6*(4), 499–528.

Bers, M. U. (2019b). Coding as another language. In C. Donohue (Ed.), *Exploring key issues in early childhood and technology: Evolving perspectives and innovative approaches* (pp. 63–70). New York, NY: Routledge.

Bruner, J. S. (1975). The ontogenesis of speech acts. *Journal of Child Language, 2*, 1–19.

Bruner, J. S. (1985). *Child's talk.* Cambridge: Cambridge University Press.

Chall, J. S. (1983). Literacy: Trends and explanations. *Educational Researcher, 12*(9), 3–8.

Chomsky, N. (1976). On the biological basis of language capacities. In R. Rieber (Ed.), *The neuropsychology of language: Essays in honor of Eric Lenneberg* (pp. 1–24). New York, NY: Plenum Press.

Ferreiro, E., & Teberosky, A. (1982). *Literacy before schooling.* Portsmouth, NH: Heinemann Educational Books, Inc.

Guzdial, M., & Morrison, B. (2016). Growing computer science education into a STEM education discipline. *Communications of the ACM, 59*(11), 31–33.

Hassenfeld, Z. R., & Bers, M. U. (2019). When we teach programming languages as literacy. (Blog post).

Jenkins, T. (2002, August). On the difficulty of learning to program. In *Proceedings of the 3rd Annual Conference of the LTSN Centre for Information and Computer Sciences* (Vol. 4, No. 2002, pp. 53–58).

Lockwood, J., & Mooney, A. (2018). Developing a computational thinking test using bebras problems. In *CC-TEL 2018 and TACKLE 2018 Workshops*, 3 September 2018. Leeds.

Papert, S. (1987). Computer criticism vs. technocentric thinking. *Educational Researcher, 16*(1), 22–30.

Puranik, C. S., & Lonigan, C. J. (2011). From scribbles to scrabble: Preschool children's developing knowledge of written language. *Reading and Writing, 24*(5), 567–589.

Resnick, M., & Siegel, D. (2015, November 10). A different approach to coding: How kids are making and remaking themselves from scratch. *Bright/Medium.* Retrieved from https://brightthemag.com/a-different-approach-to-coding-d679b06d83a

Sulzby, E. (1989). Assessment of writing and of children's language while writing. In L. Morrow & J. Smith (Eds.), *The role of assessment and measurement in early literacy instruction* (pp. 83–109). Englewood Cliffs, NJ: Prentice-Hall.

Sulzby, E., & Teale, W. (1991). Emergent literacy. *Handbook of Reading Research, 2,* 727–757.

Vygotsky, L.S. (1978). *Mind in society: The development of higher psychological processes.* London: Harvard University Press.

Whitehurst, G. J., & Lonigan, C. J. (2001). Emergent literacy: Development from prereaders to readers. *Handbook of Early Literacy Research, 1,* 11–29.

6 | A Pedagogical Approach

Coding as Another Language, CAL for short, is the name I gave to our curriculum explicitly designed to highlight the idea of "coding as a literacy." In our teaching, we understand programming languages as symbolic systems for expression. In the early childhood classroom, children are already learning about other symbolic systems. They learn about numbers and the alphabet. They learn that sequence and order matters when putting together those symbols. The word TAC is not the same as CAT. They also learn the rules for manipulating those symbols and creating new meaning. 1+1=2 but 1−1=0. By teaching coding as a symbolic system, we make a bridge between already established curricular areas, such as literacy and math, and new ones, such as computer science.

The CAL curriculum is designed for children aged 4 to 7 years old to learn coding using either KIBO robotics or ScratchJr in both formal and informal learning settings. It supports the transition through the six coding stages described in the previous chapter, by exposing children to developmentally appropriate powerful ideas of computer science as well as to principles of literacy. Guided by the Positive Technological Development (PTD) framework, which I will describe in Chapter 10, the curriculum targets the whole child by proposing activities that engage children in cognitive, socialemotional, and moral development. The learning experiences using computer programming offer opportunities for children to participate in six positive behaviors (the six Cs of PTD): collaboration, communication, community building, content creation, creativity, and choices of conduct.

The CAL curriculum is organized into units, all centered around a children's book, and are designed to engage emergent readers or early readers in expressive programming using the KIBO robotics kit or the tablet-based ScratchJr application. The curricular units, regardless of the technology used, follow a similar structure and include time spent working with coding and literacy as well as an emphasis on offscreen activities involving social interactions, creativity, and movement. Each curriculum contains five to seven lessons organized around powerful ideas of computer science, which will be explored in Chapter 8, as well as a section detailing what prior knowledge children should have, a list of all technology and non-technology materials required, vocabulary explored in the lesson, individual and group activities such as warm-up games to playfully introduce or reinforce concepts, design challenges to solidify skills, free explorations to allow students to tinker and expand their skills, expressive explorations to promote creativity, and writing activities and technology circles to share and reflect on activities. Each curriculum culminates with a final project focused on a given theme that children work on over the course of multiple sessions. This open-ended project is designed to be shared with family and friends and to allow students with varying academic abilities to succeed. The project can also be easily scaled to meet the needs of gifted or special education inclusion students. In addition, the design activities are carefully chosen to be of interest to girls and minority students, as these groups are still greatly underrepresented in engineering and technology fields, and are informed by research that identified ways to make the format and content of activities more attractive to girls and marginalized populations.

CAL is based on the following principles:

a. Coding can be a playground experience.

b. Strategies used in literacy education can be helpful for teaching children how to code.

c. Coding projects can provide opportunities for children's sensemaking and expression.

d. Problem-solving can serve as a means toward self-expression and communication.

e. Coding activities can engage children in thinking about powerful ideas from computer science, as well as from other domains, such as literacy.

Each unit contains a minimum of 12 1-hour lessons that are centered on a storybook such as *Where the Wild Things Are* by Maurice Sendak and *There Was an Old Lady Who Swallowed a Fly* by Simms Taback. For example, children might program a robot to do a Wild Rumpus dance, recalling special moments from the book they read, or they might write and animate their own alternative story endings in ScratchJr.

Simon, a second grade student in southeastern Virginia, participated in a 12-hour robotics-based curriculum with the CAL (Coding as Language) approach (Bers, 2019). Simon is a "PALS (Phonological Awareness Literacy Screening)-identified" literacy student who needs remedial literacy instruction. Despite this, his writing in his design journal to document his programming process was clear, engaging, and sophisticated (including compound sentences and narrative-style stories)—and so were the programs he wrote for the KIBO robot (including specific sequences of actions to depict his ideas). Simon composed an alternative ending to *Where the Wild Things Are* that was articulate and creative. He went on in the curriculum to compose "Simon's Special Wild Rumpus" dance, and wrote about how he and the monsters went in a rocketship and played videogames (two of his favorite things) and later programmed the same narrative with KIBO. Simon, in this new learning context, asserted a very different student identity. He was far from remedial. As a composer of program and prose, he was exceptional.

Simon, while participating in the CAL–KIBO curriculum, not only scored highly in the programming language assessment, evidencing mastery, but his writing embedded in the curriculum was also strong. There are two hypotheses for why this might be the case. First, taking literacy outside of the formal literacy block may have allowed Simon to revisit reading and writing anew, free of his remedial literacy identity (McDermott, 1996; Steele, 2003). Second, and more significantly, learning an introductory programming language through the CAL approach may have reinforced essential concepts in literacy for Simon. For example, Simon had the chance to juxtapose algorithms in programming with sequencing and story structure in literacy. It seems that the practice of scanning syntactically correct and incorrect sequences of KIBO blocks allowed Simon to explore the foundational concept of algorithms (sequencing) and apply it in other areas of his writing. Simon's case highlights the importance of allowing literacy skills and practices to spill across disciplinary lines. With the media format of robotic code, Simon was able to find new motivation to read, write, and compose—skills that he had always assumed were too advanced for him before using KIBO.

Sarah is a second grade student in a school outside of Boston, Massachusetts. She currently tests at a second grade level in literacy, and is an eager and excited novice programmer in ScratchJr. Although she knows how to revise written work, Sarah rarely revises her own writing. When she receives suggestions in writing conferences from her teacher and classmates, she addresses their questions with single-sentence additions to her narrative—in other words, the bare minimum. If something really does not make sense, she simply crosses it out and starts again. As Sarah explains to Dr. Ziva Hassenfeld, a postdoctoral researcher at my DevTech research group who is researching composition in Sarah's classroom, "I don't like writing if it's too much to write. I mean I like thinking of stories but it's annoying when I have to write it" (Hassenfeld & Bers, 2020). However, when Sarah writes her ScratchJr code, she revises in a very different way. During many programming sessions with Dr. Hassenfeld, Sarah creates a programming project that is loosely based on a writing composition that she had made earlier in the school year. In Sarah's project, she programmes two characters, fox and turtle, to have a conversation and play a game of tag.

At some point, while composing, Sarah tests her program and discovers several problems, or *bugs*. Her first problem is that the dialogue in her program does not work. She has mixed up the messaging blocks in ScratchJr. Sarah debugs this part of her program quickly by tapping the message block to change its color. Her second problem is that the voice recorder cannot make a single recording that fits what she wants to record—turtle counting to 60 during the game of tag (Sarah had recorded herself as turtle, counting, "1, 2, 3 …," and put the recording into her program). She debugs this issue by creating three different voice recordings to get her entire recording of turtle counting to 60 in the project. Finally, she encounters a third problem in her program's sequence. Sarah wrote her program in such a way that the characters count to 60 and move around the screen playing tag all at the same time. The sequence is wrong. She rewrites her program using orange "Wait" blocks to ensure that the game of tag begins *after* turtle finishes counting, and not before. Although Sarah is reticent to revise her written composition, often choosing instead to erase everything and start over, she fluently debugs her ScratchJr project with ease, and even enthusiasm.

Both of these vignettes, Simon working on his Wild Rumpus with KIBO and Sarah programming her ScratchJr conversation, are examples of how the CAL curriculum integrates coding with literacy. A conceptualization of programming that is not solely STEM-based may help combat the stigma associated with STEM disciplines and attract a wider range of children to computer science. In addition, it might help promote a predisposition to literacy. It is my strong belive that decades of scholarly work and teaching practices on language development and reading and writing instruction can provide new pathways that inform the early teaching of computer science.

We began the process for developing the CAL integrated curriculum by looking at academic frameworks for both literacy and computer science. For literacy, we chose the Common Core literacy standards (National Governors Association Center for Best Practices & Council of Chief State School Officers, 2010) and for computer science we chose the K-12 CS frameworks (K-12 Computer Science Framework Steering Committee, 2016). This framework resulted from a collaboration between the Association for Computing Machinery (ACM), the Computer Science Teachers Association (CSTA), Code.org, the Cyber Innovation Center (CIC), the National Math and Science Initiative (NMSI), more than 100 advisors within the computing community (i.e., higher education faculty, researchers, K-12 teachers, etc.), several states and large school districts, technology companies, and other organizations. This major effort allowed the development of conceptual guidelines for states and districts creating a K-12 pathway in computer science and computational thinking.

In addition, we chose to look at the curriculum for both literacies in two different states: the MA standards in literacy and digital literacy and STEM (Massachusetts Department of Elementary and Secondary Education, 2016, 2017), where Tufts University is located, and the Virginia standards (Virginia Department of Education, 2019), the first state to mandate the teaching of computer science starting in kindergarten in the U.S. Although most states share similar approaches in the early grades, we are doing lots of work with Virginia and therefore it is important to us to make sure our CAL curriculum is well aligned with Virginia state curriculum standards.

By analyzing the standards, we identified powerful ideas that were transversal and that were found in all of the documents that we looked at. The term "powerful idea" refers to a central concept or skill within a discipline that is simultaneously personally useful, inherently interconnected with other disciplines, and has roots in intuitive knowledge that a child has internalized over a long period of time (Papert, 1980). The powerful ideas from computer science addressed in the CAL curriculum include: algorithms, modularity, control structures, representation, hardware/software, design process, and debugging. The powerful ideas from literacy that are placed in conversation with these powerful ideas from computer science are: the writing process, recalling, summarizing and sequencing, using illustrative and descriptive language, recognizing literary devices such as repetition and foreshadowing, and using reading strategies such as predicting, summarizing, and evaluating. Table 6.1 shows more information.

Ms. Murray is a first grade teacher and has been teaching for eight years. She attends a one-day professional development training led by DevTech doctoral students Emily Relkin and Madhu Govind on KIBO and the CAL curriculum. Ms. Murray was nervous at first, but after playing

Table 6.1 The powerful ideas from computer science and literacy that are placed in conversation in the CAL curriculum. The computer science powerful ideas are in the left-hand column, literacy powerful ideas are in the center column, and explanations of how these ideas are connected are in the right-hand column

Powerful Ideas from Computer Science	Powerful Ideas from Literacy	Connecting the Powerful Ideas
Algorithms—series of ordered steps taken in a sequence to solve a problem or achieve an end goal	Sequencing and Summarizing—retelling a story or activity in a logical, step-by-step way	Both emphasize that order matters, and that complex tasks or activities can be broken down into step-by-step instructions in a logical and organized fashion.
Modularity—breaking down tasks or procedures into simpler, manageable units that can be combined to create a more complex process	Phonological Awareness—ability to identify and manipulate sounds at the sentence/word/syllable/phoneme (sound) level Summarizing/Sequencing—identifying the small steps or actions needed to create a larger story or process	Both involve the concept of decomposition, or breaking down a complex task into smaller tasks.

(Continued)

Table 6.1 (Continued)

Powerful Ideas from Computer Science	Powerful Ideas from Literacy	Connecting the Powerful Ideas
Control Structures—determine how a set of instructions are followed or executed within a program (e.g., repeat loops, conditional statements, events)	**Literary Devices—**techniques that writers use for a special or intended purpose (e.g., repetition, patterns) **Making Inferences—**reaching a conclusion about something using prior information	Both involve the use of more advanced techniques to communicate a set of ideas. Repetition reinforces the concept of patterns, conditionals reinforce the concept of branching logic (e.g., if X happens, then Y will happen), and events reinforce the concept of cause and effect.
Representation—the idea that concepts can be represented using symbols (e.g., programming instructions represent specific commands or actions)	**Alphabetic Understanding and Letter-Sound Correspondence—**words are composed of letters that represent sounds	Both involve the use of symbols that have different attributes (color, shape, sound, etc.) in order to represent something else.
Hardware and Software—hardware refers to the physical parts of a computing system that requires software, or instructions, in order to run	**Tools of Communication and Language—**recognizing there are a variety of ways to express one's ideas through language (e.g., oral, written, typed)	Both emphasize the process of communicating abstract thoughts through tangible means. Just like hardware and software work together as a system to accomplish tasks, the expression of thoughts and ideas through language requires a medium for communicating to the outside world, such as through spoken or written/typed word.

Design Process—the series of steps that engineers and designers use to create solutions to problems	Writing Process—the series of steps that writers use to express themselves through written communication	Both are creative processes that involve imagining, planning, creating, revising, and sharing. The processes are iterative and cyclic; there is no official starting or ending point.
Debugging—identifying problems and troubleshooting errors in order to achieve a particular outcome	Editing and Audience Awareness—revising our writing in order to effectively communicate to an intended reader	Both involve systematic analysis, testing, and evaluation to improve communication to the intended audience (computer or person). Whenever miscommunication occurs, the programmer or writer uses a variety of strategies to solve the problem.

hands-on with KIBO herself and seeing how the coding concepts relate to her literacy instruction, she became excited about implementing the CAL curriculum in her classroom. A few weeks later, Ms. Murray teaches Lesson 2: Tools of Communication. During this lesson, students play a few games of telephone, first by whispering a secret message, then by handwriting a message, and, finally, by typing a message. Ms. Murray facilitates a class discussion about different ways of communicating and why it is important to communicate clearly so that others can understand. Ms. Murray's student Dani chimes in, "That's like KIBO. We can't talk to KIBO because it doesn't know our language. We have to use the blocks to tell KIBO what to do." Ms. Murray responds, "That's exactly right. KIBO is a robot with a lot of different parts, and the blocks are the language we use to communicate with KIBO." Through this activity, Ms. Murray guides her students to understand the difference between hardware (machinery) and software (an instructional language) and applies this powerful idea to KIBO.

Another teacher, Ms. Chun, teaches an inclusion class of 22 second graders. She is thrilled by the hands-on nature of KIBO but is skeptical about the literacy connection. "Writing isn't my students' favorite thing to do in class," she claims, "but maybe this will spice things up." She begins

Lesson 5: Debugging, by creating an anchor chart of KIBO issues and solutions. Together, as a class, they brainstorm strategies for assembling KIBO and scanning the programming blocks correctly. She then adapts the lesson plan by allowing students to either revisit their former Hokey Pokey programs or to come up with new dances, as long they are able to practice different debugging strategies. At the end of the lesson, students are excited about the new tips and tricks they learned with KIBO and proceed to write about their favorite strategies in their individual design journals. During this time, Ms. Chun works together with her lowest writing group, who is still working on writing full sentences. Although they normally need encouragement to write, they are all eagerly asking for help to spell words like "retest" and "sequence." With Ms. Chun's scaffolded instruction, the students draw and write key words to help them remember their debugging strategies.

Mr. Robinson, a kindergarten teacher, has been implementing the CAL curriculum in his classroom for several months, and his students are working on the final project in Lessons 11 and 12: The Wild Rumpus. Mr. Robinson rereads the story *Where the Wild Things Are*, by Maurice Sendak, and pauses at the six wordless pages. He asks his students, "What are the Wild Things doing? If you had your own Wild Rumpus, what would you do?" Mr. Robinson guides his students through the design process as they plan and program KIBO to act out different "wild" things that might happen at their Wild Rumpus party. Remembering that the students had trouble sharing KIBOs during their last project-based activity, Mr. Robinson decides to bring back the KIBO job cards. He splits the classroom into groups of three and hands out three necklaces with name tags on them: Scanner, Assistant, and Organizer. His students Aimee, Sadie, and Tom are in a group together. "I'm going to scan KIBO first," Sadie says. Aimee and Tom play rock-paper-scissors to decide who gets to be Sadie's Assistant first for scanning the KIBO blocks. The other will be the Organizer and helps to gather and put away supplies. While the class works on their KIBO projects, Mr. Robinson chimes a bell every few minutes that informs students to switch out their name tags. He comments that the job cards ensure that everyone gets a fair turn and help to promote collaboration in his classroom.

Teachers are encouraged to use the CAL curriculum as a guiding resource and to adapt lessons and activities to their needs of their students, as well as to choose their own favorite books. The CAL curriculum is free and can be downloaded as a PDF document and accessed through a website (https://sites.tufts.edu/codingasliteracy/). In addition to a summary of each lesson, the website also includes videos and tutorials, teaching resources such as templates for design journals, and songs, and tools for teachers and researchers to evaluate the learning. When choosing a CAL curriculum, it is important to understand what kind of programming language we want children to learn. Are we looking for a screen-free experience? If so, the CAL curriculum using KIBO robotics will be more suitable. See Table 6.2 for an example of the types of skills and activities children will explore in progressive lessons in a CAL–KIBO curriculum. Are we looking for a CAL curriculum that utilizes free software? The CAL curriculum for ScratchJr might then be ideal.

Table 6.2 Sample KIBO robotics curriculum structure

Lesson Topic	Children Will Be Able to ...
1. Foundations	• Define engineer and understand that there are different types of engineers • Compare and contrast the design process and writing process • Use the design and writing processes to write a set of instructions for making something
2. Technological Tools: Robots	• Identify characteristics of a robot • Compare human languages and programming languages • Create a simple algorithm using the KIBO programming blocks
3. Sequencing	• Understand why order matters when programming a robot or telling a story • Identify the different parts of the KIBO robot
4. Programming	• Tell and retell a story clearly and effectively • Identify common errors with scanning KIBO programs and troubleshoot them • Practice scanning programs with KIBO • Learn strategies for debugging and editing
5. Debugging	• Identify common errors with scanning KIBO programs and troubleshoot them • Practice scanning programs with KIBO • Learn strategies for debugging and editing

(Continued)

Table 6.2 (Continued)

Lesson Topic	Children Will Be Able to ...
6. Cause and Effect: Level 1	● Distinguish between human senses and robot sensors ● Use the KIBO Sound Sensor with its appropriate "Wait for clap" block ● Record a sound clip successfully using the Sound Recorder module and Sound recorder blocks
7. Cause and Effect: Level 2	● Program KIBO to sing and dance to the "If You're Wild and You Know It" song
8. Repeat Loops: Level 1	● Identify patterns in code sequences and rewrite codes using repeat loops ● Use KIBO number parameters to make a program that loops a certain number of times ● Understand how repetition is used in stories and songs
9. Repeat Loops: Level 2	● Compare and contrast human senses and robot sensors ● Successfully test a KIBO program using the Light and Distance sensors
10. Repeat and If Statements	● Successfully test a conditional KIBO program using the Light and Distance sensors ● Identify situations that would require an If statement or a Repeat loop
11. Final Project: Writing the Wild Rumpus Composition	● Utilize the writing process by writing their Wild Rumpus composition ● Decide which of their ideas can and cannot be translated into KIBO programs
12. Final Project: Coding the Wild Rumpus (Three-Day Plan)	● Demonstrate the design process in full by planning, designing, and creating a final KIBO project ● Share final projects with peers, family, and community members ● Identify and show appreciation to those who have helped them with their final projects

Some ask the question, why teach a programming language to children, when coding itself might become obsolete? Many believe that computers will just understand us in natural language and therefore there is no need to learn artificial languages (e.g., Manning, 2015). While this might or might not be true, we will still need the logic, sequencing, decomposition, and problem-solving required to give instructions to a computer.

We are still far away from having machines display a full array of artificial intelligence, and humans still need to do much of the thinking. Thus, the question is not whether coding will become obsolete or not, but how we can support computational thinking, regardless of the specifics of the coding system or programming language.

CAL integrates literacy with coding. However, it is positioned as a computer science curriculum. As such, it engages children in learning how to create their own projects but also in how to think in computational ways. What does it mean to teach computer science in early childhood? What concepts and skills can young children learn and are developmentally ready to comprehend? What does it mean to engage in computational thinking at this age? The next part of the book will explore these questions.

References

Bers, M. U. (2019). Coding as another language: A pedagogical approach for teaching computer science in early childhood. *Journal of Computers in Education, 6*(4), 499–528.

Hassenfeld, Z. R., & Bers, M. U. (2020) Debugging the writing process: Lessons from a comparison of students' coding and writing practices. *The Reading Teacher, 73*(6), May/June 2020, 735–746.

K-12 Computer Science Framework Steering Committee. (2016). K-12 computer science framework. doi:10.1145/3079760.

Manning, C. D. (2015). Computational linguistics and deep learning. *Computational Linguistics, 41*(4), 701–707.

Massachusetts Department of Elementary and Secondary Education. (2016). *Massachusetts science and technology/engineering curriculum framework.* Malden, MA: Massachusetts Department of Elementary and Secondary Education.

Massachusetts Department of Elementary and Secondary Education. (2017). *Massachusetts curriculum framework for English language arts and literacy, grades pre-kindergarten to 12.* Malden, MA: Massachusetts Department of Elementary and Secondary Education.

McDermott, R. P. (1996). The acquisition of a child by a learning disability. In S. Chaiklin & J. Lave (Eds.), *Understanding practice: Perspectives on activity and context* (pp. 269–305). Cambridge, England: Cambridge University Press.

National Governors Association Center for Best Practices & Council of Chief State School Officers. (2010) Common core state standards for English Language Arts (ELA)/literacy. Washington, DC: National Governors Association Center for Best Practices, Council of Chief State School Officers.

Papert, S. (1980). *Mindstorms: Children, computers, and powerful ideas.* New York, NY: Basic Books, Inc.

Steele, C. (2003). Stereotype threat and African American student achievement. In D. Grusky (Ed.), *The inequality reader: Contemporary and foundational readings in race, class, and gender* (pp. 276–281). New York, NY: Routledge.

Virginia Department of Education. (2019). *Computer science standards of learning.* Richmond, VA: Virginia Department of Education.

PART

III

Computational Thinking

Thinking about Computational Thinking

Madison is a 7-year-old girl who has been programming with ScratchJr for one year at school and at home. As Madison begins a new project, she plans it aloud, adding new characters and actions as she goes along. She declares to her classmates that she is going to make a basketball game. Her favorite sport is basketball. As she explores the ScratchJr library of available backgrounds, she narrates her design process: "I'm going to have team-mates and a crowd cheering and a dragon. I should have it in the gym, but I want to add a snack stand." Madison enters the ScratchJr Background Paint Editor and draws a rectangle in the corner of the gym background, representing the snack stand.

Next, Madison adds nearly ten characters to her project. Some she chooses from the character library; some she draws herself. As she formulates her design she expresses an understanding of the tool: "I want the kitten to pass the ball to the girl. So, I'll have to program the ball to move forward." Clearly, Madison understands that ScratchJr is not magic—the characters have potential to do many things, but will only *actually* do what she *programs* them to do. She is in control and must use the programming blocks in the correct sequence to get the characters to carry out the desired actions.

Later, Madison wants the dragon—which she has colored purple—to dribble the ball, jump, and shoot. This requires knowledge of sequencing and order, cause and effect, and an awareness of the debugging process, in case the characters do something different than she intended. Madison programs the dragon to move right five times to the basketball hoop, then hop. The basketball's program proves trickier. At first, she programs it to move right then hop in a repeat loop. This results in a rigid motion that does not look like dribbling. "No! I want it to move forward and bounce

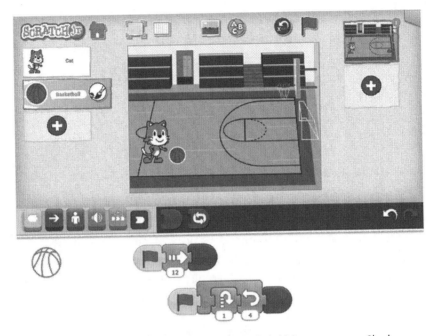

Figure 7.1 Illustration of Madison's basketball dribbling programs. She has two programs starting simultaneously with the "Green flag": 1) the first program makes the ball move forward across the screen, and 2) the second program makes the ball bounce up and down.

at the same time!" Madison exclaims. After several different combinations, she has a breakthrough: "It can do two programs at once! Cool!" She writes two separate but simultaneous programs for the ball, one that tells it to move right, and one that tells it to hop (see Figure 7.1).

Madison has debugged her program and refined her problem-solving skills by separating the ball's actions to create a logical program sequence. The ball is successfully "dribbled" toward the hoop for the dragon's game-winning point. Immediately after, a crowd of animal fans cheer via Sound blocks that Madison had pre-recorded. Madison smiles proudly at her masterpiece.

As Madison was working on her project, she explored powerful ideas such as sequencing, debugging, modularization, and design. These are some of the core concepts of computational thinking. This chapter will focus on the growing literature and initiatives in this area. While most definitions focus on computational thinking as a problem-solving pro-cess, the approach I present extends beyond this notion by considering computational thinking as an expressive process. While Madison was solving many problems to make her basketball game, she was also telling a story about how a dragon could dribble a ball while a crowd of animal fans cheered. It was her desire to tell that story about her favorite sport that kept her going when she encountered challenges to solve.

In the 1960s, Alan Perlis, the computer scientist known for his work on the ALGOL programming language and one of the founding fathers of the discipline, argued that all college students need to learn programming and the "theory of computation" (Grover & Pea, 2013; Guzdial, 2008; Perlis, 1962). Given that computers back then were as big and obscure as the rooms that held them, this insight was surprising. Although Perlis took a leadership role in molding the then nascent field of computer science into an academic discipline, and it was during his term as president of the Association for Computing Machinery (ACM) that the first ACM Curriculum Committee on Computer Science was established, he strongly believed that everyone—not just computer scientists—would benefit from learning how to program. In his "Epigrams in Programming," Perlis wrote, "perhaps if we wrote programs from childhood on, as adults we'd be able to read them" (Perlis, 1982, p. 8). This assertion was based on his belief that "most people find the concept of programming obvious, but the doing impossible" (Perlis, 1982, p. 10).

What Perlis referred to as the "concept of programming" is close to our current understanding of computational thinking. Although Perlis was not a developmental scientist or an early childhood educator, he probably knew that even young children could grasp the concepts of sequencing, patterns, modularity, cause and effect, and problem-solving when presented with them in a way that made sense. At the time, Seymour Papert was busy exploring how to create a programming language that children could use, so the "doing" would not be impossible, as Perlis had argued.

Computational Thinking as Expression

Building on the knowledge gained while working with Piaget, Papert collaborated with Wally Feurzeig and others to create LOGO. This was the first programming language designed for children and explicitly aimed at helping them think in new, computational ways. The term "computational thinking" grew out of this pioneering work, and it meant both solving problems algorithmically and developing technological fluency (Bers, 2010; Papert, 1980). Children who could think like a computer were children who could use a computer to express themselves in a fluent way.

Papert's choice of the word "fluency" was explicitly aimed at referencing language when thinking about computation. A person fluent in a language can use it to recite a poem, write an academic paper, or socialize at a party. A technologically fluent person can use a computer to make an animation, write a speech, model a simulation, or program a robotic creature. As with learning a second language, fluency takes time to achieve and requires hard work and motivation.

Individuals become technologically fluent when they can use technology to express themselves creatively, in a fluent way, effortlessly, and smoothly, as one does with language (Bers, 2008). In the process of using the language of computation (LOGO, ScratchJr, KIBO, or any other programming language), one learns to think in different ways. Seymour Papert's computational thinking involved problem-solving, but also the notion of expression. I call this the "computational thinking as expression" metaphor, as opposed to the more traditional "computational thinking as problem-solving."

The notion of computational thinking encompasses a broad set of analytic and problem-solving skills, dispositions, habits, and approaches most often used in computer science, but that can serve everyone (Barr, Harrison, & Conery, 2011; Barr & Stephenson, 2011; Computer Science Teachers Association, 2020; Lee et al., 2011). In 2006, Jeannette Wing's influential article "Computational Thinking" appeared in the *Communications of the ACM* and caught the attention of many researchers, computer scientists, and educators across the U.S. (Wing, 2006). Wing created quite a stir by arguing that *computational thinking,* a problem-solving skill set rooted in computer science, is a universally applicable skill that should be part of every child's analytical ability.

According to Wing (2006), computational thinking is defined as "solving problems, designing systems, and understanding human behavior, by drawing on the concepts fundamental to computer science" (p. 33). Computational thinking includes a range of mental tools that are inherent to the field of computer science, including thinking recursively, using abstraction when figuring out a complex task, and using heuristic reasoning to discover a solution (Wing, 2006).

Computational thinking represents a type of analytical thinking that shares similarities with mathematical thinking (e.g., problem-solving), engineering thinking (designing and evaluating processes), and scientific thinking (systematic analysis) (Bers, 2010). While the act of engaging in computational thinking is rooted in computer science, Wing argued that it is pertinent to everyone: "It represents a universally applicable attitude and skill set everyone, not just computer scientists would be eager to learn and use" (Wing, 2006, p. 33). Wing asserts that just as the printing press facilitated the spread of the three Rs (reading, writing, and arithmetic), computers facilitate the spread of computational thinking.

Many researchers and educators have cited this 2006 "call to action" paper, as it urges that computational thinking be taught to pre-college students and noncomputer science majors. However, although it brought newfound light to the importance of learning how to code, which was introduced in the early '80s by Seymour Papert, it also limited computational thinking to a problem-solving process that complements mathematical and engineering thinking, obscuring the relevance of expression and communication in the act of programming. Students who learn to code with a playground approach engage in computational thinking as a problem-solving process, but also as an expressive process. They develop a new literacy.

Brennan and Resnick (2012) broke down computational thinking into a three-dimensional framework that comprises *concepts*, *practices*, and *perspectives*. At a higher level, computational thinking practices refer to techniques applied by humans to express themselves by designing and constructing computation. Not surprisingly, this definition of the term from Papert's disciples brings back the relevance of expression in the process of computer programming.

Although computational thinking has received considerable attention over the past several years, there is little agreement on what a definition for computational thinking might encompass (Allan et al., 2010; Barr & Stephenson, 2011; Grover & Pea, 2013; National Academies of Science, 2010; Relkin, 2018; Relkin & Bers, 2019; Shute, Sun, & Asbell-Clarke, 2017). The importance of computational thinking, regardless of its definition, took center stage in 2010 following a stark report titled "Running on Empty: The Failure to Teach K-12 Computer Science in the Digital Age" (Wilson, Sudol, Stephenson, & Stehlik, 2010). This report revealed very low numbers for women in computing, and revealed that more than two-thirds of the country had only a few computer science courses at the secondary school level.

Since then, public and private organizations, motivated by a shortage of programmers in the industry, began to work on frameworks and initiatives to foster computational thinking and address these issues before college. For example, that same year (in 2010), the International Society for Technology in Education (ISTE) and the Computer Science Teachers Association (CSTA) led a National Science Foundation (NSF) project entitled "Leveraging Thought Leadership for Computational Thinking in PK-12." One of the activities of this project was to construct a clearer definition of computational thinking to be applied in the school curriculum. In addition to summarizing many of the skills introduced by Wing, this project also included a list of attitudes toward dealing with computing problems in the face of complexity and ambiguity (Barr, Harrison, & Conery, 2011).

In 2011, Wing published another article in which she redefined computational thinking as "thought processes involved in formulating problems and their solutions so that the solutions are represented in a form that can be effectively carried out by an information-processing agent" (Wing, 2011). Within the playground approach that I propose, this definition gets tweaked. The goal of the thought processes involved in computational thinking is not necessarily problem formulation, but expression. Problem formulation might be a path to expression, but not the end in itself. Ideas are not problems, and we might want to use the power of computers to share and test our ideas. Wing describes the computational thinker as "an information-processing agent." In contrast, I refer to this thinker as an "expressive agent." This is someone who has the internal and external resources and the required fluency to put those ideas into computational media to share with others. Thus, the coding stages presented in Chapter 5 reflect this. For example, it is possible for a child to have a low level of progress in the fluency stage, but a high level of progress in the purposefulness stage. This means that they might not have mastered the full syntax and grammar of the programming language, but with what they do know, they are able to effectively analyze, synthesize, and translate abstract concepts into code. The opposite is also true: a child can have a high level of progress in the fluency stage, but a low level of progress in the purposefulness stage. This means that they might have mastered the syntax and grammar of the programming language, but figuring out how to abstract, synthesize, and translate abstract concepts into code is difficult for them.

A key difference in these two instances is the matter of expression: in the former case, a child's expression is limited by their mastery of programming language, but with what syntax and grammar they understand, they can navigate coding expression effortlessly. Meanwhile, the latter child may have no difficulty with manipulating the full syntax and grammar of a programming language, but struggles to personally process concepts into code.

What is important is that problem formulation here does not necessarily exist as a path to expression. While the two can be linked, one's ability to express one's self in code and provide purpose to programming extends beyong problem-solving skills.

The "problem-solving" and "expression" metaphors for describing computational thinking complement each other. However, when the public discourse is too tilted toward the former, which is seen in initiatives that introduce coding as a series of logic puzzles for students to solve, it is important to counterbalance it with the latter.

In an interview, Mitchel Resnick says (Kamenetz, 2015, para. 8),

> If you have kids put blocks together to solve the puzzle, that can be useful for learning basic computing concepts. But we think it's missing an important part of what's exciting about coding. If you present just logic puzzles, it's like teaching them writing by only teaching grammar and punctuation.

In terms of textual literacy, it would be like only giving children crossword puzzles to solve and expecting them to become fluent writers.

Beyond STEM

Researchers, practitioners, funding institutions, and policy makers have traditionally associated computer programming and computational thinking with problem-solving. Thus, translated into the educational curriculum, computer science is grouped with science, technology, engineering, and math: STEM. In STEM education programs, computational thinking is defined as a set of cognitive skills for identifying patterns, breaking apart complex problems into smaller steps, organizing and creating a series of steps to provide solutions, and building a representation of data through simulations (Barr & Stephenson, 2011). This traditional approach doesn't allow room for integrating the tools of mind associated with language and expression; it ignores that coding is a literacy. Furthermore, it forgets the work of the many researchers who have proposed that learning a programming language may also be closely related to literacy, akin to acquiring a new foreign language (National Research Council, 2010; Papert, 1980; Solomon, 2005).

The approach I present in this book treats computational thinking as a means of expression and communication. In previous work, I have shown that conceptualizing of coding as a literacy, and correspondingly using strategies typically used to teach a new language, leads to positive learning outcomes regarding sequencing, a foundational skill for literacy (Kazakoff & Bers, 2011, 2014; Kazakoff, Sullivan, & Bers, 2013). For example, we found that children in prekindergarten had significant increases in their picture story sequencing skills after completing just a one-week robotics and programming curriculum (Kazakoff, Sullivan, & Bers, 2013). Currently, I am exploring, through fMRI techniques, the hypothesis that engaging in programming activities has similarities to engaging in language comprehension and production (Bers & Fedorenko, 2016; Fedorenko, Ivanova, Dhamala, & Bers, 2019; Ivanova et al., 2019). We are aiming to understand the cognitive and neural basis of learning computer science and developing computational thinking.

To date, there is a lack of research looking at this interdisciplinary issue. Our nation is moving forward with policy decisions regarding the introduction of computer science in education, but we lack the basic data that will provide the evidence needed to make informed choices. For example, as of the date of writing the second edition of this book, 47 states and the District of Columbia have policies in place that allow computer science to count as a mathematics or science credit in high schools—and that number is on the rise—and three states (Texas, Georgia, and Oklahoma), have approved legislation that allows computer science to fulfill a foreign language requirement (State of Computer Science Education, 2018). Basic research must inform the debate about the role of computer science in the school curriculum. The jury is still out regarding the balance between the metaphors of problem-solving and expression in this effort.

Computational Thinking and Coding

Computing professionals and educators have the responsibility to make computation available to thinkers of all disciplines (Guzdial, 2008). This responsibility could be easily tackled if the linkage to language and expression were greater than it currently is. Furthermore, over the past few years, there has been growing enthusiasm about integrating STEM with the arts. The STEAM (Science, Technology, Engineering, *Arts*, and Mathematics) movement was originally spearheaded by the Rhode Island School of Design (RISD) but is now widely adopted by schools, businesses, and individuals (Rhode Island School of Design, 2016; Yakman, 2008). Adding the arts to STEM-based subjects, such as computer programming and engineering, may enhance student learning by infusing opportunities for creativity and innovation (Robelen, 2011). Furthermore, STEAM represents more than just the visual arts; it includes a broad spectrum of the humanities, including the liberal arts, language arts, social studies, music, culture, and more (Maguth, 2012).

Research shows that there are many everyday "nonacademic" examples of exercising computational thinking skills (Wing, 2008; Yadav, 2011). These everyday activities draw on the same type of problem-solving inherent in computer science troubleshooting, but do not involve programming. Wing (2008) presents a series of examples, including: sorting LEGO (using the concept of "hashing" to sort by color, shape, and size), cooking a meal (using "parallel processing" to manage cooking different types of food at different temperatures for different amounts of time), and looking up a name in an alphabetical list (linear: starting at the beginning of the list; binary: starting at the middle of the list).

Recently, unplugged games were developed and have grown in popularity. Robot Turtles (Shapiro, 2015) was released in 2013 and is designed for young children aged 3–8 years to start thinking in computational ways while playing a traditional turn-based board game. How can young players think in computational ways without a programming language or even a computer? In Robot Turtles, by using a variety of "obstacle cards" such as ice walls, crates, and stone walls, the players make a maze on the board that their turtles need to navigate to get to their respective jewels. Children place their turtles in the corners of the game board and their jewels somewhere amidst the maze. The kids play instruction cards one at a time on their turn (such as, turn right, turn left, and move forward) to navigate the obstacles, while an adult plays as the "computer" to ensure that children's actions match the code cards that they have selected. When they get to their jewel, they win. If they make a mistake at any time, they can just tap the bug card (a whimsical cartoon bug that also represents a "bug" or problem in the code) to fix it and make changes (see Figure 7.2). Because every

Figure 7.2 The Robot Turtles board game in the middle of a four-person game.

player is trying to get to their own jewel, every player can find their own way to win. There are multiple paths for reaching a goal and for solving a problem successfully.

The powerful ideas that children encounter while playing this game, such as sequencing and debugging, breaking one big problem into smaller steps, and planning and testing a strategy, all tap into the core of computational thinking. In my own work at the DevTech research group at Tufts University, we have also used low-tech strategies to promote computational thinking: singing and dancing, card games, bingo, and Simon Says. Any approach that encourages sequencing and problem-solving is a good precursor for computational thinking.

This low-tech or unplugged approach to computational thinking is growing. Many people claim that when working with young children it is not necessary to engage them in coding, as computational thinking can be achieved through other activities that involve sequencing and problem-solving (e.g., Bell, Witten, & Fellows, 1998). I do not agree with this perspective. If computational thinking is to be defined not only as a process of problem-solving, but as a process of expression and creation, we need to provide tools that enable the creation of an external artifact. We need a language for expression. Programming languages are the tools for computational thinking. In contrast to most other tools, programming languages provide instant feedback and guide us when troubleshooting and debugging, which is essential in computational thinking.

Software and apps have also been created to encourage computational thinking. For example, LightBot, a highly rated educational video game (https://lightbot.com/), also uses the idea of navigating a maze (Biggs, 2013; Eaton, 2014). Players arrange symbols on the screen to command LightBot to walk, turn, jump, switch on a light, and so on. The maze and the list of symbols become more complicated as the game progresses.

However, while this kind of software promotes computational thinking and runs on a computer, it doesn't engage in the full range of experiences that a programming language does. It focuses on problem-solving, but not expression. It facilitates exploration of computational concepts in a limited way. It doesn't support creative projects; it is a playpen, not a playground. As a playpen, it serves a purpose (i.e., practicing skills, mastering discrete concepts, isolating skills), but it shouldn't be confused with a playground and its open-ended opportunities.

Programming languages can become playgrounds in which children code. If designed in a developmentally appropriate manner, children can code in a playful way. In the process, they develop computational thinking. But they need to learn the grammar and syntax of the programming language to become fluent. Like writing in Spanish, English, or Hebrew, the language of choice doesn't matter if we are fluent in it and can use it for self-expression and communication. Likewise, programming languages, when one has achieved fluency, support personal expression and communication. Technological fluency is developed only after many attempts at problem-solving. In my approach, problem-solving is not the goal of teaching a programming language or of promoting computational thinking, but is a necessary step so that others can see and understand who we are and what we are making.

Of course, the teaching of programming languages can be complemented by other strategies and activities that, in early childhood, can serve as precursors. As we saw in the previous chapter, the CAL curriculum takes advantage of many low-tech materials as well as singing, acting, drawing, etc. to engage children in computational thinking. Despite this, I strongly believe that if we want to engage children at any age in the full potential of computational thinking, we must also provide them with opportunities to code. Can we think in textual ways without knowing how to read or write? Can we be literate without those skills? I don't think so. We must start in early childhood, just like we did with reading and writing.

I have devoted my academic career to understanding coding as literacy and, therefore, thinking about how to design playground-style experiences that are developmentally appropriate for young children. Through my research at the DevTech research group, we have shown that learning to program with tools like KIBO and ScratchJr allows young children to practice sequencing, logical reasoning, and problem-solving (Kazakoff, Sullivan, & Bers, 2013; Portelance & Bers, 2015; Sullivan & Bers, 2015). We have seen that when beginning in prekindergarten, learning to program a robot significantly improves a child's ability to logically sequence picture stories (Kazakoff, Sullivan, & Bers, 2013). Our findings are consistent with other research that shows the positive effect that learning computer programming and computational thinking can have on skills such as reflectivity, divergent thinking, and cognitive, social, and emotional development (Clements & Gullo, 1984; Clements & Meredith, 1992; Flannery & Bers, 2013).

Coding in the playground is possible and can promote computational thinking. However, the approach to designing the programming languages (see Chapter 13) and the learning environments (see Chapter 14) needs to be developmentally appropriate. The playground approach to coding provides opportunities to encounter a complex system of ideas that is logically organized and utilizes abstraction and representation—as well as the skills and habits of mind to put those powerful ideas to use—by making personally meaningful projects. The next chapter will explore those powerful ideas in the early childhood context.

References

Allan, W., Coulter, B., Denner, J., Erickson, J., Lee, I., Malyn-Smith, J., & Martin, F. (2010). Computational thinking for youth. *White Paper for the National Science Foundation's Innovative Technology Experiences for Students and Teachers (ITEST) Small Working Group on Computational Thinking (CT)*. Retrieved from http://stelar.edc.org/sites/stelar.edc.org/files/Computational_Thinking_paper.pdf

Barr, D., Harrison, J., & Conery, L. (2011). Computational thinking: A digital age skill for everyone. *Learning & Leading with Technology, 38*(6), 20–23.

Barr, V., & Stephenson, C. (2011). Bringing computational thinking to K-12: What is involved and what is the role of the computer science education community? *ACM Inroads, 2*(1), 48–54.

Bell, T. C., Witten, I. H., & Fellows, M. R. (1998). Computer science unplugged: Off-line activities and games for all ages. Computer Science Unplugged.

Bers, M. (2008). *Blocks to robots: Learning with technology in the early childhood classroom.* New York, NY: Teachers College Press.

Bers, M. U. (2010). The tangible K robotics program: Applied computational thinking for young children. *Early Childhood Research and Practice, 12*(2). 1–20.

Biggs, J. (2013, June 26). Light-bot teaches computer science with a cute little robot and some symbol-based programming. Retrieved from Tech-Crunch.com/2013/06/26/light-bot-teaches-computer-science-witha-cute-little-robot-and-some-symbol-based-programming

Brennan, K., & Resnick, M. (2012). New frameworks for studying and assessing the development of computational thinking. In *Proceedings of the 2012 Annual Meeting of the American Educational Research Association.* Vancouver, Canada.

Clements, D. H., & Gullo, D. F. (1984). Effects of computer programming on young children's cognition. *Journal of Educational Psychology, 76*(6), 1051–1058. doi:10.1037/0022-0663.76.6.1051.

Clements, D. H., & Meredith, J. S. (1992). *Research on logo: Effects and efficacy.* Retrieved from http://el.media.mit.edu/logo-foundation/pubs/papers/research_logo.html

Computer Science Teachers Association. (2020). *Standards for Computer Science Teachers.* Retrieved from https://csteachers.org/teacherstandards

Eaton, K. (2014, August 27). Programming apps teach the basics of code. *The New York Times.* Retrieved from www.nytimes.com/2014/08/28/technology/personaltech/get-cracking-on-learning-computer-code.html

Fedorenko, E., Ivanova, A., Dhamala, R., & Bers, M. U. (2019). The language of programming: A cognitive perspective. *Trends in Cognitive Sciences, 23*(7). doi:10.1016/j.tics.2019.04.010.

Flannery, L. P., & Bers, M. U. (2013). Let's dance the "robot hokey-pokey!": Children's programming approaches and achievement throughout early cognitive development. *Journal of Research on Technology in Education, 46*(1), 81–101.

Grover, S., & Pea, R. (2013). Computational thinking in K-12: A review of the state of the field. *Educational Researcher, 42*(1), 38–43.

Guzdial, M. (2008). Paving the way for computational thinking. *Communications of the ACM, 51*(8), 25–27.

Ivanova, A., Srikant, S., Sueoka, Y., Kean, H., Dhamala, R., O'Reilly, U. M., Bers, M. U., & Fedorenko, E. (2019, October). The neural basis of program comprehension. *Poster session presented at the Society for Neuroscience 2019*, Chicago, IL.

Ivanova, A. A., Srikant, S., Sueoka, Y., Kean, H. H., Dhamala, R., O'Reilly, U-M., Bers, M. U. & Fedorenko, E. (2020). Comprehension of computer code relies primarily on domain-general executive resources. *BioRxiv*, 2020.04.16.045732.

Kamenetz, A. (2015, December 11). *Engage kids with coding by letting them design, create, and tell stories.* Retrieved from https://ww2.kqed.org/mindshift/2015/12/15/engage-kids-with-coding-by-letting-them-design-create-and-tell-stories/

Kazakoff, E. R., & Bers, M. U. (2011, April). The impact of computer programming on sequencing ability in early childhood. *Paper presented at American Educational Research Association Conference(AERA)*, 8–12 April, 2011, Louisiana: New Orleans.

Kazakoff, E. R., & Bers, M. U. (2014). Put your robot in, put your robot out: Sequencing through programming robots in early childhood. *Journal of Educational Computing Research, 50*(4), 553–573.

Kazakoff, E. R., Sullivan, A., & Bers, M. U. (2013). The effect of a classroom-based intensive robotics and programming workshop on sequencing ability in early childhood. *Early Childhood Education Journal, 41*(4), 245–255. doi:10.1007/s10643-012-0554-5.

Lee, I., Martin, F., Denner, J., Coulter, B., Allan, W., Erickson, J., Malyn-Smith, J., & Werner, L. (2011). Computational thinking for youth in practice. *ACM Inroads, 2*(1), 32–37.

Maguth, B. (2012). In defense of the social studies: Social studies programs in STEM education. *Social Studies Research and Practice, 7*(2), 84.

National Academies of Science. (2010). *Report of a workshop on the scope and nature of computational thinking.* Washington, DC: National Academies Press.

National Research Council (U.S.). (2010). *Report of a workshop on the scope and nature of computational thinking.* Washington, DC: National Academies Press.

Papert, S. (1980). *Mindstorms: Children, computers and powerful ideas.* New York, NY: Basic Books.

Perlis, A. (1962). The computer in the university. In M. Greenberger (Ed.), *Computers and the world of the future* (pp. 180–219). Cambridge, MA: MIT Press.

Perlis, A. J. (1982). Epigrams on programming. *SigPlan Notices, 17*(9), 7–13.

Portelance, D. J., & Bers, M. U. (2015). Code and tell: Assessing young children's learning of computational thinking using peer video interviews with ScratchJr. In *Proceedings of the 14th International Conference on Interaction Design and Children (IDC '15).* ACM, Boston, MA.

Relkin, E. (2018). Assessing young children's computational thinking abilities (Master's thesis). Tufts University, Medford, MA. Retrieved from ProQuest Dissertations and Theses database. (Accession Order No. 10813994).

Relkin, E., & Bers, M. U. (2019). Designing an assessment of computational thinking abilities for young children. In L. E. Cohen & S. Waite-Stupiansky (Eds.), *STEM for early childhood learners: How science, technology, engineering and mathematics strengthen learning* (pp. 85–98). New York, NY: Routledge.

Rhode Island School of Design. (2016). Public engagement: Support for STEAM. Retrieved July 27, 2016, from http://stemtosteam.org/

Robelen, E. W. (2011). STEAM: Experts make case for adding arts to STEM. *Education Week, 31*(13), 8.

Shapiro, D. (2015). *Hot seat: The startup CEO guidebook.* Sebastopol, CA: O'Reilly Media, Inc.

Shute, V. J., Sun, C., & Asbell-Clarke, J. (2017). Demystifying computational thinking. *Educational Research Review, 22,* 142–158. doi:10.1016/j.edurev.2017.09.003.

Solomon, J. (2005). Programming as a second language. *Learning & Leading with Technology, 32*(4), 34–39.

State of Computer Science Education. (2018). Retrieved from advocacy.code.org/

Sullivan, A., & Bers, M. U. (2015). Robotics in the early childhood classroom: Learning outcomes from an 8-week robotics curriculum in prekindergarten through second grade. *International Journal of Technology and Design Education, 26*(1), 3–20.

Wilson, C., Sudol, L. A., Stephenson, C., & Stehlik, M. (2010). *Running on empty: The failure to teach K-12 computer science in the digital age.* New York, NY: The Association for Computing Machinery and the Computer Science Teachers Association.

Wing, J. (2006). Computational thinking. *Communications of the ACM, 49*(3), 33–36.

Wing, J. (2008). Computational thinking and thinking about computing [PowerPoint Slides]. Retrieved from www.cs.cmu.edu/afs/cs/usr/wing/www/talks/ct-and-tc-long.pdf

Wing, J. (2011). *Research notebook: Computational thinking—What and why? The Link Magazine,* Spring. Carnegie Mellon University, Pittsburgh, PA. Retrieved from http://link.cs.cmu.edu/article.php?a=600

Yadav, A. (2011). Computational thinking and 21st century problem solving [PowerPoint Slides]. Retrieved from http://cs4edu.cs.purdue.edu/_media/what-is-ct_edps235.pdf

Yakman, G. (2008). STEAM education: An overview of creating a model of integrative education. In *Pupils' Attitudes towards Technology(PATT-19) Conference: Research on Technology, Innovation, Design & Engineering Teaching.* Salt Lake City, UT.

8 | Powerful Ideas in the Early Coding Curriculum

This chapter focuses on the powerful ideas of computational thinking (core content and skills) as well as the habits of mind or practices that a young programmer develops. Seymour Papert coined the term "powerful ideas" to refer to a central concept and skill within a domain (i.e., computer science) that is at once personally useful, interconnected with other disciplines, and has roots in intuitive knowledge that a child has internalized over a long period. Papert claims that powerful ideas afford new ways of thinking, new ways of putting knowledge to use, and new ways of making personal and epistemological connections with other domains of knowledge (Papert, 2000).

While the curriculum might use a particular programming environment, such as ScratchJr or KIBO, the powerful ideas and habits of mind, if they are indeed powerful, should be useful when coding with any language. Furthermore, these ideas can also be encountered when engaging in low-tech or unplugged activities aimed at promoting computational thinking.

Computational thinking involves the ability to abstract from computational instructions to computational behaviors and to identify potential "'bugs'" (Wing, 2006). The challenge for early childhood education is that powerful ideas need to be defined in a developmentally appropriate way and explored at different levels of depth, in a spiral manner, in the sequence of PreK-2. For example, understanding algorithmic thinking in PreK might focus on linear sequencing, while in second grade it extends to loops. Children will understand that within a sequence there are patterns that repeat themselves.

What are the powerful ideas in an early childhood curriculum focused on coding and computational thinking? Inspired by already existing computational thinking curriculum such as the framework and resources for educators launched by Google in 2010 (Google for Education, 2010), the work of Karen Brennan and Mitchel Resnick with Scratch (2012), and my work with KIBO (Sullivan & Bers, 2015) and ScratchJr (Portelance, Strawhacker, & Bers, 2015), I propose the following seven developmentally appropriate powerful ideas for early childhood computer science education: algorithms, modularity, control structures, representation, hardware/software, design process, and debugging. These are found in most computer science standards and frameworks, although they sometimes have different names. After defining each one, I will present examples of how they integrate into early childhood curricula.

Algorithms

An algorithm is a series of ordered steps taken in a sequence to solve a problem or achieve an end goal. Sequencing is an important skill in early childhood; it is a component of planning and involves putting objects or actions in the correct order. For example, retelling a story in a logical way or ordering numbers in a line is sequencing.

Sequencing skills extend beyond coding and computational thinking. Young children might start by sequencing steps of tasks found in daily life such as brushing their teeth, making a sandwich, or following the classroom schedule. As they grow, they discover that different algorithms might achieve the same result (e.g., different paths lead to school; there are a few ways to tie shoes), but that some algorithms are more effective and efficient than others (e.g., certain paths to school might be faster). They can start to evaluate and compare competing algorithms by looking at measures such as ease of implementation, performance, and storage requirements (e.g., fewer steps involved in tying shoes is better).

Understanding algorithms involves understanding abstraction (i.e., identifying relevant information to define what constitutes a step in the sequence) and representation (i.e., depicting and organizing information in an appropriate form). As children mature and encounter different programming languages, they might discover that some algorithms run in parallel. At this stage, it is possible to untangle the concept of sequence from algorithm, but, in early childhood education, there is an advantage in teaching these concepts together.

Modularity

Modularity is breaking down tasks or procedures into simpler, manageable units that can be combined to create a more complex process. In sum, the powerful idea of modularity involves subdividing jobs and engaging in decomposition. In early childhood, decomposition can be taught anytime a complex task needs to be broken down into smaller tasks. For example, having a birthday party involves inviting guests, making food, setting the table, etc. Each of these tasks can be broken down even further: inviting guests involves making invitations, putting the cards in envelopes, putting stamps on each envelope, etc. When coding, understanding modularity facilitates the design and testing of projects, so that programmers can focus on one piece at a time. As children grow older, they also discover that different people can work on different parts of a project at the same time and bring all the parts together later. They learn different approaches to make modularization most efficient.

Control Structures

Control structures determine the order (or sequence) in which instructions are followed or executed within an algorithm or program. Children learn about sequential execution in the early years, and later they become familiar with multiple control structures that involve repeat functions, loops, conditionals, events, and nested structures. Loops can be used to repeat patterns of instructions, conditionals to skip instructions, and events to initiate an instruction.

To understand control structures, young children need to be familiar with patterns. But, at the same time, learning how to program reinforces the concept of patterns. Different programming languages employ different paradigms for working with patterns: ScratchJr and KIBO implement repetition by using loops, while others, like LOGO, use recursive function calls. As children mature, they start to understand the difference between these paradigms and might learn to combine control structures to support complex execution.

Control structures provide a window into understanding the computational concept of making decisions based on conditions (e.g., variable values, branching, etc.). For example, when children program their KIBOs using the Light Sensor, they can make a program to detect if there is light and, if there is, to then tell the KIBO to keep moving forward. Events provide a way to understand the computational concept of one thing causing another to happen. Cause and effect is widely explored in early childhood and using these kinds of control structures reinforces it.

Representation

Computers store and manipulate data and values in a variety of ways. These data need to be made accessible, which leads us to the concept of representation. Early on, children learn that concepts can be represented by symbols. For example, letters represent sounds, numbers represent quantities, and programming instructions represent behaviors. They also learn that different types of things have different attributes—cats have whiskers, and letters use both upper and lower case forms— and they learn that data types have different functionalities. For example, numbers can be added, and letters can be strung together. Some data types are used to construct models (simulations) that produce information about how a system or object changes over time. These models, that imitate real-world processes, can be used to make predictions. For example, weather data are used to make simulations and predict when storms will hit.

KIBO and ScratchJr use color to represent different types of instructions. For example, in KIBO, blue is motion, orange is sound, etc. When these blocks are put together they represent a sequence of actions for the robot to perform. As children grow and advance to more complex programming languages, they learn about other data types, such as variables, and realize that programmers can create variables to store values that represent data.

The notion that concepts can be represented using symbols is foundational in early childhood and has strong links to both math and literacy. To code, we first need to understand that programming languages use symbols to represent actions. Understanding a programming language as a formal constructed language designed to communicate instructions (an algorithm) to a machine has strong implications for early literacy, which also involves understanding a representational system.

Hardware/Software

Computing systems need hardware and software to operate. The software provides instructions to the hardware. Some hardware is visible, such as printers, screens, and keyboards, but other hardware is not, such as the internal components of a computer (e.g., the motherboard). Robotic kits like KIBO expose those hidden components. For example, we can see the circuit board through the clear plastic casing in the KIBO body (see Figure 8.1).

Hardware and software work together as a system to accomplish tasks, such as receiving, processing, and sending information. Some hardware is specifically designed to receive, or input, data from the environment (e.g., KIBO sensors), while other hardware is designed to output, or send, data to it (e.g., the KIBO light bulb). The relationship between hardware and software becomes increasingly important in understanding the ways that components affect a system. Furthermore, young children need to understand

Figure 8.1 The transparent side of the KIBO robot. Through this clear side, children are able to explore the circuit board, wires, batteries, and the other "inner workings" of KIBO's hardware.

that hardware is programmed to perform a task and that many devices can be programmed, not just computers. For example, DVRs, cars, and watches are all programmed. Furthermore, robots are a special kind of hardware/software combination that involves an electromechanical machine guided by a computer program or electronic circuitry. The word "robot" refers to a wide range of machines, from industrial to humanoid, that can perform autonomous or pre-programmed tasks.

The five powerful ideas from computer science described above, algorithms, modularity, control structures, representation, and hardware/software, are all strongly linked to foundational concepts in early childhood education. These concepts span diverse disciplines such as literacy and math, arts and sciences, and engineering and foreign languages. By offering opportunities for children to engage with these ideas in a developmentally appropriate way while coding, we also facilitate the learning of these disciplines. It is a win-win situation.

There are two other kinds of powerful ideas that have more to do with processes, habits of mind, or practices than concepts: the design process and debugging.

Design Process

A design process is an iterative process used to develop programs and tangible artifacts that involves several steps (Ertas & Jones, 1996). For example, traditionally, the engineering design process includes identifying a problem, looking for ideas, and developing solutions, and may also include sharing solutions with others (Eggert, 2010; Ertas & Jones, 1996). The process is notably open-ended in that a problem may have many possible solutions (Mangold & Robinson, 2013).

For working in early childhood, we have adapted the design process and developed a series of steps: ask, imagine, plan, create, test and improve, and share (see Figure 8.2). The design process is an infinite cycle: there's no official starting or ending point. Children can begin at any step, move back and forth between steps, or repeat the cycle over and over.

For example, when programming KIBO to dance the Hokey Pokey, some children may spend a long time in the testing phase, dancing and singing along with their robot until they get their program right. Once they share their program with a friend and receive feedback, they may want

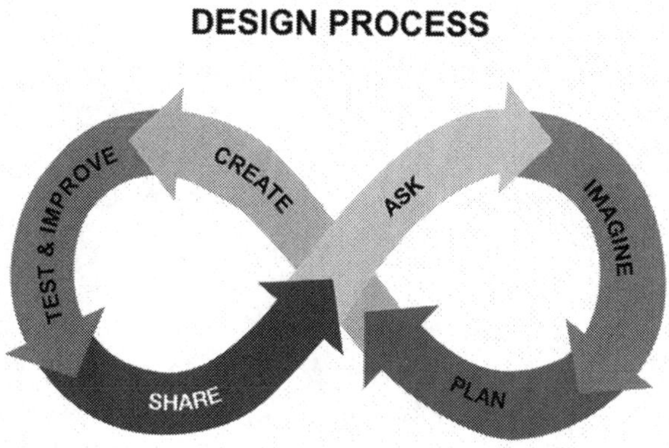

DESIGN PROCESS

Figure 8.2 The steps of a simplified design process that can be used with young children.

to go back to the testing and improving phase to include a dance step that they missed. Others may choose to plan each step of their Hokey Pokey program on paper or in a design journal before testing out any ideas. As children become more familiar with the design process, they become instilled with the ability to iteratively create and refine their work, to give and receive feedback to others, and to continually improve continually a project through experimenting and testing. This leads to iterative improvement, involves perseverance, and has strong associations with some aspects of executive functions, such as self-control, planning and prioritizing, and organization. Since the design process is such a core idea, it will be explored further in Chapter 9.

Debugging

Debugging allows us to fix our programs. It involves systematic analysis and evaluation using skills such as testing, logical thinking, and problem-solving in an intentional, iterative step-by-step way. When a code doesn't work as intended, troubleshooting strategies can help. Sometimes the problem is not the software, but the hardware, and other times it is in the connection between the two. For example, when children program KIBO to respond to a noise, they often complain that the robot doesn't work. When checking their programming blocks, all necessary wooden blocks are there. However, when checking the robot, they realize that they forgot to attach the Sound Sensor. They quickly learn to check both hardware and software. Once children understand how to debug their systems, they start to develop common troubleshooting strategies that can be used on a variety of computing systems. As children grow, their understanding of the interconnected parts of a system allows them to follow and create systematic problem-solving processes. Learning how to debug is an important skill that is similar to checking your work in math or editing in literacy. It teaches the powerful lesson that things do not just happen to work on the first try, but, in fact, that many iterations are usually necessary to get it right.

Papert writes in *Mindstorms:*

> Learning to be a master programmer is learning to become highly skilled at isolating and correcting "bugs," the parts that keep the program from working. The question to ask about the program is not whether it is right or wrong, but if it is fixable. If this way of looking at intellectual products were generalized to how the larger culture thinks about knowledge and its acquisition, we all might be less intimidated by our fears of "being wrong."
>
> (Papert, 1980, p. 23)

In the coding playground, systematic debugging is part of the fun.

Table 8.1 shows how each of the powerful ideas presented hereis related to common topics taught in early childhood education.

We encounter powerful ideas through experiences. In the coding playground, a curriculum of powerful ideas provides thematic freedom to relate computer programming and computational thinking to other academic subjects. This is a spiral curriculum (Bruner, 1960, 1975), a teaching approach in which each powerful idea is revisited as children mature and at increasingly sophisticated levels. After a decade and a half of work with young children and coding, my DevTech research group has developed curricula that provide opportunities for encountering each of the powerful ideas described earlier in multiple ways. Our curricular units are focused on a unique theme but engage children in exploring all the powerful ideas discussed in this chapter. Some curricula are designed for KIBO, others for ScratchJr (see Figure 8.3).

Table 8.1 Powerful ideas and early childhood education. This table shows the powerful ideas from computational thinking and how they align with traditional early childhood concepts and skills

Powerful Idea	Related Early Childhood Concepts and Skills
Algorithms	<ul><li>Sequencing/order (foundational math and literacy skill)</li><li>Logical organization</li></ul>
Modularity	<ul><li>Breaking up a large job into smaller steps</li><li>Writing instructions</li><li>Grouping a list of instructions into a given category or module to complete a larger project</li></ul>
Control Structures	<ul><li>Recognizing patterns and repetition</li><li>Cause and effect</li></ul>
Representation	<ul><li>Symbolic representation (i.e., letters represent sounds)</li><li>Models</li></ul>
Hardware/Software	<ul><li>Understanding that "smart" objects don't work by magic (i.e., cars, computers, tablets, etc.)</li><li>Recognizing objects that are human-engineered</li></ul>
Design Process	<ul><li>Problem-solving</li><li>Perseverance</li><li>Editing/revision (i.e., in writing)</li></ul>
Debugging	<ul><li>Identifying problems (checking your work)</li><li>Problem-solving</li><li>Perseverance</li></ul>

The following vignette describes a child's encounter with the powerful idea of debugging. During her thesis work, Megan Bennie, a Master's student at the DevTech research group, was studying children's approaches to debugging. Her thesis work explored the strategies and tactics children engage in while debugging coding errors using KIBO robotics (Bennie, 2020).

Peyton is a 6-year-old visiting Tufts University for a special play session with Megan. Peyton knows she will be solving fun "debugging missions," special coding games in which children work to repair common errors. Megan developed these games to explore how children find and fix problems with broken KIBO code. As Megan reads aloud the debugging

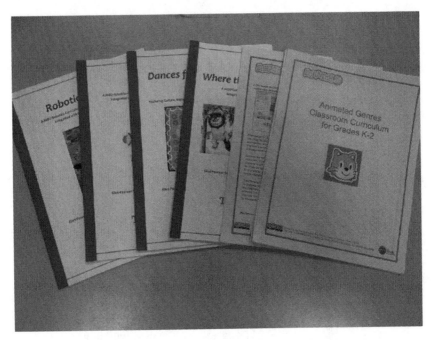

Figure 8.3 Examples of the range of DevTech curricula that have been developed for KIBO and ScratchJr exploring themes of dance, culture, identity, and more.

mission about KIBO's adventure to the zoo, Peyton's eyes widen with excitement and she seems eager to help KIBO. Peyton turns to the KIBO body and assures KIBO, "Don't worry KIBO, I will help you!" Peyton begins by scanning the original, broken KIBO code that Megan has pre-assembled. Peyton asks Megan to help her scan so that they can move faster. As Peyton scans the "End" block she hears KIBO make a noise and flash its red light. Peyton exclaims, "Oh no, KIBO only does that when it doesn't understand."

Megan and Peyton talk about Peyton's ideas for why KIBO may be confused. Peyton points to the blocks and wants to pretend that she is KIBO. Megan reads the code to her and Peyton makes it to the zoo. Peyton wonders why she understands the code as it is read to her, but KIBO does not understand when it scans the code. Peyton is determined to fix the problem, and decides to read the code for herself one block at a time. Megan and Peyton tap the "Begin" block together and move along the code one block at a time. This is one of the most commonly observed approaches to debugging an error in code; Peyton debugs by "tracing" through the code to find the problem (Bennie, 2020). Peyton's finger lingers on a block near the end of the code and discovers that a block is missing. Peyton enthusiastically runs to the box filled with KIBO blocks and grabs the missing "End repeat" block. Peyton is overwhelmed with excitement while she scans her code; she is confident that this will get KIBO to the zoo. As KIBO starts running the program, Peyton claps and cheers for KIBO when it reaches the zoo, and she turns to Megan for a high five. Peyton is so excited that she decides to draw her KIBO program with crayons to show her parents when they pick her up from the play session.

Although Peyton was focused on debugging, other powerful ideas of computer science also played a major role. For example, she used modularity to break down the program into its separate parts; the error that she found in the repeat loop involved knowledge of control structures; and when she first began debugging, she considered whether the bug seemed like a hardware or a software problem. Peyton integrated many powerful ideas fluently and simultaneously to solve her debugging mission.

The concept of debugging was explored in a different way by Dr. Ziva Hassenfeld, a postdoctoral researcher in my DevTech research group. Ziva is working with a second grade classroom to explore how children create and revise compositions in code and in written language (Hassenfeld & Bers, 2019). Specifically, she is interested in how children *edit*, which involves fixing mechanical errors like spelling and grammar, and *revise*, which involves adding stylistic or clarifying details to a composition.

Seven-year-old Lila is behind her grade level literacy benchmarks. She works very, very hard at writing. Ziva is working with Lila on her first composition. In composing this story, Lila reread her work three different times, but did not make any edits or revisions. When she encountered a challenge, like how to spell a certain word, she usually asked Ziva for help. After 23 minutes, Lila showed Ziva her work: "*He gets a Legoset/for he birthday/he bildt it then he/playds with oul (all)/he (his) Legoset he gets/he othr presnt.*" From this composition, it is difficult to understand the complex story that Lila was imagining when she first told Ziva her idea. Lila also explained that she wanted to add more to the story, but after 23 minutes of writing she was ready to stop.

Later that week, Lila wrote her first programming composition with ScratchJr. This time, she completed the first scene of her story within 3 minutes. After selecting her characters (two friends named Apple and Banana, and a school bus), and picking a background (a schoolyard), Lila announced, "Okay now let's start programming!" Within minutes, she had programmed the school bus to move across the screen to where Apple was standing. She tapped the "Green flag" to watch and evaluate her program, and exclaimed "Yay! Just right!" As she continued to code, she encountered challenges, just like when she was writing. When she could not remember which block caused a character to disappear, this time, instead of asking for help from Ziva, she tried a few different blocks, and through this *debugging* process she figured out the right block on her own. Lila rewatched her entire program several times, and almost every time she decided that she didn't like something, and continued to debug and change her code. After programming for a few more minutes, she was happy with her composition and shared it with Ziva. This time, she was able to finish all the parts of the story in her mind.

Lila's commitment to working hard at her entire story, as she wished it to be expressed in her ScratchJr program, was in marked contrast to her reticence to *revise*, and even *edit*, in her writing composition. Because ScratchJr allowed Lila to rewatch her program composition, unlike written work which she had to carefully read through (a different literacy skill from composition), Lila was able to engage in the revision process with her programming composition in a way she couldn't with her writing composition.

Will this motivation and willingness to engage with the difficulties of fixing problems transfer from one compositional medium to the other? Can we develop approaches that, by focusing on powerful ideas involved in computational thinking, can also promote textual thinking?

As shown in these examples, exploring computational ideas such as algorithmic thinking, debugging, and control structures and discussing how they are analogous to literacy concepts such as story structure, awareness of audience, and tools of communication, can provide a pathway for children to understand both computer science and liuteracy in new ways. The concept of powerful ideas allows us to design curriculum in which algorithmic thinking is connected to sequencing in stories, debugging is connected to revision, and control structures are linked to cause and effect in storytelling. Both writing and programming are framed for the children as tools for self-expression and creative communication.

References

Bennie, M. (2020). *Thinking strategically, acting tactically: The emotional decisions behind the cognitive process of debugging in early childhood.* (Unpublished Master's thesis). Tufts University, Medford, MA.

Brennan, K., & Resnick, M. (2012). New frameworks for studying and assessing the development of computational thinking. In *Proceedings of the 2012 Annual Meeting of the American Educational Research Association* (pp. 1–25). April, Vancouver, Canada.

Bruner, J. (1960). *The process of education.* Cambridge, MA: Harvard University Press.

Bruner, J. S. (1975). Entry into early language: A spiral curriculum: The Charles Gittins memorial lecture delivered at the University College of Swansea on March 13, 1975. University College of Swansea.

Eggert, R. (2010). *Engineering design* (2nd ed.). Meridian, ID: High Peak Press.

Ertas, A., & Jones, J. (1996). *The engineering design process* (2nd ed.). New York, NY: John Wiley & Sons, Inc.

Google for Education. (2010). *Exploring computational thinking.* Retrieved from www.google.com/edu/resources/programs/exploring-computational-thinking/index.html#!home

Hassenfeld, Z. R., & Bers, M. U. (2020). Debugging the writing process: Lessons from a comparison of students' coding and writing practices. *The Reading Teacher, 73*(6), 735–746.

Mangold, J., & Robinson, S. (2013). The engineering design process as a problem solving and learning tool in K-12 classrooms. In *Published in the Proceedings of the 120th ASEE Annual Conference and Exposition.* Georgia World Congress Center, Atlanta, GA.

Papert, S. (1980) *Mindstorms: Children, Computers and Powerful Ideas.* NY: Basic Books.

Papert, S. (2000). What's the big idea? Toward a pedagogy of idea power. *IBM Systems Journal, 39*(3.4), 720–729.

Portelance, D. J., Strawhacker, A. L., & Bers, M. U. (2015). Constructing the ScratchJr programming language in the early childhood classroom. *International Journal of Technology and Design Education, 29*(4), 1–16.

Sullivan, A., & Bers, M. U. (2015). Robotics in the early childhood class-room: Learning outcomes from an 8-week robotics curriculum in pre-kindergarten through second grade. *International Journal of Technology and Design Education. 26*(1), 3–20.

Wing, J. M. (2006). Computational thinking. *Communications of the ACM, 49*(3), 33–35.

The Coding Process

Jamie is working on a KIBO robot that will help her clean her room. Jamie, who is 5 years old, has a messy room; toys are everywhere on the floor. She doesn't like it when her mom makes her clean her room, so she *asks* herself: how can I make KIBO help me? She then goes on to *imagine* different ways that this could happen. For example, she could program KIBO to beep every time it runs into a toy on the floor to alert her to pick it up. Or, even better, she could build a plow out of LEGO and attach it to KIBO and somehow program it to pick up the toys. Or she could just have KIBO running around randomly pushing to the side any toys it encounters.

There are so many possibilities, and some are more complex than others. Jamie needs to make a *plan* and choose an approach. She takes some time to decide and, finally, she goes for a combination of her ideas: she will make her KIBO always go forward and turn right on an infinite loop and, when it encounters an object that blocks its Light Sensor, it will beep. Then she will attach a giant plow to KIBO's front, and manipulate it to pick up the toy.

Now the fun part starts. Jamie is ready to *create* her project. As she starts working on it, she encounters many challenges. Sometimes, she is able to solve them on her own; other times they are so difficult that she chooses to change her plan. As she programs KIBO and builds her plow, she *tests* it along the way. There is always something to *improve*. She doesn't give up. She really wants her project to work. After spending almost one hour on her KIBO cleaning robot, she decides that it is ready and calls her mom. She wants to *share* the product of such hard work.

Jamie's mom is amazed. She watches as Jamie's cleaning KIBO robot travels through the room, running into both furniture and toys, stopping sometimes and others not, beeping sometimes and others not, and getting

Figure 9.1 Jamie's cleaning KIBO robot. She designed KIBO to travel through the room, cleaning items up by pushing them out of the way with the LEGO plow.

stuck under socks and clothes on the floor (see Figure 9.1). She also watches as Jamie runs behind KIBO, with a LEGO construction (the "plow," explains Jamie), bending down and picking up the toys that KIBO chooses to stop and beep on. Jamie's mom can't believe the amount of time and the quality of thought her daughter put into this project. It was certainly more time-consuming than just picking up the toys, but Jamie's mom is proud of her daughter. She knows that this is not about judging KIBO's performance as a cleaner, but about supporting her daughter's creativity.

As Jamie worked on her project, she went through the six steps of the design process that we have identified as developmentally appropriate for young children: asking questions, imagining solutions, planning a project to address the solution, creating a prototype, testing and improving it, and sharing it with others. Although Jamie seemed to follow each step in a sequential, organized way, her process was messy. She moved back and forth between steps, she asked new questions while testing, and she imagined new solutions as she was making her robot.

This chapter describes the design process involved in programming. It starts with a question that gives birth to an idea and ends with creating a final project that can be shared with others. The design process makes computational thinking visible: coding becomes a tool of expression and communication. When coding happens while working with robotics, as in Jamie's story, the design process shares similarities with the engineering design process. Starting in kindergarten, every child in the U.S. is supposed to be learning about this, according to state and national frameworks (e.g., ISTE Student Standards, 2016; Massachusetts Department of Elementary and Secondary Education, 2016). My friends at the Tufts University Center for Engineering Education and Outreach (CEEO) have been pioneers in bringing these ideas into the world and are dedicated to improving engineering in K-16 (ceeo.tufts.edu). Through collaboration with a number of companies, such as LEGO, the CEEO also works to create educational engineering tools. Their focus is on researching how kids and adults learn and apply engineering design concepts and processes. In 2003, my colleagues at the Museum of Science, Boston launched the nationwide Engineering is Elementary project (www.eie.org) and they have been very successful at spreading knowledge and creative resources for teachers interested in bringing engineering design into their schools.

The engineering design process is a methodical series of steps that engineers use when creating functional products and processes. The process is highly iterative and steps often need to be repeated many times before moving on. Furthermore, at each stage there are decisions to make, challenges to solve, and frustrations to manage. This process has been adapted here for K-2 learners and condensed into eight steps. For example, the Massachusetts frameworks identify the following steps: 1) identify the need or problem; 2) research the need or problem; 3) develop possible solutions; 4) select the best possible solutions; 5) construct a prototype; 6) test and evaluate the solutions; 7) communicate the solutions; and 8) redesign. As we have seen in the previous chapter, my DevTech research group has further revised the process to make it developmentally appropriate for children. We only include six steps that are easy for young children to remember and that start with asking a question, not necessarily identifying a problem: 1) ask; 2) imagine; 3) plan; 4) create; 5) test and improve; and 6) share. While in previous years we chose to visualize the design process as a cycle (see Figure 9.2), we found that some teachers tended to believe

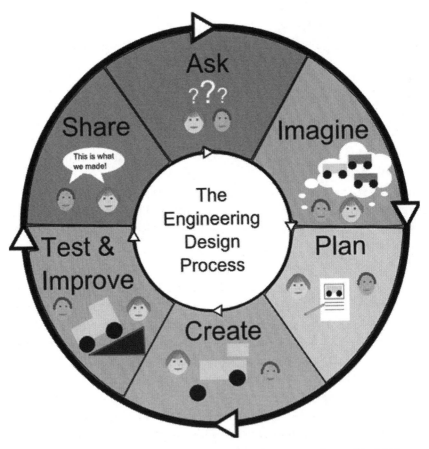

Figure 9.2 Design Process Cycle from DevTech research lab, used in 2018 and earlier.

DESIGN PROCESS

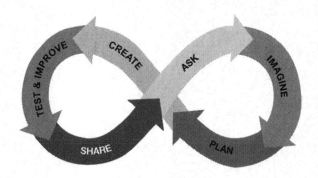

Figure 9.3 Infinity-Loop Design Process Cycle from DevTech research lab, used in 2019 and later.

that once the process was completed once, the job was done. They had difficulty understanding that the design process, like most processes, required many iterations. Therefore, we decided to change the visual to an infinite loop (see Figure 9.3). This cycle visually communicates that design work does not have a clear start or end point. Now, adults and children using this cycle have more flexibility as to which step they start and end on, and engage in the design process with more persistence to complete their task.

Like the engineering design process, the computational design process gives students another tool for systematic thinking. However, the major difference is the purpose of the activity. While the engineering process focuses on problem-solving and solutions (i.e., the first step involves identifying a problem and one of the last steps is communicating a solution), the process involved in "coding as literacy" starts with imagination and curiosity (i.e., asking a question) and culminates with pride and ownership of the work in a community context (i.e., sharing) (Bers, 2019a, 2019b).

The computational design process (like the engineering design process, the scientific method, and the writing process) introduces students to several orderly steps (see Figures 9.4 and 9.5). However, although there is a sequence, each step is interrelated with the others, such that one is likely to go back and forth between steps. Designing is a messy activity, and while

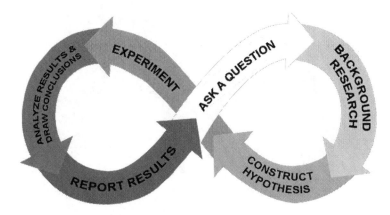

Figure 9.4 Infinity-Loop representation of the Scientific Method.

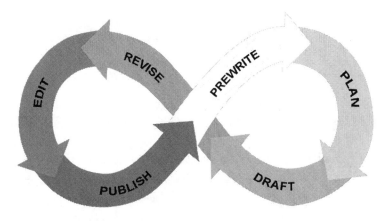

Figure 9.5 Infinity-Loop representation of the Writing Process.

design processes provide frameworks for organizing activities, they are not always neatly followed in practice.

However, all those processes begin with existing knowledge (content knowledge in the case of science, or knowledge about a need or problem in the case of engineering), and gradually become more specific in the search for *additional knowledge* (in the case of science), or a *solution* (in the case of engineering), or a *project* (in the case of computer science). Similarly, the writing process also starts with existing knowledge (our ideas or data on a piece of paper) and gradually becomes more specific as we write, rewrite, and edit drafts in iterative ways, culminating in a final work to share with a reader (see Figure 9.6).

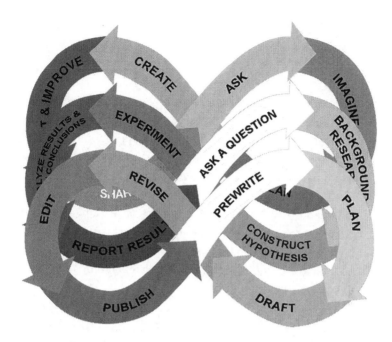

Figure 9.6 Illustration of how the design process overlaps with the scientific method and the writing process. The design process starts with existing knowledge and questions and seeks to build and improve designs. Similarly, the scientific method and the writing process follow the same approach in terms of building on what we know to create and improve something new.

Often, when giving a talk about the similarities between these processes, which have in common the need for background knowledge and skills, creativity, productivity, iteration, and communication, listeners make connections to a process that they use in their own daily work. For example, when discussing with entrepreneurs, many of them show me the similarities of this approach to creating a business plan; when chatting with marketing experts, they often share their experiences creating a marketing strategy. Educators find similarities with the process of developing curriculum and, of course, software developers with writing code. Architects, landscapers, artists, writers, performers, composers, contractors, mechanics: these professionals, who are in the business of making things, go through a design process.

We live in a world made of things. Thus, the process of making those things is of crucial importance and needs to be explored in early childhood. My colleague and collaborator in the ScratchJr project, Mitchel Resnick, writes,

> There is a constant interplay between making new things in the world and making new ideas in your head. As you make new things, and get feedback from others (and from yourself), you can revise, modify, and improve your ideas. And based on these new ideas, you are inspired to make new things. The process goes on and on, with making and learning reinforcing one another in a never ending spiral. This spiral is at the heart of the kindergarten approach to learning—and the creative process. As children create towers with blocks and pictures with finger paint, they get ideas for new towers and new pictures. And, over time, they develop intuitions about the creative process itself.
>
> (Resnick, 2001, p. 3)

Resnick calls this process the "creative thinking spiral" (Resnick, 2008), an iterative process that cyclically reinforces creative thinking. As in the other processes discussed earlier, Resnick identifies different steps (i.e., imagine, create, play, share, and reflect), but emphasizes playfulness along with problem-solving. As children experience the creative thinking spiral, they learn to develop their own ideas, try them out, test the boundaries, experiment with alternatives, and communicate their products.

Young Designers

Little children have big ideas. These are often hard to tackle on a project that they can complete on their own, which poses a challenge. On the one hand, we want to help them follow their ideas and ask big questions, but we do not want them to become frustrated when they realize (at the planning step) that they need to trim the ideas down into a manageable piece of work. On the other hand, we do not want to hinder their creativity, nor protect them from failure. We learn from failure, and we learn from iteration.

In solving this challenge, the core ideas of the design process come in handy. We work with children to identify a question or problem that they can easily describe using succinct language. We engage them in doing research to understand the big question and the small questions associated with it. We brainstorm different potential ways to address the question, and we help them evaluate pros and cons. We guide them in choosing the most feasible possible solution, and we encourage them to plan how to implement it.

Planning doesn't come easy for most young children, so we use different tools, such as design journals or peer interviews, to guide them through. We provide them with tools to make a prototype. Once it is done, children test it themselves. We encourage them to get out of their comfort zone and test it with others, as well. This always reveals new problems to solve, as others explore and play with the prototype in a different way than the child who created it in the first place did. Children find many problems with these first prototypes, and we provide the time, space, resources, and support needed to refine them. We cherish multiple iterations of problem-solving based on feedback. Finally, they feel it is ready to be shared with others. It was hard work. Learning is hard.

Alan Kay, a pioneer in the development of the personal computer, coined the phrase "hard fun" to describe an activity that engages us because it is both enjoyable and challenging. In the coding playground, we provide opportunities for children to have "hard fun," and we support the management of frustration. These are very young children, some of whom are still in the "tantrum stage." Some teachers set up a culture in which succeeding the first time is a rarity and a sign that the child did not challenge himself or herself enough. Others remind students that a project will fail a hundred times before it works, thus anticipating the inevitable. This creates a safe learning environment. It happens to everyone; we learn from failure. Some of the best teachers I have seen over the years invite laughter over failure; just as children laugh at their mistakes on the playground, they can find silliness in their mistakes in the classroom. Having fun and setting up an environment in which laughter is commonly heard is, in my experience, one of the best ways to help children manage frustration when working with technology (Bers, 2008).

Tools for Designers

How do we scaffold the design process for young children? Over the years, my DevTech research group has developed various strategies to guide children through the different steps (e.g., Bers, González-González, Belen Armas Torres, 2019; Elkin, Sullivan, & Bers, 2018; Govind, Relkin, & Bers, 2020). However, we must be careful; we do not want to take the fun out of it. Coding is a playground. If the design process becomes too scripted, the playfulness might disappear. We give children a design journal and set up the classroom routine with opportunities to talk about ideas. We reserve time to answer questions about their project's implementation early in the process. We also invite children to interview each other on video about their projects and to discuss the challenges that they encounter along the way. We engage them in documenting the design process. We sometimes share those videos and materials with parents as part of the child's portfolio.

Design journals, as well as video interviews, make transparent to the children their own thinking, as well as the project's evolution. This is also the case for parents and educators. However, children do not always welcome design journals, as they can impose a systematic approach, and some children do not like to plan. Those children might belong to a group of learners that Papert and Turkle have characterized as tinkerers and bri-coleurs (Turkle & Papert, 1992), who engage in dialogues and negotiations with the materials as they work with them. Their ideas emerge as they design, build, and program, not beforehand. As Papert and Turkle write, "The bricoleur resembles the painter who stands back between brush-strokes, looks at the canvas, and only after this contemplation, decides what to do next" (Turkle & Papert, 1992, p. 6).

The playground approach to coding supports different learning and designing styles. Some children want, and need, to plan. Others enjoy working bottom-up and messing around with the materials to come up with ideas. Tinkerers and planners complement each other and can also learn from each other. However, there is value in reinforcing the concept of the design process and breaking down the major task of making something. Processes are as important as products. When we ask children to share their projects, we remind them that we want to see their code, not only their final artifacts. We want them to tell us the story of how this product came to be. Just like in any other domain of early childhood education, we want them to show us their work, including the successes and the failures encountered in the learning journey.

In my book *Blocks to Robots* (Bers, 2008), I describe how making the design process visible is conducive to "teachable moments," those times in which students share a prototype that is not working or a failed strategy. Teachable moments offer fantastic opportunities for debugging. Debugging, the methodical process of finding and solving bugs, is one of the powerful ideas discussed in Chapter 6.

Learning on Demand

Mario, 7 years old, is working on a ScratchJr game. He created a bunch of flying pigs that make an explosion when they bump into the sun. He is using two pages. On the first page, five pigs are flying in the sky. On the next, there is a bright sun (see Figure 9.7). Mario can't make the pigs go to the next page. During technology circle, he shares his not-working program and explains the problem to his classmates. Immediately, he gets different ideas for how to solve (or "debug") his project.

This approach provides technical information on demand. It is based on the emerging needs of students and presents an alternative to lecture-type introductions. It also fosters a learning community where peer interaction

Figure 9.7 The first iteration of Mario's ScratchJr program that features five flying pigs. Mario hopes that the pigs will fly from one page to the next to create an explosion once they near the sun, however he has not yet learned the "Go to next page" End block yet.

is supported. It supports the development of different roles and forms of participation in the classroom culture. Technology circles can be called as often as every 20 minutes at the beginning of a project, or only once at the end of a day of work, depending on the needs of the children and the need of the teacher to introduce new concepts or reinforce old ones.

The challenge with technology circles is that children often ask questions that the teacher is not prepared to answer. This is an opportunity for modeling what programmers do when they do not know the answer. The teacher can first disclose her or his lack of knowledge and say, "Well, I'm not sure. Let's try!" or she can ask the children if someone knows the answer. If neither approach works, the teacher can then assure the children that she or he will find out by asking an expert or checking online, and will bring back the answer next time (Bers, 2008).

Seeking information, solving problems, and learning how to find help and resources are important activities that workers in the information technology industry (and workers in most other professions) do daily. The design process that engages children in the journey from having an idea to sharing a project provides opportunities for modeling useful lifelong learning habits. On the way, children develop emotional resources that they can later apply to all domains of life. The next chapter will explore the potential for personal growth when coding.

References

Bers, M. (2008). *Blocks to robots: Learning with technology in the early childhood classroom.* New York, NY: Teachers College Press.

Bers, M., González-González, M., & Belen Armas Torres, M. (2019). Coding as a playground: Promoting positive learning experiences in childhood classrooms. *Computers & Education: An International Technology Journal, 138,* 130–145. doi:10.1016/j.compedu.2019.04.013.

Bers, M. U. (2019a). Coding as another language: A pedagogical approach for teaching computer science in early childhood. *Journal of Computers in Education, 6*(4), 499–528.

Bers, M. U. (2019b). Coding as another language. In C. Donohue (Ed.), *Exploring key issues in early childhood and technology: Evolving perspectives and innovative approaches* (pp. 63–70). New York, NY: Routledge.

Elkin, M., Sullivan, A., & Bers, M. U. (2018). Books, butterflies, and 'bots: Integrating engineering and robotics into early childhood curricula. In L. English & T. Moore (Eds.), *Early engineering learning* (pp. 225–248). Singapore: Springer. doi:10.1007/978-981-10-8621-2_11.

Govind, M., Relkin, E., & Bers, M. U. (2020). Engaging children and parents to code together using the ScratchJr app. *Visitor Studies.* doi:10.1080/10645578.2020.1732184.

International Society for Technology in Education (ISTE). (2016). *Standards for students.* Retrieved from www.iste.org/standards/standards/for-students-2016

Massachusetts Department of Elementary and Secondary Education. (2016). *2016 Massachusetts science and technology/engineering curriculum framework.* Retrieved from www.doe.mass.edu/frameworks/scitech/2016-04.pdf

Resnick, M. (2001). Lifelong kindergarten. *Presentation delivered at the Annual Symposium of the Forum for the Future of Higher Education,* Aspen, Colorado.

Resnick, M. (2008). Sowing the seeds for a more creative society. *Learning & Leading with Technology, 35*(4), 18–22.

Turkle, S., & Papert, S. (1992). Epistemological pluralism and the revaluation of the concrete. *Journal of Mathematical Behavior, 11*(1), 3–33.

10 Personal Growth through Coding

Brandon has been struggling with his KIBO robot for at least 10 minutes. He built a KIBO lion that will run after a gazelle, as he saw a documentary last night at home about wildlife in Africa. He is trying to make KIBO move forward in a straight line, but every time he presses the button, KIBO turns. Brandon is persistent and doesn't want to give up; he is also too proud, and too shy, to ask for help. He wants to do it by himself. He has done it before, when working on another project. He keeps scanning the "Forward" block, but the robot keeps turning. Tom, his best friend, comes over and Brandon shows him the problem. Together they try again, but the KIBO lion doesn't go forward. Tom is puzzled and encourages Brandon to approach the teacher. Brandon is afraid. Mrs. Garcia said many times, "If you don't know how to do something, ask a friend first. Do not come to me." Tom reassures him. They will go together.

Mrs. Garcia smiles, takes a quick look at the robot, and points out to the boys the little green dot showing through the clear case of one of the motors, but not the other. Brandon suddenly gets it. Both motors need to have the green dots showing. He thanks the teacher and walks away with his KIBO. Tom is still confused, so Brandon explains to him how the green dots indicate the directionality of the motors. One of the motors was set to move differently than the other, which is why KIBO was turning instead of going straight. Brandon reassembles the motors and this time the KIBO lion works just the way he wants.

Brandon and Tom were doing a lot more than problem-solving. They were helping each other, working together, choosing a path of action (i.e., asking the teacher), and supporting each other in their weaknesses. They were displaying empathy and emotional connection to each other.

I developed a framework called Positive Technological Development (PTD) (Bers, 2012) to describe and identify these kinds of positive behaviors through the use of technology: collaboration, communication, community building, content creation, creativity, and choices of conduct. These are the six Cs. Some of the Cs support behaviors that enrich the intrapersonal domain (content creation, creativity, and choices of conduct); others address the interpersonal domain and look at social aspects (collaboration, communication, and community building). These behaviors are associated with personal assets (also using a six Cs labeling model) that have been described by decades of research on positive youth development (PYD) looking at the dynamic relations between individuals and contexts needed for thriving (Lerner, Almerigi, Theokas, & Lerner, 2005) (see Figure 10.1). While the six Cs proposed by PYD focus on developmental assets, the six Cs of PTD focus on behaviors. Together, these 12 Cs provide a framework for understanding how technology can be designed and used to promote positive behaviors and how, in turn, those behaviors can promote developmental assets. Of course, the learning culture, rituals, and values of a classroom will have an impact on how those behaviors get implemented through concrete practices.

PTD is a natural extension of the computer literacy and the technological fluency movements that have influenced the world of education

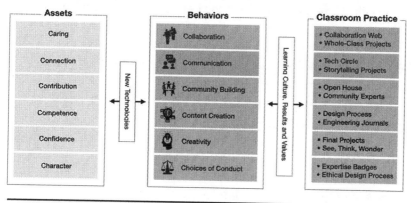

Figure 10.1 The PTD framework, including assets, behaviors, and classroom practices.

and technology, but it also incorporates psychosocial, civic, and ethical components. PTD examines the developmental tasks of a child growing up in our digital era, and provides a model for designing and evaluating technology-rich youth programs. The explicit end goal of educational programs guided by a PTD framework is not only to teach children how to code or to think in computational ways, but to engage them in positive behaviors. Within the PTD framework, the vision of coding as literacy that empowers individuals can be implemented.

In the PTD framework presented above, context plays a big role. There is nothing in the design of KIBO that prompts children to collaborate with each other. The secret ingredient is in the classroom culture and the curriculum: a setup that favors conversations around small tables and a teacher who invites children to help each other and promotes cooperative activities. It is not the technology, but the learning environment in which that technology is used, that promotes collaboration. For example, if Mrs. Garcia's goal was to promote efficiency and speed in problem-solving, she probably would have given children a different instruction than "ask a friend for help before asking me." Mrs. Garcia's goal for her robotics class was to support personal growth. When planning her classroom routines and curriculum, Mrs. Garcia asks herself, "What kind of developmental processes need to be facilitated?"

This question pervades all areas of study: math and science; literacy and social studies; music and movement; coding and engineering. The PTD framework provides a lens to approach these questions in a structured way by using the Cs model. In the next sections I will address each of the six Cs as they relate to coding and young children. In each section, I connect a C referring to one of the positive behaviors with a C referring to a positive personal asset: collaboration and caring, communication and connection, community building and contribution content creation and competence, creativity and confidence, choices of conduct and characterand. In total, these Cs form the backbone of the PTD framework.

Collaboration and Caring

The PTD framework focuses on collaboration to promote caring, defined in this context as the willingness to respond to the needs of other individuals, to assist others, and to use technology as a means to help others.

Collaboration is a process where two or more people work together to realize their shared goals. This can be challenging in early childhood; however, educational research has found that working in pairs or small groups can have beneficial effects on learning and development, particularly in the early years and primary education (Rogoff, 1990; Topping, 1992; Wood & O'Malley, 1996). Furthermore, research shows that when children are using computers, they are more likely to ask other children for advice and help, even if an adult is present, thus increasing collaboration toward positive socialization (Wartella & Jennings, 2000), and they are also more likely to engage in new forms of collaboration (New & Cochran, 2007). However, for a typically developing young child, the turn-taking, self-control, and self-regulation required to effectively collaborate on a project is difficult. In the past decade, kindergarten teachers in the U.S. have reported that many of their children lack effective self-regulatory skills (Rimm-Kaufman & Pianta, 2000).

Research with young children has shown many ways to foster peer collaborations through coding, particularly when teachers think carefully about the way that they design curriculum and how to group children. For example, a recent study conducted in my DevTech research lab showed how young children in second grade could work effectively in pairs to interview one another about their ScratchJr programming projects (Portelance & Bers, 2015). Other research explored the impact of curriculum structure during robotics and coding activities on young children's peer-to-peer collaborations. We found that a less-structured robotics curriculum was more successful for promoting peer interactions (Lee, Sullivan, & Bers, 2013).

To support collaboration, my DevTech research group has developed a low-tech pedagogical tool, called a "collaboration web," to help children become aware of their collaborative patterns (Bers, 2010b). At the beginning of each day of work, along with their design journals and their robotic kits, children are given a personalized printout with their photograph in the center of the page and the photographs and names of all other children in the class arranged in a circle surrounding their own photo. Throughout the day, when the teacher prompts students to do so, each child draws a line from his or her own photo to the photo of the children he or she has collaborated with. For this purpose, collaboration is defined as getting or giving help with a project, programming together, lending or borrowing materials, or working together on a common task.

At the end of the week, children write or draw "thank-you cards" to the children with whom they have collaborated the most to show that they care about them.

Richard Lerner, in his book *The Good Teen*, remembers his grandmother's definition of caring. He recalls her response when showing her his report card: "This is very nice. Getting good grades is important. But what is really important is being a mensch!" (2007, p. 165). This Yiddish word refers to a good person, someone who thinks not only of himself but of others, someone who cares about issues and people outside his immediate world, someone who listens, someone with a "big heart," someone who has compassion.

The PTD framework's goal is to engage children in collaborative endeavors to become mensches. In the process, we promote coding, learning about computer science, developing computational thinking, and learning in general; furthermore, from a positive developmental perspective, the goal of collaboration is to form caring relationships. As the great Jewish scholar and rabbi Abraham Joshua Heschel said, "When I was young, I admired clever people. Now that I am old, I admire kind people" (Heschel, 2017). It is my vision that through coding activities that promote collaboration, we can help young children admire kind people and behave kindly. Fortunately for us, the worldwide community of professional coders also tends to value this. Online groups and collaborative initiatives keep growing and are very active.

Communication and Connection

In the playground, there is a lot of talking. Children talk while playing, talk while climbing, and talk while running: the playground is not a quiet place. A silent playground is not a healthy playground. Talking is one of many forms of communication for which the PTD framework advocates. Within this approach, we encourage young children to talk out loud when coding, either to themselves or to others.

When children talk to themselves they are externalizing their ideas and thoughts. When they talk to others they are often sharing a challenge. Research shows that children benefit from these types of peer interactions (Rogoff, 1990). When children talk to one another, they engage in a process of language socialization in which they are learning how to talk and respond to one another (Blum-Kulka & Snow, 2002). Rogoff (1990) highlights Piaget's (1977) argument that children's discussions with adults are less productive for cognitive development than their discussions with their peers. This may be because the superior role of adults might intimidate children from freely expressing their ideas, while conversations with peers can provide the opportunity for reciprocal exchanges, thus promoting the types of social interaction conducive to cognitive development. This informs our curricular implementation of technology circle time to provide scaffolded opportunities for children to talk with each other about their projects.

Communication can be defined as an exchange of data and information. The PTD framework highlights the importance of communication to promote connection between peers or between children and adults. When designing coding experiences with the playground approach, we ask ourselves, "What are the communication mechanisms that will support the formation and sustainment of positive connections?" Activities such as the technology circles provide an answer. Children stop their work, put their projects on the table or floor, and come together to share their learning process. Technology circles present a good opportunity for problem-solving as a community. A different method to foster communication that we have used over the years is peer video interviews or "Code and Tell" sessions. In "Code and Tell" sessions, teachers partner students so that they can interview one another about their projects, their coding process, and the challenges that they have faced along the way (Portelance & Bers, 2015).

Studies have shown that when playing together at a computer, children speak twice as many words per minute than during other non-technology-related play activities such as playdough and building blocks (New & Cochran, 2007). Research also found that children spend nine times longer talking to peers while working with computers then they do when working on puzzles (Muller & Perlmutter, 1985). How can we leverage these findings when creating coding opportunities for young children? Experiences that effectively provide ways for children to communicate not only facilitate social interaction but also promote language and literacy. This is an essential developmental task for younger children.

Community Building and Contribution

The previously discussed Cs of communication and collaboration support the establishment and sustainment of social relationships when engaging young children in coding experiences. The Cs of community building and contribution take this a step further. They remind us that we must also provide mechanisms for giving back to others, to make our world a better place. Richard Lerner's work shows that when young people are "competent" and "confident," when they have a strong sense of "character" and they can "connect" with and "care" about others, they will also be able to "contribute" to society. All six Cs are interrelated but, according to Lerner, the C of contribution makes them all come together and is "the glue that creates healthy human development" (2007, p. 183). While contribution is an internal asset, a natural capacity of all human beings, coding experiences can facilitate community building.

With young children, community-building techniques may focus on scaffolding support networks that promote each child's contribution to the learning environment (Bers, 2010b). In the spirit of the Reggio Emilia approach (started in municipal infant-toddler centers and preschools in Reggio Emilia, Italy, after World War II), children's projects can be shared with the community via an open house, demonstration day, or exhibition (Rinaldi, 1998). An open house for coding projects provides authentic opportunities for children to share and celebrate the processes and products of their learning with others who are invested in their learning, such as family, friends, and community members.

Teachers may also choose to assign coding projects focused on the idea of societal contribution and community building. This prompts children to make projects with the explicit purpose of contributing to their community. For example, a public school in Somerville, MA, implemented a KIBO robotics curriculum on the theme "Helping at Our School" (Sullivan, 2016). Throughout the curriculum, children learned about robots that perform helpful jobs in the real world (such as hospital robots and robots that clean, like the Roomba, etc.). As a final project, children worked in groups to build and program their own "Helpful KIBO Robots" to do helpful classroom jobs like picking up trash, teaching important ideas, and demonstrating respectful behaviors and school rules (Sullivan, 2016) (see Figure 10.2). As a literacy, coding can provide the intellectual and material tools so that children, as they grow up, can fully participate in the ultimate type of community building: the civic society, with its legal and governmental systems.

In summary, the six Cs of the PTD framework are: collaboration, communication, community building, content creation, creativity, and choices of conduct. All of our curriculum units are marked with color-coded

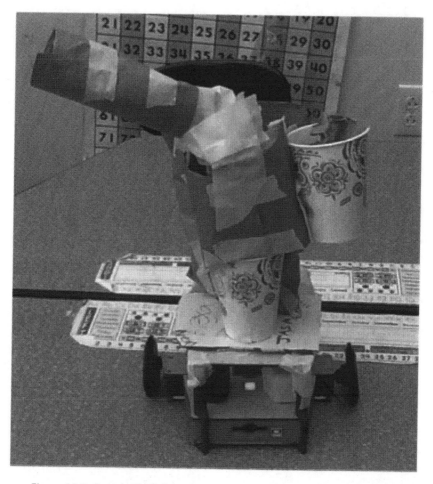

Figure 10.2 Sample "Helpful KIBO Robot." This robot was designed by a child to carry trash that is thrown out through the "trash chute" on top and stored in the paper cups. It is programmed to navigate across the classroom to the garbage and recycling bins in order to help keep the class clean.

symbols representing each of the Cs of PTD (see Figure 10.3). These symbols are defined at the start of every curriculum, with clarifying examples given. They are designed to remind us about the positive experiences that children can have while coding, just as they have in the playground.

In my DevTech research group, we created a set of PTD tools to help teachers, researchers, and designers to ask questions and to engage in guided observations to implement the 6Cs. The PTD cards are a set of cards

Lesson 11: Activities

WILD RUMPUS COMPOSITION (20 min)

First ask students to take out their Design Journals and write down their top three activities they would have in their own Wild Rumpus. *You might first provide an example: In my Wild Rumpus, I would have an awesome dance party, some howling at the moon, and making s'mores. Ask students: What three things would you have in your Wild Rumpus?* Students should refer back to these three ideas throughout the final project.

Students will engage in the Writing Process to plan out their Wild Rumpus composition using their Design Journals. Based on their three ideas, explain to students they will write a story about their Wild Rumpus. Below are examples of things to include in their composition, as well as writing tips:

- Identify the audience and purpose of writing *(Who will be reading your ideas for your Wild Rumpus? What might they want to know about your project?)*
- Use prewriting strategies to generate ideas before writing Use organizational strategies to keep track of the different project components
- Organize writing to include a beginning, middle, and end *(How does the Wild Rumpus start, what happens during it, and how does it end?)*

Organize writing to include a beginning, middle, and end (How does the Wild Rumpus start, what happens during it, and how does it end?)

WRITING VS. CODING (10 min)

This activity provides a chance for students to reflect on the constraints and affordances of each medium, writing and coding. Have students come together in a technology circle. *Ask students:*

- *What activities did you include in your Wild Rumpus?*
- *Are there certain activities you wrote about that you can code with KIBO?*

Figure 10.3 A screenshot of a lesson from the Coding as Another Language (CAL) curriculum. Each activity in the lesson is visually labelled with symbols along the right that identify the Cs of PTD that are supported in the activity. For example, in the "Wild Rumpus Composition" activity, children engage in creativity, communication, and content creation. In the "Writing vs. Coding" activity, children engage in community building.

with instructions to foster discussion amongst educators or any adults who plan to bring technology into a learning setting for children. The cards are designed to be used for collaborative, interactive evaluation of a technological tool or technology-rich learning setting using the PTD framework and the six Cs. They can be printed back-to-back, cut out, and used in the classroom with children, or amongst educators (see Figure 10.4). The following vignette describes a common way that early childhood practitioners can use the PTD cards to inform their teaching practice.

Early childhood teachers Sonya, Monika, and Jen are attending a professional development workshop where they are learning about integrating the KIBO robotics kit into their classrooms. After presenting the PTD framework, the workshop facilitator hands out PTD cards to small groups of

Figure 10.4 PTD cards.

teachers and tasks them with evaluating the extent to which KIBO embodies the six Cs of PTD. Sonya, Monika, and Jen receive the Collaboration card and take turns expressing their opinions.

Sonya comments first. "I think KIBO is an excellent tool for collaboration because several children can work with the robot at once and create a project together." Monika does not agree. She comments, "You know, it only takes one child to program KIBO. I know that at least some of the kids in my class would rather have KIBO to themselves than share it with others." Jen takes a middle ground. She feels that KIBO can embody collaboration but points out, "I think the teacher has to provide an environment that fosters collaboration."

Their next task is to think of ways that they can modify the technology or environment to best facilitate collaboration. Sonya is again the first to comment. She says, "I can picture giving each child a special job or role when programming KIBO, and then have all the children work together towards a common goal." Monika focuses on the classroom itself. She proposes, "Let them play with KIBO in an open space instead of on desks—that way, more children will be able to work together." Jen suggests that children be given the opportunity to get feedback on their projects from their peers and then collaborate to improve their projects.

By the end of this discussion, all three teachers agree that KIBO embodies the collaboration aspect of PTD. This activity allowed the educators to envision and address potential challenges that can arise when teaching with the KIBO platform. Exercises such as this can be applied to virtually any classroom technology to help educators think critically and to better understand the tools and environments that foster PTD.

We also developed two PTD Engagement Checklists: one to evaluate children in a variety of settings where they are engaging with technology; the other to evaluate the learning environment and the teacher/facilitator while children are working within the space (Bers, Strawhacker, & Vizner, 2018). Adults may use the checklists as often as they wish during each lesson, or as infrequently as once per unit. The checklists are divided into six sections (each one representing a behavior described in the PTD framework) and measured using a five-point Likert scale. For example, under the C of choices of conduct, the checklist for evaluating children asks observers to rate how often "Children handle tools/materials with care." Observers can evaluate choices of conduct using the environments and facilitators' checklist by rating how often "Tools/materials are offered that require children to use with care." I encourage you to explore both the PTD cards and the PTD Engagement Checklists: sites.tufts.edu/devtech/ptd/.

The next part of the book will present, in more detail, the two programming languages that I have worked on over so many years: ScratchJr and KIBO. It will also describe both design principles and teaching strategies for bringing coding into early childhood.

Content Creation and Competence

The act of coding facilitates content creation. The child becomes a producer, as opposed to a consumer (Bers, 2010a). Brandon learned how to make his KIBO lion move straight forward. But, most importantly, he learned computational ways of thinking and behaving. He learned that he can create the projects he imagines, even if it is hard and he needs to ask for help. A child who can program individual projects is likely to develop a sense of competence and a sense of mastery. And, like a chain reaction, the more competence a child masters, the more the child will be able to do, which sharpens skills and leads to even more competence (Bers, 2012).

When children program, they engage in a series of interrelated steps that might or might not be linear: the design process. They identify a final goal, they formulate an action plan, they make an initial attempt to meet their goals, they test and evaluate, they revise their ideas by assessing what went wrong and what they could do better, and they formulate new attempts to compensate for failure (Bers, 2010a). This iterative design experience may promote and support intentional self-regulation. This set of complex and abstract metacognitive processes is sometimes referred to in the literature as executive functions that enable self-regulated learners to set goals, strategize, and self-monitor in order to process the information around them (Blair, 2002).

Nobel Laureate economist James Heckman (Cunha & Heckman, 2007; Heckman & Masterov, 2007) identified skills involved in successful academic performance that are not measured by conventional indices of intellectual ability (e.g., "IQ" tests), such as motivation and goal setting, strategic thinking, identifying and recruiting the resources needed for problem-solving, and compensating when goals are blocked or when failure occurs. Although there are clearly cognitive components involved in these skills, Heckman and colleagues call these abilities "non-cognitive skills" in order to differentiate them from the specific cognitive abilities measured on conventional mental ability tests. In turn, other scholars have used terms such as "life skills" (Lerner, 2007) or "fundamental pragmatics of life" (Baltes, 1997; Freund & Baltes, 2002) to capture the essence of this set of motivational, cognitive, emotional, behavioral, and social skills.

Competence is not an innate asset; opportunities to create content and become producers of our own artifacts help us gain and reinforce competence. In this book, I make the case that coding is one of such opportunities to master not only powerful ideas of computer science, but also ways of thinking computationally. Within the playground approach to coding that I present in this book, coding means engaging children in making personally meaningful projects while developing new skills. When this happens successfully, we can see children developing a sense of confidence.

Creativity and Confidence

The fifth C of the PTD framework, creativity, has a strong relationship with the fourth one, content creation. The act of coding goes beyond using the technical skills to solve challenges or puzzles devised by others, that many current initiatives that promote coding have made popular (Resnick & Siegel, 2015). Coding, as a literacy, must support creative expression.

Despite early worries that computers might stifle creativity (Cordes & Miller, 2000; Oppenheimer, 2003), research has found that when used well, programming environments help creativity bloom (Clements & Sarama, 2003; Resnick, 2006, 2008). A creative person can imagine new ways of using the tool of computer programming and grows confident in those new skills. Confidence can be defined as the perception that one can achieve desired goals through one's actions. Confident coders believe in their ability to make the projects that they want to make. If they encounter problems along the way (and they surely will), they know they can try many different paths to problem-solve. Children who are confident coders have the needed skills to create a project, the ability to find help when necessary, and the perseverance to work hard when faced with technical difficulties.

Researchers have found self-efficacy (or self-efficacy beliefs) to be a necessary component for successfully using technologies to complete tasks (Cassidy & Eachus, 2002; Coffin & MacIntyre, 1999). Competence and confidence often go hand in hand: the more competent someone is, the more likely that person will feel confident. In turn, confidence can reinforce competence.

An important aspect of confidence is the belief that we can improve our skills. Stanford professor Carol Dweck (2006) calls this a "growth mindset," as opposed to a "fixed mindset." Individuals who believe that their talents can be developed (through hard work, good strategies, and input from others) have a growth mindset. They tend to achieve more than those with a more fixed mindset (those who believe their talents are innate gifts).

The process of teaching children to code with a playground approach reinforces the growth mindset. Coding invites problem-solving and perseverance, and it invites children to ask for help and to give help. It encourages the belief that children can do better in each iteration of their own designs.

Choices of Conduct and Character

The last C in the PTD framework is choices of conduct. The process of making choices builds character. Like the playground, coding experiences can provide the freedom for children to make authentic choices and to experience consequences. In this book, I propose that programming languages, amongst other technologies, can become ethical playgrounds to explore moral identities.

Some of these consequences happen at a micro, individual level. For example, Brandon chose the actions for his KIBO lion (i.e., pursuing the gazelle). Other consequences happen at the macro, social level. Children in a classroom can choose to adhere to the teacher's guidelines regarding projects or can do something else and discover the consequences. Furthermore, we live in a time when we are surrounded by news media about people choosing to use their coding skills in positive or in negative ways, to help or to harm society. There is controversy about hackers and computer scientists like Edward Snowden, who has been called a hero, a whistle-blower, a dissident, a patriot, and a traitor (Bamford, 2014; Gellman, Blake, & Miller, 2013). When one is a competent and confident producer, once has a choice of how to apply those skills. Thus, the C of choices of conduct is truly important to help young children start thinking about the ethical and moral choices associated with the power of literacy.

Although young children might not be aware of the complexities of these issues, it is never too early to bring up the fact that coding is a tool and, like any other tool, it can be used for good or bad, just like a hammer that can be used to build but also to destroy. When a child first learns how to use a hammer, we explain the precautions that tool requires and we indicate the need to be responsible. The same goes for coding. As a literacy, it is an intellectual tool with tremendous power.

Character is about the actions we take. It implies having a moral purpose and a sense of responsibility (Colby & Damon, 1992; Damon, 1990). Character informs the choices we make and, at the same time, these choices have an impact on our character. This perspective is strongly influenced by Piaget's belief that moral development emerges from action; that is to say, individuals construct their knowledge about morality as a result of interactions with the environment and experiences, rather than pure imitation (Kohlberg, 1973; Piaget, 1965). Morality is not learned by simply internalizing the norms of a group but, rather, by a developmental process that involves personal struggles to arrive at fair solutions and the development of a moral identity (Kohlberg, 1973).

Programming can provide opportunities for young people to explore moral identities (Bers, 2001). Sometimes, these opportunities are carefully planned. For example, I have developed and implemented several projects in which children create robots to represent cherished religious and moral values. Young children and families from Jewish day schools and Catholic schools in the U.S. have explored how robotics can be used to think about not only engineering and computer science, but also moral identities (Hassenfeld & Bers, 2018; Igoe, 2020). If you are interested in learning more, I suggest reading about the Mi Ani project in Watertown, MA (Bers, Matas, & Libman, 2013), and the Conciencia project in Buenos Aires, Argentina (Bers & Urrea, 2000).

References

Baltes, P. B. (1997). On the incomplete architecture of human ontogeny: Selection, optimization, and compensation as foundation of developmental theory. *American Psychologist, 52*(4), 366–380.

Bamford, J. (2014). Edward Snowden: The untold story. *WIRED Magazine*, August.

Bers, M. (2001). Identity construction environments: Developing personal and moral values through the design of a virtual city. *The Journal of the Learning Sciences, 10*(4), 365–415. Mahwah, NJ: Lawrence Erlbaum Associates, Inc.

Bers, M. U. (2010a). Beyond computer literacy: Supporting youth's positive development through technology. *New Directions for Youth Development, 128*, 13–23.

Bers, M. U. (2010b). The tangible K robotics program: Applied computational thinking for young children. *Early Childhood Research and Practice, 12*(2), 1–20.

Bers, M. U. (2012). *Designing digital experiences for positive youth development: From playpen to playground.* Cary, NC: Oxford University Press.

Bers, M. U., Matas, J., & Libman, N. (2013). Livnot u'lehibanot, to build and to be built: Making robots in kindergarten to explore Jewish identity. *Diaspora, Indigenous, and Minority Education: Studies of Migration, Integration, Equity, and Cultural Survival, 7*(3), 164–179.

Bers, M. U., Strawhacker, A. L., & Vizner, M. (2018). The design of early childhood makerspaces to support Positive Technological Development: Two case studies. *Library Hi Tech.* doi:10.1108/LHT-06-2017-0112.

Bers, M. U., & Urrea, C. (2000). Technological prayers: Parents and children exploring robotics and values. In A. Druin & J. Hendler (Eds.), *Robots for kids: Exploring new technologies for learning experiences* (pp. 194–217). New York, NY: Morgan Kaufman.

Blair, C. (2002). School readiness: Integrating cognition and emotion in a neurobiological conceptualization of children's functioning at school entry. *American Psychologist, 57*(2), 111.

Blum-Kulka, S., & Snow, C. E. (Eds.). (2002). *Talking to adults: The contribution of multiparty discourse to language acquisition.* Mahwah, NJ: Erlbaum.

Cassidy, S., & Eachus, P. (2002). Developing the computer user self-efficacy (CUSE) scale: Investigating the relationship between computer self-efficacy, gender and experience with computers. *Journal of Educational Computing Research, 26*(2), 133–153.

Clements, D., & Sarama, J. (2003). Young children and technology: What does the research say? *Young Children, 58*(6), 34–40.

Coffin, R. J., & MacIntyre, P. D. (1999). Motivational influences on computer-related affective states. *Computers in Human Behavior, 15*(5), 549–569.

Colby, A., & Damon, W. (1992). *Some do care: Contemporary lives of moral commitment.* New York, NY: Free Press.

Cordes, C., & Miller, E. (Eds.). (2000). *Fool's gold: A critical look at computers in childhood.* College Park, MD: Alliance for Childhood. Retrieved from http://drupal6.allianceforchildhood.org/fools_gold

Cunha, F., & Heckman, J. (2007). The technology of skill formation. *American Economic Review, 97*(2), 31–47.

Damon, W. (1990). *Moral child: Nurturing children's natural moral growth.* New York, NY: Free Press.

Dweck, C. S. (2006). *Mindset: The new psychology of success.* New York, NY: Random House.

Freund, A. M., & Baltes, P. B. (2002). Life-management strategies of selection, optimization and compensation: Measurement by self-report and construct validity. *Journal of Personality and Social Psychology, 82*(4), 642–662.

Gellman, B., Blake, A., & Miller, G. (2013). Edward Snowden comes forward as source of NSA leaks. *The Washington Post, 6*(9), 13.

Hassenfeld, Z. R., & Bers, M. U. (2018, November 28). Computer programming: An unexplored path to Jewish literacy [Blog post]. Retrieved from https://ejewishphilanthropy.com/computer-programming-an-unexplored-path-to-jewish-literacy/

Heckman, J. J., & Masterov, D. V. (2007). The productivity argument for investing in young children. *Applied Economic Perspectives and Policy, 29*(3), 446–493.

Heschel, A. J. (2017). *The mystical element in Judaism.* Skokie, Illinois: Varda Books.

Igoe, K. J. (2020, January 22). Can a screen-free robot teach coding—And build character? [Blog post]. Retrieved from https://alum.mit.edu/slice/can-screen-free-robot-teach-coding-and-build-character

Kohlberg, L. (1973). Continuities in childhood and adult moral development revisited. In P. B. Baltes & K. W. Schaie (Eds.), *Life-span developmental psychology* (pp. 179–204). New York, NY: Academic Press.

Lee, K., Sullivan, A., & Bers, M. U. (2013). Collaboration by design: Using robotics to foster social interaction in kindergarten. *Computers in the Schools, 30*(3), 271–281.

Lerner, R. M. (2007). *The good teen: Rescuing adolescence from the myths of the storm and stress years.* New York, NY: Three Rivers Press.

Lerner, R. M., Almerigi, J., Theokas, C., & Lerner, J. (2005). Positive youth development: A view of the issues. *Journal of Early Adolescence, 25*(1), 10–16.

Muller, A. A., & Perlmutter, M. (1985). Preschool children's problem-solving interactions at computers and jigsaw puzzles. *Journal of Applied Developmental Psychology, 6*, 173–186.

New, R., & Cochran, M. (2007). *Early childhood education: An international encyclopedia* (Vols. 1–4). Westport, CT: Praeger.

Oppenheimer, T. (2003). *The flickering mind: Saving education from the false promise of technology.* New York, NY: Random House.

Piaget, J. (1965). *The child's conception of number.* New York, NY: W. W. Norton & Co.

Piaget, J. (1977). Les operations logiques et la vie sociale. In J. Piaget (Ed.), *Sociological studies* (pp. 270–286). London: Routledge. (Original work published 1951).

Portelance, D. J., & Bers, M. U. (2015). Code and tell: Assessing young children's learning of computational thinking using peer video interviews with ScratchJr. In *Proceedings of the 14th International Conference on Interaction Design and Children (IDC '15).* ACM, Boston, MA.

Resnick, M. (2006). Computer as paintbrush: Technology, play, and the creative society. In *Play = learning: How play motivates and enhances children's cognitive and social-emotional growth* (pp. 192–208). New York, NY: Oxford University Press.

Resnick, M. (2008). Sowing the seeds for a more creative society. *Learning & Leading with Technology, 35*(4), 18–22.

Resnick, M., & Siegel, D. (2015, November 10). A different approach to coding: How kids are making and remaking themselves from Scratch [Web blog post]. *Bright: What's new in education.* Retrieved June 29, 2017, from https://brightreads.com/a-different-approach-to-coding-d679b06d83a

Rimm-Kaufman, S. E., & Pianta, R. C. (2000). An ecological perspective on the transition to kindergarten: A theoretical framework to guide empirical research. *Journal of Applied Developmental Psychology, 21*(5), 491–511.

Rinaldi, C. (1998). Projected curriculum constructed through documentation—Progettazione: An interview with Lella Gandini. In C. Edwards, L. Gandini, & G. Forman (Eds.), *The hundred languages of children: The Reggio Emilia approach—Advanced reflections* (2nd ed., pp. 113–126). Greenwich, CT: Ablex.

Rogoff, B. (1990). *Apprentices in thinking: Cognitive development in a social context.* New York, NY: Oxford University Press.

Sullivan, A. (2016). *Breaking the STEM stereotype: Investigating the use of robotics to change young children's gender stereotypes about technology & engineering* (Unpublished doctoral dissertation). Tufts University, Medford, MA.

Topping, K. (1992). Cooperative learning and peer tutoring: An overview. *The Psychologist, 5*(4), 151–157.

Wartella, E. A., & Jennings, N. (2000). Children and computers: New technology—Old concerns. *The Future of Children: Children and Computer Technology, 10*(2), 31–43.

Wood, D., & O'Malley, C. (1996). Collaborative learning between peers: An overview. *Educational Psychology in Practice, 11*(4), 4–9.

IV

New Languages for Young Children

ScratchJr

Lilly is in first grade. She has been using ScratchJr for the last two months during English class. Last week, Mrs. Brown read a story called *Are You My Mother?* by P. D. Eastman. Lilly loved the story of the little bird encountering different animals and asking them if they were her mother. After story time, Mrs. Brown gave the children iPads and invited them to work with a friend to animate the story using ScratchJr. Lilly found her partner, Sam. They loved the idea! They spent some time discussing what scenes they were going to create because they wanted to match the story to the available pages in ScratchJr. They decided to make the bird talk with the dog first, then go to the next page to talk with the cat, and finally the bird would talk with a steam shovel.

While Sam wanted to draw the characters on his own, Lilly wanted to use the iPad to take pictures of the book's drawings and import them into the already existing ScratchJr library. After some back and forth, Sam agreed to this proposal, but only if he could use the ScratchJr paint editor to add some stripes to the cat. He thought the book's illustrations needed some spicing up. Once both children agreed on the look of the main characters, it was time to start programming. Lilly wanted the bird to ask the dog, "Are you my mother?" and the cat to respond with a "meow." She set out to put together her ScratchJr program by snapping together the "Say" blocks, which allow characters to express themselves via speech bubbles. When trying out her program, Lilly noticed that the cat and the bird were speaking at the same time, unlike conversations in real life where, according to Lilly, "You're supposed to wait for the other person to talk before you respond." She started tinkering with different blocks until she discovered what she thought was a perfect solution to this problem: she connected a "Wait" block after each "Say" block in her program.

The function of the "Wait" block, which looks like the face of a clock, is to pause the program for a period. The way Lilly placed these blocks into her program caused intervals of time between the characters' speech bubbles. As a result, the conversation between the bird and the cat felt more natural. Sam liked this solution. During whole-class technology circle time, Lilly and Sam were proud to share their project with their classmates. Many other students wanted to know how they got their characters to talk to each other. Beaming, Lilly showed the class the code and carefully explained how she programmed the amount of time that the characters would "wait" before saying their lines. It was a trial and error process. At the end of this activity, Mrs. Brown showed the children how to share their interactive stories with their parents via email so that they could see their projects at home.

Lilly and Sam are two children from over 13 million around the world who are learning to code and who are creating their own interactive stories with the free ScratchJr app. ScratchJr was launched in July 2014 (Bers & Resnick, 2015), and from then until Febuary 2020 it was downloaded over 13 million times, and it records an average of over 280,000 worldwide users per week. ScratchJr is used in 191 countries across the globe (Bers, 2018). As of today, we are proud that ScratchJr can be downloaded to iPads, Android tablets, Amazon kindle tablets, and Chromebooks, and we are tirelessly working on making the application available on other platforms. Translations in Spanish, Dutch, French, Catalan, Italian, and Thai are also available, and we are actively adding new languages to improve localization. Our goal is to provide a free programming language for every young child to learn to code, to think in new ways, and to use technology for self-expression in a playground style.

The rapid growth and penetration of ScratchJr in early childhood education, such as in Lilly and Sam's first grade classroom, shows that teachers want and need technological playgrounds for young children. While Mrs. Brown did not have time allocated in her day for a computer or programming class, she was able to creatively integrate ScratchJr into her English class. Before ScratchJr, she might have asked children to recreate the *Are You My Mother?* story with crayons and paper. Now, with ScratchJr, she could incorporate coding into this activity. Children engaged with literacy and with programming skills simultaneously. Furthermore, they wove together their creativity and problem-solving with their excitement and pride, sharing their projects with peers at school and parents at home.

Like many creative endeavors, ScratchJr started with a question: how can we make a programming language developmentally appropriate for young children? We were inspired by Scratch, designed for children aged 8 and up by Mitch Resnick and his team at the MIT Media Lab, which is used by millions of young people around the world (visit scratch.mit.edu to find out more).

After observing my own three children, who were young at the time, trying to program on their own with Scratch, I realized the need to make some important design changes. They understood the basic programming concepts, but it was hard for them to manipulate the interface. They were lost with the many choices of programming commands that they couldn't read or comprehend. With an adult mediating the experience, they could happily use Scratch, but they could not work on their own. This troubled me. Children do not need an adult to hold their hand in the playground. They can figure out how to use the equipment and how to navigate the social rules. They might need help for the more challenging tasks but, generally speaking, playgrounds are designed so that children can play and experiment on their own. I wanted a programming language that would enable the same experience of freedom and exploration and the same sense of mastery, without an adult stewarding every action.

Resnick and I decided to collaborate on the ScratchJr project, and brought to our team old friends and colleagues Paula Bontá and Brian Silverman from the Playful Invention Company (PICO) in Canada. The adventure began in 2011 when we received a grant from the National Science Foundation to start the research and design process (NSF 1118664). In addition, we received generous support from the Scratch Foundation, which was developed to provide support and raise funds for the Scratch ecosystem. It took us three years to get ready to launch ScratchJr. We wanted an age-appropriate programming language for children aged 5–7. We wanted a digital playground to create interactive stories and games using graphical blocks. We wanted to do it right. Therefore, we sought out the best design partners available at each stage of development for guidance and valued input, including early childhood educators, parents, principals, and children themselves.

The Tool

ScratchJr is a digital playground for coding. We spent a great amount of time working in partnership with graphic designers so that the interface would convey playfulness. The color scheme sets a playful tone, the graphics are bright and whimsical, and the programmable actions are fun. Children drawn to artistic endeavors can design characters and backgrounds. Children drawn

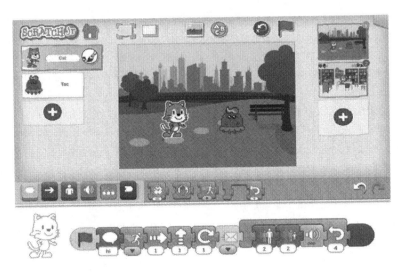

Figure 11.1 The ScratchJr interface.

to animations can explore the range of programming concepts systematically or by tinkering. Children can snap together graphical programming blocks to make their characters move, jump, dance, and sing. They can modify characters in the paint editor, create colorful backgrounds, add their own voices and sounds, and even take photos of themselves to insert into their stories.

ScratchJr has a user's library of projects, a main project editor, and tools for selecting and drawing characters and background graphics (Figure 11.1). At the center of the project editor is the story page, the scene under construction. New characters, text, and settings can be added by clicking large buttons labeled with icons: for example, a cat silhouette, the letter A, and a mountain range. Pages (thumbnails of which appear on the right-hand side) can be created and played in sequence as multi-scene stories.

The blue palette of programming instructions lies along the center of the editor. Children display one instruction category at a time by clicking selectors on the left. Dragging instruction blocks from the palette into the scripting area below activates them. Snapping blocks together creates programs that are read and played from left to right. The "Green flag" ("Play") and red "Stop" buttons respectively start and interrupt the programmed animation.

The programming blocks are organized into six categories represented by different colors: yellow Trigger blocks, blue Motion blocks, purple Looks blocks, green Sound blocks, orange Control flow blocks, and red End blocks (see Table 11.1).

Table 11.1 ScratchJr programming block categories. For more detailed descriptions of individual programming blocks see www.scratchjr.org/learn.html

Block Category	Sample Block	Category Description
Trigger blocks	"Start on green flag"	These blocks can be placed at the beginning of a script in order to make that script execute when a certain event happens. For example, when the "Start on green flag" block is placed at the beginning of a script, the script will execute whenever the "Green flag" at the top right of the screen is tapped.
Motion blocks	"Move right" (1 step)	These blocks make characters move up, down, left, and right. They can also make characters go back to the place they started, rotate, and hop.
Looks blocks	"Grow"	These blocks change how characters look. This set includes blocks that change the size of the character, add a speech bubble with user-defined text, and show or hide the character.
Sound blocks	"Play pop"	Sound blocks play a sound in ScratchJr's library. Children can also record a sound and save it in a new Sound block.
Control flow blocks	"Wait"(1/10th second)	Unlike Motion or Looks blocks, which visibly change the characters on the stage, Control flow blocks change the nature of a character's program. For example, a sequence of blocks can go inside of a "Repeat" block and then the user can change the number on this block to determine how many times the given script will execute.
End blocks	"Repeat forever"	These blocks can be placed at the end of the program and determine whether something happens when the program finishes executing.

Figure 11.2 A script in ScratchJr comprising six programming blocks. This script will start when the user presses the "Green flag." When the script runs, the corresponding character will hop twice, then grow by two times, and then shrink by two times back to its original size.

When put together as a jigsaw puzzle, these programming blocks allow children to control their character's actions on the screen. For example, the following image shows a programming script for a character hopping twice and then growing and shrinking (see Figure 11.2).

The design of the block shapes prevents syntax errors. The jigsaw puzzle pieces have visual properties that correspond to their syntactic properties. For example, the "Repeat forever" block can only appear at the end of a program. Since nothing should follow a "Repeat forever" command, the right side of this block is rounded so that another jigsaw piece cannot attach to it (see Figure 11.3).

A programming script runs as a sequence from left to right instead of the traditional top-to-bottom format of most programming languages,

Figure 11.3 "Repeat forever" block with rounded right side.

including Scratch. This choice reinforces print-awareness and English liter-acy skills. As a character's script runs, the app highlights each block as it is executed, representing the instructions given to that character on the stage.

When the app opens to the project screen, the Motion blocks are shown within the blocks palette in the middle of the screen (Figure 11.4). Children can drag as many Motion blocks as they like from the palette to the programming area below it and then connect them to create scripts. To program with blocks from other categories, children may tap one of the color-coded buttons on the left side of the palette. For example, if a child taps the purple button, the Motion blocks on the palette are replaced with Looks blocks. In this way, children have access to over 25 programming blocks, without being overwhelmed by options on the screen. Text show-ing the name of each block can be revealed by tapping it, which supports word recognition.

The programming blocks span concepts from simple sequencing of motion to control structures. Most of the powerful ideas of computer sci-ence described in Chapter 6 can be encountered when making a ScratchJr project. In addition, children can use ScratchJr for other activities beyond coding. They can create and modify characters in the paint editor, record

Figure 11.4 The circled blue Motion blocks are shown within the blocks palette in the middle of the screen.

their own voices and sounds, and even insert photos of themselves that they take in the paint editor using the camera option. Then they can incorporate those media-rich materials into their projects to personalize them. ScratchJr comes with a small basic set of graphics compared to the hundreds available in Scratch. This decision was motivated by our overarching theme that "less is more" in order to ease children's difficulty in navigating vast arrays of options. Furthermore, it encourages them to create their own new graphics that might relate to classroom-specific themes. Children can edit the included images or draw their own in an embedded scalable vector graphics editor. Data shows that 11 percent of all projects created by children include either a character or background that was created in the paint editor. Furthermore, the most common character added in ScratchJr, encompassing 33 percent of the characters added during sessions, is "User Asset," or a character created or altered in some way in the paint editor. This demonstrates users' desire to add personal and unique aspects to their projects.

ScratchJr has a feature called "the grid" that overlays the animation stage (see Figure 11.5). It can be toggled on and off, and is most helpful when used during programming (as opposed to when presenting a project). The grid was designed to help children understand the units of measurement

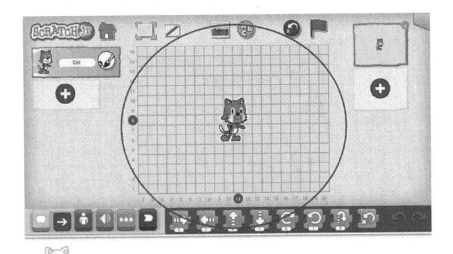

Figure 11.5 ScratchJr has a grid feature.

for each programming block. It addresses the countable unit of measurement for linear movement. For example, a character programmed to "Move right 10" glides ten grid cells rather than ten pixels or some other arbitrary unit.

The grid is similar to the upper-right quadrant of the Cartesian coordinate system, with discrete rather than continuous units of measure. Its numbered axes prompt counting and provide a marker to track counting. Children may use several methods to relate the numbers on the axes to the number representing a desired amount of motion along that axis.

Motion created by a single script always parallels either the vertical or horizontal axis, ensuring that the grid-cell unit of measure always corresponds to the distance the character will move. In using the grid, several possible strategies for programming movement of a given distance facilitate exploration of increasingly sophisticated number and programming concepts. For example, to move a character three grid squares, a child could sequence three "Move 1" blocks, using the default parameter value for this block. The child could also use a single "Move 1" block and click the script or the "Play" button three times. Finally, the child could change the number parameter, creating a "Move 3" block (see Figure 11.6). The grid's cells and numbered axes allow for strategies varying in complexity, from

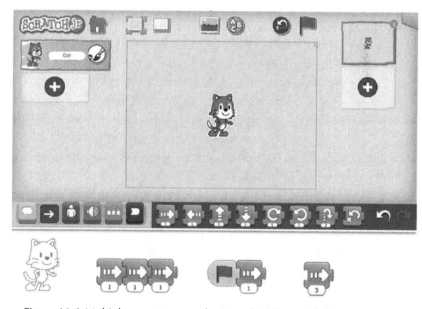

Figure 11.6 Multiple ways to move the ScratchJr kitten with blue Motion blocks.

estimating and adjusting, to counting, to basic arithmetic. The design of the grid was influenced by our goal to facilitate the integration of ScratchJr with other curricular disciplines: in this case, math.

Furthermore, several design decisions were made for seamless integration with literacy. The ability to create up to four independent "pages" and to integrate text and speech into a project allows children to create their own storybooks with a beginning, middle, and end. When creating these projects, children think in terms of "if this happens, then this happens." By programming with ScratchJr, they can begin to understand the basic components of a story while also reinforcing sequencing skills.

While working with ScratchJr, children encounter powerful ideas and develop skills that can be applied across domains such as sequencing, estimation, prediction, composition, and decomposition. "How many?" or "How far?" are questions commonly heard when children are using ScratchJr. Furthermore, experienced teachers invite children to predict what will happen when they run each iteration of their program, and to think about whether the changes they have made will result in their intended outcome. ScratchJr provides immediate feedback about the accuracy of their estimations and predictions. That is the beauty of a programming language: computational thinking can be tested and feedback received (Bers & Sullivan, 2019; Relkin & Bers, 2019).

Many of ScratchJr's design features support problem-solving by reducing unnecessary low-level cognitive burdens, therefore freeing up mental resources for high-level processes, such as troubleshooting a script that produces unexpected outcomes. These design decisions keep the challenge at an appropriate level and may help young children devote sufficient cognitive resources to the many high-level thinking processes involved in imagining and creating a program. When the goal of coding is expression, this is much needed.

In order to facilitate the teaching of ScratchJr, we have developed curriculum for beginner, intermediate, and advanced students. Although the powerful ideas that we teach at each level remain similar, with the exception of orange control structures, we teach each of them with a different level of depth. For example, beginner students explore algorithms through simple linear sequencing, while intermediate students can explore looping sequences using "Repeat" blocks, and advanced learners can engage with parallel sequences of two or more simultaneous programs. However, at each expertise level, we introduce new ScratchJr blocks (see Table 11.2). For example, children in a beginner ScratchJr curriculum use blue Motion blocks

Table 11.2 Table comparing the blocks we recommend teaching at the beginner, intermediate, and advanced levels of ScratchJr instruction

	Beginning	**Intermediate**	**Advanced**
ScratchJr (28 blocks)	• Start—Green Flag Block • Blue Motion Blocks (Right, Left, Up, Down, Turn Right, Turn Left, Hop) • Pink Character Blocks (Say, Grow, Shrink, Reset Size, Hide, Show) • Green Pop Block • Red End Block	**All the beginner blocks +** • Start—On Tap Block • Blue Go Home Block • Green Recorded Sound Block • Orange Set Speed Block • Orange Wait Block • Orange Repeat Block • Red Repeat Forever Block • Red Go To Page Block	**All the beginner + intermediate blocks +** • Start—On Bump Block • Start—On Message Block • Send Message Block • Stop Block • Parallel Programming

to program a collage of characters that perform a dance or move around the screen. In an intermediate curriculum, children might combine the now-familiar blue blocks with new green Sound "Recording" blocks and yellow "Start on tap" blocks to create interactive characters that speak when touched. Finally, children in an advanced curriculum combine all their previous knowledge and add orange message blocks to program the characters to realistically interact with each other, depicting a game, a conversation, or a story.

Our Design Process

We started our design and development process by observing how young children used Scratch, which is designed for older children, and noting their difficulties. We spent many hours in local kindergartens, and first and second grade classrooms to understand the limitations for our intended age range, 5 to 7 years old (Flannery et al., 2013). For example, we noted that children were getting lost with so many possibilities for programing commands. Thus, we learned early on about the need to simplify and offer a more limited programming palette. We also noticed that movement happened too fast and children had a difficult time understanding the relationship between the programming blocks and their resulting actions. We, therefore, decided to slow down processes, so that every block would take time before the triggering of the action. Teachers pointed out that as children were learning how to read and write in English from left to right it might be a good idea to mirror this directionality in ScratchJr. In contrast, Scratch is programmed from top to bottom to mimic other established and more advanced programming languages. Based on these findings we started the design of our first ScratchJr prototypes, Alpha and Beta.

Throughout each stage of development, we conducted user testing with young children, parents, and educators. While this approach might have slowed down the development process, it ensured that we created a programming language that each of these groups, with their diversity of needs and wants, would find useful. We worked with hundreds of teachers and children through informal after-school sessions, educator workshops, experimental classroom interventions, and at-home play sessions. Additionally, we conducted online surveys and face-to-face focus groups to obtain feedback. These provided valuable insights for our design team.

Alpha, the initial prototype, was web-based. It required children and teachers to log in to a private server. This version addressed our overarching goals of scaling down the Scratch programming environment to appeal to a younger audience (e.g., less text on the screen, more inviting and colorful graphics, large programming blocks with simple commands, etc.). However, the username system was poorly received as teachers had difficulty keeping track of students' login credentials, and students forgot them. Furthermore, most of the children could not type with accuracy anyway. By using the Alpha web-based prototype, most children ended up with multiple accounts and lost their work, while teachers were frustrated because they spent most of their time with the school's technical administration team, rather than focusing on the children learning programming concepts.

Through focus groups and surveys, we heard loud and clear that most teachers wanted to have a ScratchJr version that did not require internet access. Many schools had slow connectivity that caused lags and errors as students worked, creating frustration for both students and teachers. Others did not have connectivity at all. Teachers wanted a stand-alone application.

Furthermore, they wanted a tablet version, not a desktop or laptop computer version. It is conceivable that this wish was partially spurred by the growing popularity in 2011 and 2012 of Apple iPad tablets and touch-screen devices, but our research also showed that students had considerable difficulty manipulating mice and touch pads when using ScratchJr on computers.

We released the Beta version of ScratchJr as a tablet interface for iPads, which did show improvements in children's ability to quickly and fluently create projects. However, due to technical issues, classrooms still needed access to wireless internet. We created an experimental Admin Panel, a master-user web page for teachers that grouped all student accounts and completed work in one location. While there were some successes with this method (for example, it was easy for teachers to view all students' work at once), the Admin Panel was overwhelming to use, as each classroom had hundreds of projects by the end of a single unit. Furthermore, log in credentials were still required and problematic.

While our technical team was working on the platform issues, we experimented with different kinds of programming blocks and the grouping of the blocks into categories. Teachers suggested setting the Rotate character" block at 12 steps so that it could perform a full rotation. This number corresponds with an analog clock, a topic typically covered in first and second grade. We also explored the different tool options. Children provided extensive feedback on the camera functionality in the paint editor, the sound recording feature in the Sound blocks palette, the colorful highlighting of blocks as they are running within a program, and the drag-to-copy feature that allows characters and their code to be shared across multiple pages in a single project. Parents applauded our decision to have no internet links or "pop-ups" anywhere in the app (so children could not accidentally get online), except for the email-sharing feature to send projects to family members or other devices. The sharing feature has played an important role in fostering a ScratchJr community in which children can share what they have made in school with friends and family at home.

In conjunction with our design team, h24 Creative Studio, we experimented with different looks and metaphors for the interface. For example, Figures 11.7, 11.8, and 11.9 show the different interface aesthetics we experimented with, from a digital feel to a traditional notebook to a wooden surface.

Figure 11.7 ScratchJr interface 1 "digital feel" design.

Figure 11.8 ScratchJr interface 2 "notebook" design.

Figure 11.9 ScratchJr interface 3 "wooden" design.

All along the design process, we struggled with an important decision: the look of the ScratchJr kitten. We explored different ideas until we were all happy (see Figure 11.10).

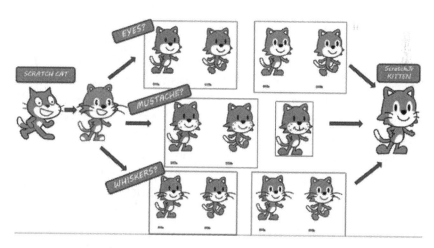

Figure 11.10 The ScratchJr kitten was influenced by the Scratch cat of the Scratch programming language developed in 2007. The kitten went through many iterations until the team agreed on what it looks like today.

By July 2014, after a successful Kickstarter campaign to raise funds to complement our already existing grant, we launched the current version of ScratchJr as a native tablet app. We removed the username and Admin Panel systems and we developed a simple one-to-one device-sharing model. Projects can now be shared via email or via Apple's AirDrop feature. This was a compromise for school and home use. As creators of ScratchJr, we immersed ourselves in a journey that took us through the different steps of the design process. It was fun.

ScratchJr Today

After the release of ScratchJr for iPads, teachers around the world started to ask for an Android version, so we expanded our team. At the time, Mark Roth, a managing director and software engineer at Two Sigma Investments, and a proud father of two boys, had just learned of ScratchJr. Disappointed to hear that there was no Android version yet, he approached Resnick to volunteer his spare time with the team. Together with Kevin Hu, another software engineer at Two Sigma, the team released a Beta version in November 2014 and a final version in March 2015. Today, the Android version is officially supported by the Scratch team, works on Android 5.0 + (Lollipop or higher) with 7-inch screens or larger, and has seen over 3,000,000 downloads (and is growing rapidly).

Mark worked on this project because he believes it is important for people around the world to have access to tools that allow creative minds to explore. He knows that Android is a more common platform outside the U.S., so he decided to help out by volunteering his time. Using the Android version, we then created a version for Amazon tablets in January 2016 and further expanded it by making ScratchJr compatible with Chromebook devices in March 2016. Making ScratchJr available on many different devices has allowed the application to have a more global impact. ScratchJr is actively used in 191 countries worldwide (out of 196), and is used the most in the U.S., the U.K., Australia, Canada, Sweden, China, France, Spain, Japan, and the Netherlands.

Furthermore, in December 2015, we launched PBS KIDS ScratchJr in collaboration with PBS KIDS, so that children could create their own interactive stories and games using over 150 characters and backgrounds from popular children's television programs produced by PBS KIDS, such as *Wild Kratts*, *WordGirl*, *Peg + Cat* and *Nature Cat* (www.pbs.org/about/blogs/news/pbs-kids-launches-free-scratchjr-app-helping-young-children-learn-to-code-and-code-to-learn/). The app was developed as part of the Corporation for Public Broadcasting (CPB) and the PBS Ready To Learn Initiative with funding from the U.S. Department of Education and, at the time of writing this book, had over 1 million downloads.

The ScratchJr team began collecting analytics data in January 2016, which has provided a more comprehensive overview of how children and educators are using the application. From January 2016 until Febuary 2020, over 48.6 million projects have been created, and over 64.8 million existing projects have been opened again and edited, indicating that users are working on improving and altering the same projects over time. Additionally, over 1.5 million projects have been shared with others via email or Apple AirDrop. In this relatively short time span, over 936 million programming blocks have been used, the most popular blocks being "Forward," "Start on green flag," "Up," "Backward," and "Say." The "Say" block is used so that characters within a project can communicate with each other—the notion that it is in the top five most-used blocks on ScratchJr shows that children are using the app to build upon their storytelling skills. Furthermore, users around the world spend a consistent average of 13 minutes per session creating projects in ScratchJr. Additionally, ScratchJr maintains an 80 percent rate of returning users, while still bringing in a consistent 20 percent rate of new users each month. ScratchJr is certainly growing rapidly, and those who use it keep coming back to program more. By the time you are reading this book, these numbers will have increased.

A Playground on the Screen

Children's projects show the depth of their creativity. A popular kindergarten activity with ScratchJr involves designing and creating collages with embedded animations about their favorite places, activities, or special people in their lives. Children exploring storytelling have used classic storybooks by Eric Carle, Mo Willems, and Maurice Sendak for inspiration, and then programmed their own original multipage stories. These projects allow children to imagine new endings to favorite tales, or even to invent new narratives of their own. For example, children have created versions of *Little Red Riding Hood* where Little Red and the Wolf became friends, or fantasy stories about dragons and wizards travelling to another planet to save Earth. Older children, inspired by game mechanics in mazes, Tetris, and Frogger, delight in building projects that are interactive. Children explore perspective-taking and user-centered design by developing simple interactive games, and testing them out with their friends and family.

ScratchJr provides the opportunity for a digital coding playground. As evidenced by the diversity of experiences described earlier, children can playfully program their own stories, games, and animations. Furthermore, when working on their own, children have chosen to program the artwork they themselves created. This is something that is happening spontaneously in the ScratchJr playground. Children use their imagination and art skills, along with their coding and problem-solving strategies.

ScratchJr is an open-ended programming environment that engages children in the six positive behaviors (six Cs), proposed by the Positive Technological Development (PTD) framework. Thus, it engages children in making their own projects (i.e., *content creation*). Throughout this iterative creation process, children develop computational thinking concepts, skills, and practices. Furthermore, they exercise their own *creativity*. In the process of solving technical problems in creative ways, children develop confidence in their learning potential. Clever or creative projects may be difficult to make, and the process can be frustrating. Just like in the playground, where children need to learn to play on the monkey bars without throwing tantrums, children using ScratchJr must learn how to manage their own frustration—an important step toward the development of confidence in their ability to learn new skills.

Classrooms that foster a culture in which it is expected that things may not work and might be difficult, can facilitate this process (Portelance & Bers, 2015; Strawhacker, Lee, & Bers, 2017). As children program different projects, they gradually realize their ability to find solutions by trying multiple times, by using different strategies, or by asking for help (Bers, 2010). In addition to supporting their creativity, my research has found that classrooms with a culture where teachers and students learn alongside each other, rather than following strict instructions from an educator, result in higher learning outcomes and a stronger understanding of ScratchJr programming concepts in children (Strawhacker & Bers, 2019).

The PTD framework calls for coding experiences that promote *collaboration*. This is tricky when working on a device that has only one screen. Although children can work in groups, the design of the tablet itself puts only one child in control. Children can discuss their ideas as a team, within the limitations of their developmental abilities. Young children are learning how to work together as they get out of the phase of parallel play. Having one single object to manipulate amongst a group of multiple children might pose some challenges. There is no design feature in ScratchJr specifically conceived to promote collaboration between children. The platform is a tablet designed for a single user. Thus, as seen earlier, collaboration is not about the tool, but about the teaching strategies that surround it.

The same is true for *communication*: while the playground structure fosters interaction because children need to negotiate space, a tablet directs the attention to itself. Although two children might be sitting next to each other working on ScratchJr, it is not the tool that will promote conversation, but the pedagogical choices and teaching strategies used with it. This emphasizes the importance of designing a curriculum that is aligned with the PTD framework. For example, by encouraging students to describe their projects to one another, their classroom culture fosters communication in more than one media form (Portelance & Bers, 2015). It is too easy to forget that when teaching to code in early childhood, we must also teach children how to communicate.

Along the same lines, the playground itself doesn't foster a sense of community, but the neighborhood can put in place practices to help build community around the playground. *Community-building* activities, popularized in early childhood by the Reggio Emilia approach, promote each child's contribution to the wider community. In ScratchJr we added a "sharing" capability so that children can share their projects with teachers and loved ones. We are also working on an online support network for adult users. Furthermore, we are organizing ScratchJr family days that bring together parents, children, siblings, and grandparents to work together on their coding projects and to learn from each other (Govind, Relkin, & Bers, 2020).

The PTD framework reminds us of the importance of making *choices of conduct*. In the playground, children are often faced with challenges: should they cut the line for the slide or patiently wait their turn? Should they take home the nice yellow truck forgotten in the sandbox, or leave it because there is a chance that its owner will come and get it later? While these dilemmas are presented every day in the playground, in a coding environment, it is harder to observe them. There are the obvious classroom situations, such as being a good partner and sharing the tablet with some-one else, but there are also subtler ways.

For example, after Johnny is done with his project, should he make himself available to help others in the classroom or should he quietly do something else? Should Mary constantly ask for help when she encounters a difficult problem, or should she first try her best, so as not to monopolize her teacher's attention? It is not the ScratchJr programming app that will invite children to make choices of conduct to provoke examination of val-ues and exploration of character traits. It is, once again, the pedagogical choices of the teacher and the setup of the learning environment.

ScratchJr provides multiple ways of doing the same thing—thus, the need to choose. Just like in the playground, coding must provide oppor-tunities for children to experiment with "what if" questions and consider the potential consequences of their own choices. These moral and ethi-cal dimensions are present in all realms of life, even when coding. When designing ScratchJr, we carefully kept the playground metaphor in sight. When we found ourselves limited by the tool itself, we developed curricu-lum and activities to help teachers and parents to create playful learning environments to promote the six Cs of PTD. However, although we tried our best, we are limited by the onscreen format of the tablet. Much of the magic of what happens in the playground is because children are free to move around and experiment with their bodies, and not just their minds.

To address this challenge, we developed a curricular guide for proj-ects incorporating multiple tablets. Our goal was to create opportunities for children to focus their attention *off* the screen and *on* one another. By working together to create a cohesive story or game using multiple tab-lets, children also engage more deeply in the design process and expand their ScratchJr coding skills. For example, one group of students created a "Whack-Animal" game, in which they programmed ScratchJr characters to appear and disappear at different times. Students then placed the tablets around the room and pressed the Green flag on all the tablets to start the game. Players would race around the room and win points by tapping only on the animal characters when they appeared on the screen (see Figure 11.11). The "Whack-Animal" game, along with other sample projects and step-by-step instructions, can be found in the Collaborative ScratchJr Project Guide on the DevTech website: https://sites.tufts.edu/devtech/files/2018/07/Collaborative-ScratchJr-Project-Guide.pdf. The vignette following Figure 11.11 illustrates how this kind of project can be implemented in practice.

Figure 11.11 Six children play the game ScratchJr "Whack-Animal." The children have programmed the same project on many different tablets so that they can race around the table tapping an animal as it appears. An extra tablet keeps track of the score.

Mr. Rivera is a second grade teacher. He introduced ScratchJr to his students in the fall, as an afternoon choice activity. It is now spring, and most of his students have become very familiar navigating the ScratchJr interface and creating simple projects. Noting that his students have been asking repeatedly for "more coding time," Mr. Rivera is eager to integrate ScratchJr into another part of the day, perhaps into one of his science lessons. His class is wrapping up an astronomy unit, so Mr. Rivera incorporates a multi-tablet ScratchJr element into their final unit project. His students get really excited. They work in pairs to design their own planet Earth and program their Earth character to move from the left side of the screen to the right side.

Once everyone is ready to share, Mr. Rivera plans a special "Trip Around the Sun." The students pretend to be astronauts and dress up in handmade space suits, then they gather on the space-themed carpet, their tablets in hand. They place their tablets in a circle, while Mr. Rivera, who's dressed up as the sun, sits in the middle of the circle. One by one, each pair plays their program, waiting patiently for one program to end before beginning the next, which symbolizes the Earth rotating around the sun. One student, Nadia, exclaims,

> Wait a minute! These three tablets all have a snowy Earth! They should be placed next to each other. And these planets over there—they have flowers and trees just like we have in spring. Maybe we should group the tablets by season.

The other students agree and switch their positions around the circle. At the end of class, Mr. Rivera records a video of their final project to send to his students' families, remarking how the activity sparked lots of conversation about seasons and planets and enabled students to be creative thinkers and storytellers.

This collaborative ScratchJr project is an example of how a playground experience can also happen if screens are used in creative ways. However, tangible, physical objects can be more easily conducive to a playground type of experience that involves the use of our bodies. The ability to play in space and manipulate tangible objects might contribute to an understanding of more complex, abstract ideas. Furthermore, objects in the playground do not mediate children's interactions, face-to-face communication, or eye contact. In contrast, tablets do. Through my other project, KIBO, I was able to address some of these issues. The next chapter will expand on this.

References

Bers, M. U. (2010). The tangible K robotics program: Applied computational thinking for young children. *Early Childhood Research and Practice, 12*(2), 1–20.

Bers, M. U. (2018). Coding and computational thinking in early childhood: The impact of ScratchJr in Europe. *European Journal of STEM Education, 3*(3), 08. doi:10.20897/ejsteme/3868.

Bers, M. U., & Resnick, M. (2015). *The official ScratchJr book*. San Francisco, CA: No Starch Press.

Bers, M. U., & Sullivan, A. (2019). Computer science education in early childhood: The case of ScratchJr. *Journal of Information Technology Education: Innovations in Practice, 18*, 113–138.

Flannery, L. P., Kazakoff, E. R., Bontá, P., Silverman, B., Bers, M. U., & Resnick, M. (2013). Designing ScratchJr: Support for early childhood learning through computer programming. In *Proceedings of the 12th International Conference on Interaction Design and Children (IDC '13)* (pp. 1–10). ACM, New York, NY. doi: 10.1145/2485760.2485785.

Govind, M., Relkin, E., & Bers, M. U. (2020). Engaging children and parents to code together using the Scratchjr app. *Visitor Studies.* doi:10.1080/10645578.2020.1732184.

Portelance, D. J., & Bers, M. U. (2015). Code and tell: Assessing young children's learning of computational thinking using peer video interviews with ScratchJr. In *Proceedings of the 14th International Conference on Interaction Design and Children (IDC '15)*. ACM, Boston, MA.

Relkin, E., & Bers, M. U. (2019). Designing an assessment of computational thinking abilities for young children. In L. E. Cohen & S. Waite-Stupiansky (Eds.), *STEM for early childhood learners: How science, technology, engineering and mathematics strengthen learning* (pp. 85–98). New York, NY: Routledge.

Strawhacker, A., & Bers, M. U. (2019). What they learn when they learn coding: Investigating cognitive domains and computer programming knowledge in young children. *Educational Technology Research and Development, 67*(3), 541–575. doi:10.1007/s11423-018-9622-x.

Strawhacker, A. L., Lee, M. S. C., & Bers, M. U. (2017). Teaching tools, teachers' rules: Exploring the impact of teaching styles on young children's programming knowledge in ScratchJr. *International Journal of Technology and Design Education.* doi:10.1007/s10798-017-9400-9.

12 | **KIBO**

Ezra, Mark, and Sarah are in kindergarten. During their social studies unit, they have been learning about Alaska and the Iditarod sled dog race that happens every March. They chose a musher, a strong man or woman who leads the dogs on a sled across Alaska, and followed the path on the internet, cheering for their team to win the race. They learned the names of each of the dogs, their needs and habits, and the different things that mushers must carry to survive the harsh weather.

On their classroom wall, there is a huge map of Alaska, marked with the different checkpoints across the state of Alaska, from Willow to Nome. Ezra, Mark, and Sarah learned geography by studying the race and its different routes. They also learned the Iditarod's history through a book that Mrs. Dolan read aloud to them. In 1925, a diphtheria epidemic threatened Nome, and Nome's supply of antitoxin had expired. The nearest antitoxin was found in Anchorage, about 500 miles away, near Willow. The only way to get the antitoxin to Nome was by sled dog. A safe route was organized and the 20-pound cylinder of serum was sent, first by train and then by 20 mushers and more than 100 dogs. The dogs ran in relays. Since then, every year the Iditarod sled dog race reenacts this event, and the children in Mrs. Dolan's kindergarten class learn about it.

Ezra, Mark, and Sarah studied Alaska's towns and geography. They learned about the hard terrains and the easy paths. They have been doing research on the subject for over two weeks and today is the time to put all their knowledge to the test; not by passing an exam or completing a worksheet, but by recreating the Iditarod race with KIBO robots.

Mrs. Dolan gave them the challenge to build and program their robots to travel from one checkpoint to another, starting in Willow and ending in Nome, carrying all the things mushers must carry, as well as the pretend serum for the sick children. Each team receives a piece of thick cardboard with two checkpoints marked at the ends and a KIBO robot. They first need to draw the route from checkpoint to checkpoint and decorate the cardboard to resemble the geography of that region. Second, they need to build their robots with a platform that can carry everything needed, including a safe way to transport the serum until reaching the next checkpoint and passing it on to the next team. They need to do sturdy engineering because the Alaskan terrain is bumpy, and they do not want everything to fall off the robotic sled. Finally, they need to program their robots to travel safely from checkpoint to checkpoint.

Mrs. Dolan put together the cardboard on the library floor making a huge map of Alaska. They needed a big space to work in, so they chose the library because the classroom wasn't big enough. Mrs. Dolan assigned "jobs" to the children within each of the groups: the artist, the engineer, and the programmer. She asked them to come forward to the tables that had the needed materials. Some children complained because they did not like their assigned jobs. Mrs. Dolan assured them that all children would experience every job and spend the same amount of time at each task.

Mark walks to the art material table and grabs markers and crayons as well as recyclable materials, cotton balls, and glue. He wants to decorate the cardboard with snow, trees, mountains, and a family of foxes. Both Sarah and Ezra want to be the engineers. After some back and forth, they agree that Sarah will take on that role first and Ezra will be second. Sarah walks to the robot table and grabs three motors, three wheels, and two wooden platforms. She also picks up a KIBO light bulb and a bunch of sensors. She is still not sure what those are, but she wants to have them. Ezra, the programmer, walks to a table full of bins with different wooden blocks labeled with colors, images, and words he cannot read, with a peg on one side and a hole on the other. That is KIBO's programming language. Following Mrs. Dolan's instructions, Ezra chooses a green Begin block, to start the program, and a red End block, to end the program. And then he grabs as many other colorful blocks as he can carry in his hands.

Shortly, the three children meet again at their spot on the Alaska floor map. The library becomes noisy as each group starts their work. There is a lot to decide. Sarah builds a robot with two motors and wheels on the sides and a motor and a moving platform on top. She adds the light bulb and a few sensors: an ear to detect sound, a telescope to detect distance, and an eye to detect light. The robot is ready to go, but it must be programmed, otherwise it will not move. Mark wants the robot to follow the path he drew on the cardboard. Ezra is not sure how many blue "Forward" blocks are needed in between the green Start and the red End blocks. He puts together a sequence of four "Forward" blocks and tells Sarah to try it out. Sarah starts scanning the blocks. She holds the robot and makes sure it is "awake" by looking at the red light coming out of its scanner. She aligns the scanner light with the barcodes on the blocks and starts scanning the blocks one by one. Mark helps her by saying "yes" every time a green light on the robot turns on, signaling a successful scan. When they are done programming KIBO, they place it on the cardboard trails to see what happens.

"It is not running long enough," says Sarah. "It needs to have at least two more 'Forward' blocks." "I don't think so," replies Ezra, "I think we need five more 'Forward' blocks." A few exchanges follow, in which children are busy estimating distance and predicting how many more steps are needed, and then they decide to try things out. After some trial and error, they make it work. Now they are ready to make the journey a little bit fancier. They decide that the robot will start to move once it hears a clap, marking the fact that the serum is on board. They also decide that before arriving at the last checkpoint it will shake and turn its red light on to alert the next team to get ready.

As children start programming their KIBO sleds and practicing the relay race, the classroom becomes a playground. Different children are busy at different tasks. Some are drawing and decorating, others are programming with wooden blocks, some are using tape and plastic cups to make sturdy structures for the serum, some are experimenting with different sensors, some are doing math to calculate distances, and a few are running from checkpoint to checkpoint cheering on their robots. All of them are very engaged.

We can hear laughs and sighs of frustration, as well as lots of questions and answers. Children are interacting amongst themselves and with the adults in the room. They are fully immersed and focused in the activity. Mrs. Dolan has planned a trial run before the end of the period, because family and friends are invited to come on Friday morning, at drop-off, to see the robotic race and cheer for the different teams. Most parents can't wait to see how their young kindergartners, who mostly do not know how to read and write, can program robots.

KIBO: The Tool

KIBO is a robot kit specifically designed for children aged 4–7 years old. Young children learn by doing, thus KIBO provides opportunities for doing different things. Children can build their own robot, program it to do what they want, and decorate it with art supplies. KIBO gives children the chance to make their ideas physical and tangible—without requiring screen time from PCs, tablets, or smartphones.

The concept, prototypes, and research for KIBO were born in my DevTech research group in 2011 through generous funding from the National Science Foundation (NSF DRL 0735657). KIBO became commercially available worldwide in 2014 through KinderLab Robotics, a company I co-founded with Mitch Rosenberg (see www.kinderlabrobotics.com).

Designed with a playground approach, KIBO supports children in making almost anything: a character from a story, a carousel, a dancer, a dog sled. The possibilities are endless, as wide as children's own imaginations. The child puts together a sequence of instructions (a program) using the wooden KIBO blocks. Then, they scan the blocks with the KIBO body to tell the robot what to do. Finally, they press a button and the robot comes "alive." KIBO engages children in becoming programmers, engineers, problem-solvers, designers, artists, dancers, choreographers, and writers.

As a robotics construction kit, KIBO has hardware (the robot body, wheels, motors, a light output, a variety of sensors, and art platforms) (see Figure 12.1) and software (a tangible programming language composed of interlocking wooden blocks).

Each wooden block has a colorful label with an icon, text, and a barcode, as well as a hole on one end and a peg on the other (see Figure 12.2). These wooden blocks contain no electronic or digital components. Instead, the KIBO robot has an embedded scanner. The scanner allows users to scan the barcodes on the wooden blocks and send a program to their robot instantaneously. No computer, tablet, or other form of "screen time" is required to program with KIBO. This design choice is aligned with the American Academy of Pediatrics' recommendation that young children should have a limited amount of screen time per day (American Academy of Pediatrics, 2016). KIBO's programming language contains 21 different, individual programming wooden blocks. Some of those blocks are simple, while others represent complex programming concepts including repeat loops, conditionals, and nesting statements.

Figure 12.1 KIBO robot with sensors and light output attached.

The use of wooden blocks for KIBO was inspired by early ideas from tangible programming. In the mid-1970s, Radia Perlman, a researcher at the MIT LOGO Lab (Perlman, 1976), first introduced the idea of tangible programming, which was then revived nearly two decades later (Suzuki & Kato, 1995). Since then, several tangible languages have been created

Figure 12.2 Sample KIBO program. This program tells the robot to spin, turn a blue light on, and shake.

in several different research labs around the world (e.g., Google Research, 2016; Horn, Crouser, & Bers, 2012; Horn & Jacob, 2007; McNerney, 2004; Smith, 2007; Wyeth & Purchase, 2002).

A tangible programming language, like any other type of computer language, is a tool for telling a processor what to do. With a text-based language, a programmer uses words such as BEGIN, IF, and REPEAT to instruct a computer. With a visual language, such as ScratchJr, words are replaced with pictures, and programs are expressed by arranging and connecting icons on the screen. Tangible languages, instead, use physical objects to represent the various aspects of computer programming (Manches & Price, 2011).

With KIBO, children arrange and connect wooden blocks to give commands to their robots. The physical properties of these objects are exploited to express and enforce syntax. For example, the KIBO Begin block doesn't have a hole, only a peg, because there is nothing that can be placed before the begin; and the End block doesn't have a peg, because there is no instruction that can go after the program ends (see Figure 12.3). The language syntax in KIBO (i.e., a sequential connection of blocks) is designed to support and reinforce sequencing skills in young children.

Why is a programming language made of wooden blocks? Wooden blocks are naturally familiar and comfortable for young children and teachers and can be found in almost every kindergarten classroom. They belong to a tradition of learning manipulatives already used in early childhood classrooms to teach shapes, size, and colors (Froebel, 1826; Montessori & Gutek, 2004). Table 12.1 presents a list of currently available programming blocks for KIBO. As new sensor modules are developed, new programming blocks are also released.

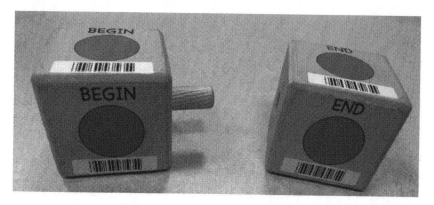

Figure 12.3 KIBO's Begin and End blocks.

Table 12.1 KIBO's block language

KIBO Block	Block Function
BEGIN	This is the first block in every program, it tells the robot to start
END	This is the last block in every program, it tells the robot to stop
FORWARD	Makes KIBO move forward several inches
BACKWARD	Makes KIBO move backward several inches
SPIN	Makes KIBO turn around in a circle
SHAKE	Makes KIBO shake from left to right
TURN LEFT	Makes KIBO turn to face the left
TURN RIGHT	Makes KIBO turn to face the right
WHITE LIGHT ON	Turns on KIBO's light bulb with a white light
RED LIGHT ON	Turns on KIBO's light bulb with a red light

BLUE LIGHT ON	Turns on KIBO's light bulb with a blue light
SING	Makes KIBO "sing" (i.e., play a series of automated tunes)
BEEP	Makes KIBO beep once
PLAY △ PLAY ○ PLAY □	Plays back a sound recorded with KIBO's Sound Recorder
WAIT FOR CLAP	When the Sound sensor is attached, this block makes KIBO stop and wait for a sound before continuing to the next action in the program
REPEAT	This block is used to open a "repeat loop" (like opening a set of parentheses). A repeat loop allows users to separate out a series of blocks for KIBO to repeat a particular number of times
END REPEAT	This block is used to close a "repeat loop" (like closing a set of parentheses)
IF	This block is used to open a "conditional statement" (like opening a set of parentheses). A conditional statement allows KIBO to decide what to do based on sensor input
END IF	This block is used to close a "conditional statement" (like closing a set of parentheses)
2 3 4 ∞ UNTIL NEAR UNTIL FAR UNTIL LIGHT UNTIL DARK LIGHT ...	In addition to the 18 blocks in KIBO's current language, there are 12 parameters that can be used to modify the "repeat loops" and "conditional statements" in order to tell KIBO how many times to repeat actions or what type of sensor input to react to

In addition to the tangible programming language, the KIBO robot comes with sensors and actuators (motors and light bulb), as well as art platforms. These modules can be interchangeably combined on the robot body.

Each sensor's aesthetic is designed to convey meaning (i.e., the ear-shaped part is a Sound sensor; the eye-shaped part is a Light sensor; and the telescope-shaped part is a distance Sensor). During the late pre-operational stage of cognitive development (ages 4–6), children extend and apply culturally learned symbol systems to interactions with the physical and social world—thus, our explicit emphasis on design features with symbolic representations.

Sensing is the ability of the robot to collect and respond to information from its environment. The Sound sensor is used to differentiate the two concepts of "loud" and "quiet." Using the Sound sensor, the robot can be programmed to do something when it is loud, and do something else when it gets quiet, or vice versa. The Light sensor is used to differentiate the two concepts of "dark" and "light." The robot can be programmed to do something when it is bright out, and do something else when it gets dark, or vice versa. Finally, the Distance sensor is used to detect whether the robot is getting nearer to something or further from it. The robot can be programmed to do something when it gets near something, and do something else when it moves away from it. The Sound Recorder module includes both input and output properties (see Figure 12.4). The Sound Recorder allows KIBO to record sound (input), and it can also be programmed with a corresponding block to play back the sound (output). The light output is shaped like a light bulb and is made of a different color plastic (transparent) than the sensors, so children do not get confused between the concepts of inputs and outputs (see Figure 12.5).

The use of sensors is well aligned with most early childhood curricula that engage children in exploring both human and animal sensors. For example, in most early childhood classrooms young children are already exploring their own five senses (sight, sound, taste, touch, and smell) and they can apply this knowledge to an exploration of KIBO's robotic sensors. They can liken their own sense of sound, for example, to KIBO's Sound sensor.

Three motors are included with the robot, two can be connected to the opposite sides of the robot, for mobility, and one motor can be located on top, for rotation of an attached element such as the art platform. Children

Figure 12.4 KIBO's Sound Recorder and corresponding blocks.

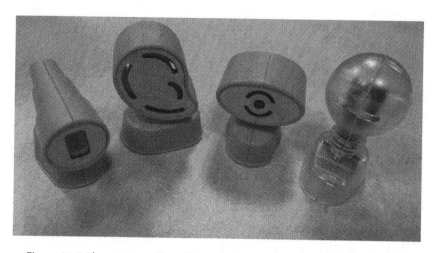

Figure 12.5 Three sensors (from left: Distance, Sound, and Light) and one light-bulb.

Figure 12.6 Art supplies and KIBO's art platforms and whiteboard.

can decide which motors they want to connect, but they cannot control the speed of the motors. This design feature highlights the importance of creating flexible and stimulating learning environments, and at the same time prevents the overload of young children's working memory and limited attention span.

The KIBO kit also contains art platforms and Expression modules for artistic exploration (see Figure 12.6). These can be used for children to personalize their projects with craft materials and foster STEAM (Science, Technology, Engineering, Arts, and Mathematics) integration. The art platforms are attached to the top of KIBO, can be static or mobile, and provide a place for children to creatively use different materials. Additionally, the motorized art stage allows for more versatility in robotic design. For example, children can construct kinetic sculptures and animated dioramas. The Expression module includes a whiteboard, markers, and flagpole. Children can decorate the whiteboard with pictures and words or they can create their own flag out of paper or fabric to insert into the flagpole. In addition to these core components, KIBO can be enhanced with several extension modules, including a Free-Throw extension set with a catapult arm that allows children to explore physics and force by programmatically launching a ping pong ball; a Brick Building extension set that is compatible with building kits like LEGO to decorate KIBO's body; and a Marker extension set that allows children to affix makers to KIBO's body to program and create works of visual art through code. New extension sets and modules are periodically added on the KinderLab Robotics website (www.kinderlabrobotics.com).

KIBO: The Process

In the beginning, back in 2011, KIBO had a different name. We called it KIWI (Kids Invent With Imagination). Students in my DevTech research group chose that acronym. However, later, we discovered potential copyright conflicts with that name, so we switched it to KIBO. We liked the sound of it. We also thought it was a way to remind children of the words kids and 'bot (from robot).

KIBO went through many prototypes before it made it out into the world. The NSF funded research on each of the iterations (DRL-1118897, DRL-0735657), and we received additional money from a successful Kickstarter campaign. At every stage of development and testing we collaborated with early educators, children, and specialists to create an age-appropriate robotic kit that would be intuitive and engaging, but also challenging enough to support new learning.

We wanted KIBO to support developmentally appropriate practices, often shortened to DAP, in early childhood (Bredekamp, 1987). DAP is a teaching approach grounded in research on how young children develop and learn, and in what is known about effective early education (Bredekamp, 1987; Copple & Bredekamp, 2009). We also wanted it to become a playground for tangible coding in which children could encounter powerful ideas from computer science and develop computational thinking, while engaging with the six positive behaviors of the Positive Technological Development (PTD) framework. Based on this, KIBO was designed to be:

- Age appropriate: its design features should establish reasonable expectations of what is interesting, safe, achievable, and challenging for young children.

- Individually appropriate: it can be used by children with different learning styles, background knowledge, exposure, and skills in the technological domain, and different developmental abilities and self-regulatory skills.

- Socially and culturally appropriate: the use of KIBO can be integrated with multiple disciplines and can support the teaching of interdisciplinary curricula that meet state and nationally mandated frameworks.

Our early research with KIBO was informed by doing pilot studies where we used commercially available robotics kits such as LEGO WeDo and LEGO MINDSTORMS, both designed for older children. We learned from observing children's challenges and discoveries, and from talking with teachers about their experiences. Most of that early research is summarized in my book *Blocks to Robots* (Bers, 2008). For some of the studies, we used the commercially available software that came with those kits; for others, my then-student Mike Horn connected the LEGO MINDSTORMS yellow brick to a tangible programming language that he developed as part of his doctoral work, called TERN (Horn, Crouser, & Bers, 2012). Later on, two other students in my group, Jordan Crouser and David Kiger, extended this project and created the language CHERP (Creative Hybrid Environment for Robotic Programming) (Bers, 2010). Both TERN and CHERP required a standard webcam connected to a desktop or laptop computer to take a picture of the program, which included blocks or puzzle pieces with circular barcodes easily readable by a vision software. The computer then converted the picture into digital code. We conducted lots of research to understand what worked and what didn't with those robot kits, and also what needed to change (Sullivan, Elkin, & Bers, 2015).

From pilot testing and focus groups, we learned that KIBO needed parts that could be physically and intuitively easy to connect, and it would be best if it was programmed without a computer. We also heard that children and teachers wanted to attach a variety of crafts and recycled materials to the core robotic parts to make different types of creations, both stationary and mobile. Based on these general principles, we developed a list that identified desired design features and, through NSF funding, hired a consultant team to develop an initial prototype that instantiated these ideas. The first KIBO prototype (then called KIWI) was programmed

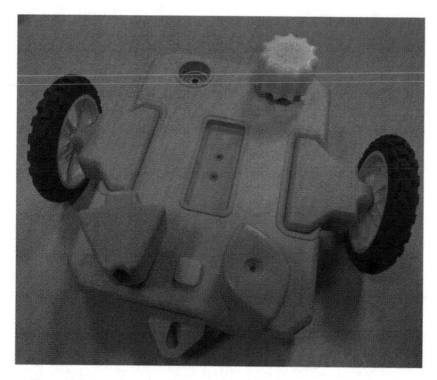

Figure 12.7 KIWI prototype.

with CHERP and required the use of a computer and a webcam to take pictures of the blocks and to then send the program to the robot through a USB cable. This robot was constructed out of solid wood and opaque blue plastic for the modules (see Figure 12.7).

We hand built the first ten prototypes and tested them in focus groups, professional development workshops, and the classroom (Bers, Seddighin, & Sullivan, 2013; Sullivan & Bers, 2015; Sullivan, Elkin, & Bers, 2015). We asked teachers about our design choices for KIBO, as well as its suitability for: 1) teaching foundational engineering concepts of sturdy building and construction; 2) teaching foundational coding concepts such as sequencing, repeat loops, and conditional branching; and 3) teaching open-ended creativity and artistic design.

Teachers were generally excited and were drawn to the use of wood and the simplicity of our first design. However, they also pointed out several impediments for using this original design in a sustained and feasible way in the classroom. Teachers indicated that programming the robot should use minimal or no computer equipment. Teachers felt that this was important from both a logistical standpoint (e.g., most teachers did not have enough computers in a kindergarten classroom and had limited access to those resources) and from a developmentally appropriate standpoint (e.g., teachers worried about screen time and about children manipulating a keyboard and mouse).

In 2013, data were collected from 32 early childhood educators on their attitudes, opinions, and experiences to inform the redesign of the prototype (Bers, Seddighin, & Sullivan, 2013). Results show that this first version of KIBO was successful in engaging children in foundational pro-gramming skills. However, its robotic parts were too easy to assemble and did not sufficiently engage children in engineering problem-solving or creative artistic design.

From early testing with that first prototype, we learned a lot and hired a new team of consultants, as well as engaged many volunteers, teachers, and students to work with us on the next prototype. This sec-ond prototype had a 3D printed KIBO body, as opposed to one made of wood. It also included an embedded scanner, eliminating the need to use a computer. This directly addressed the teachers' concerns about availability of computers in early childhood classrooms and screen time for young children. Additionally, instead of having a "magical black box" with the electronic components inside the robot's body, the newer KIBO prototype had a clear plastic bottom, allowing children to see the wires, batteries, microprocessor, and other parts involved in making the robot function (see Figure 12.8).

Furthermore, in order to address the need of more "engineering," we designed the wheels to connect to the motors in two different ways, prompting children to test how changing the wheels' orientation makes the robot move differently. The shapes and looks of both sensors and light output components were also redesigned to address earlier pilot testing with children. For example, we changed the Distance sensor, which was originally a blue shape unrecognizable as a telescope, to look like a telescope. In addition, we included the use of art platforms to provide more ways for children to build and create, extending the use of KIBO to incorporate arts, crafts, and recycled materials along with the robotic components.

Figure 12.8 Transparent underside of KIBO robot.

The Complexity of Simplicity

As the new prototype was built, the circuit board, robotic components, and robot body changed in their looks and functionality. However, the new prototype kept its core design principle: simplicity. KIBO has a "plug and play" connection system. The robot parts or modules can connect and disconnect intuitively and easily. They are functional with no further steps other than plugging them in. Additionally, KIBO's design forces the correct orientation of parts.

Each basic programming instruction corresponds to one robotic action. Each robotic component corresponds to one function. For example, only one module is needed for each action (i.e., the Motor module is needed to move the robot's gears, connectors, etc.). This design choice supports correspondence, a cognitive developmental milestone for young children that is a foundational skill for later academic success.

There are a limited number of ways to construct and program KIBO. The robot has a limited number of component types and a limited number of possible combinations for these components. There are limited control points for the child (e.g., children can tell the robot to go forward or backward, but not how fast). Sensors sense the presence or absence of stimuli, but not the degree of variation within the stimuli. This design principle was guided by studies that show that children of this age typically have limited working memory capacity, and are only just beginning to hold multistep instructions in their heads (Shonkoff, Duncan, Fisher, Magnuson, & Raver, 2011).

The aesthetic features of KIBO have remained purposefully plain throughout each prototype iteration. The "unfinished" look invites children to complete the robot using their own imaginative creations. Much like a blank canvas or unsculpted clay, KIBO inspires children to add to it. This supports a variety of sensory and aesthetic experiences.

The robot is designed to be easily manipulated by a young child without falling apart. Pieces are large enough to be assembled safely by young children (i.e., there's nothing that they can swallow). KIBO remains intact while being handled and used in ways typical of 4-year-olds (e.g., dropping, running into walls, etc.). This supports children developing fine motor skills and extending their self-regulation practices.

The design of KIBO is aimed at shifting the problem-solving focus away from low-level problems (i.e., syntax and connection errors) toward high-level problem-solving (i.e., creating a program that matches a goal). The robot body has the right weight and size to be manipulated by a young child's hands and the size of the robot allows it to be shareable to promote social interaction. This allows children to engage in problem-solving in a developmentally appropriate way that takes into consideration their ability for self-regulation. Furthermore, it promotes a journey toward computational literacy that enables the use of the robot for personal expression and communication.

KIBO can be easily integrated with literacy. The programming language pairs iconic images with simple words and allows children to explore sequencing, a foundational skill for literacy development. DAP calls for interdisciplinary curriculua and KIBO supports integrated learning. For example, children encounter concepts such as number, size, measurement, distance, time, counting, directionality, and estimation. At the same time, they are learning and applying new vocabulary words, communicating with teachers and peers, and writing and drawing notes in their design journals.

From the Lab to the World

Over the years, my DevTech research group conducted many studies with the 3D printed KIBO prototypes. This research showed that beginning in prekindergarten, children could master basic robotics and programming skills, while the older children (first and second grade) could master increasingly complex concepts in the same amount of time (Sullivan & Bers, 2015). We iteratively redesigned the prototypes based on pilot studies with children and teachers (Sullivan, Elkin, & Bers, 2015).

Alongside KIBO, we developed curriculum, teaching materials, and assessments tools. These materials include games, songs, and activities (many of which can be explored without the use of the robot or blocks) that reinforce the computational and engineering concepts introduced through KIBO. We have developed nearly a dozen curriculum units that integrate KIBO with STEM disciplines as well as social sciences, literacy, and the arts. These curriculum units are aligned with national and international STEM standards. Some examples are: *How Things Move* (explores foundational physics connections related to motion, light, and friction, while engaging children in engineering and computational thinking); *Sensing the World Around Us* (looks at how sensors work, particularly the three KIBO sensors: Light, Distance, and Sound); *Dances from Around the World* (engages children in making and programming robots that perform dances from around the world); *Patterns All Around Us* (integrates a study of math and patterns with robotics). All of these curricular resources are available for anyone to access for free online at our DevTech website (sites.tufts.edu/devtech).

As time went on, the word about our KIBO prototype started to spread. When giving talks, I was often asked by parents and teachers, researchers and practitioners: "How can I get a KIBO robot kit?" For some time, I did not have a good answer, because KIBOs were only hand-built prototypes in our DevTech lab. I grew frustrated and often found myself wondering what the point of my research was if we couldn't make it available to others.

During conversations with the NSF, I learned about the Small Business Innovation Research (SBIR) program that could help me take my research on KIBO out of the lab and into a commercial enterprise. I knew I had to partner with someone with a different set of skills, as I did not know much about what makes a business viable. During a walk in Walden Pond, near Boston, my friend Mitch Rosenberg, veteran executive at several robotics start-ups, decided to join me to pursue a longtime dream of his: improving STEM education.

Together we co-founded KinderLab Robotics, Inc., with the goal of commercializing KIBO and making it available worldwide. KinderLab Robotics received initial funding from the NSF through SBIR Phase I, Phase IB, and Phase II grants. In addition, a successful Kickstarter campaign allowed us to supplement those funds and KIBO was first made commercially available through KinderLab Robotics in 2014.

KIBO Today

Since its launch in 2014, KIBO has made it into private and public schools, museums and libraries, after-school programs, and summer camps, both in the U.S. and abroad. KIBO has been used to teach a variety of curricular topics ranging from science to literacy and even social-emotional concepts, and pilot studies have been done with children on the autism spectrum.

At a local public school in Somerville, MA, early childhood teachers implemented a robotics curriculum in grade K-2 with the goal of fostering prosocial behaviors and community building. Students also programmed their robots to demonstrate respectful behaviors and school rules that kids often forget. For example, one student created a robot that reminded students to listen to their teacher during circle time. Another student created a robot to demonstrate walking through the hallway quietly and making lots of noise only when it reached the playground.

In a summer camp, KIBO was used to bring literacy and the arts to life in a playful way. In this one-week camp, students read a different book each day and programmed their robots to "act out" their favorite scenes from each book as well as alternative endings. As a final project, children read the iconic children's book *Where the Wild Things Are* by Maurice Sendak. Children designed and built their own KIBO monsters inspired by the story and programmed them to act out the "Wild Rumpus" scene (i.e., a wild monster party).

In another KIBO class, students explored robotics and programming with the theme of "Superheroes" (Sullivan, Strawhacker, & Bers, 2017). They began with a group discussion answering the question, "What makes someone a hero?" Initially, children focused on superabilities such as flying, super strength, and invisibility. These are the characteristics that their favorite cartoon superheroes like Superman and The Incredibles have. However, when prompted to think further, children came to this conclusion: superheroes strive to "do good" in the world. The class came up with a long list of what they called "everyday heroes" that included firefighters, teachers, doctors, and even their parents and friends. They also discussed all the ways that they could be "school superheroes," such as by helping their teachers, playing with someone at recess who is alone, and respecting one another. They created KIBO Superhero Bots inspired by the real everyday heroes they learned about, as well as their favorite fantasy-inspired superhero abilities. For example, many children used sensors to give their Super KIBO "super senses" that allowed it to perform extraordinary tasks. One boy used the KIBO's Sound sensor to tell a story about how his robot hero listens for people calling for help and then goes to help them. In all of these examples, the robotic technology was used not only to explore engineering, coding, and design, but also core ideas about what makes us not only human, but good humans. In fact, in these examples, all of the six Cs of the PTD framework come into play.

However, if we want to reach children in this way, we first need to work with their teachers. Thus, a few years ago, together with then-doctoral student Amanda Sullivan, we launched the Early Childhood Technology (ECT) graduate certificate program at the Eliot-Pearson Department of Child Study and Human Development at Tufts University. This blended online-and-in-person learning program is designed to help busy professionals working with children in diverse learning settings to get started with developmentally appropriate technology, engineering, and robotics activities. The program, grounded on the research conducted at the DevTech research group, focuses on technological tools for playful learning and the design of educational and technological spaces for children. Abby, a kindergarten teacher in the public school system in the Deep South and an ECT student, is focusing with her students on a unit about community helpers. She is delighted when she notices her students playing with KIBO during an indoor recess session. As her students play, they imagine that KIBO is one of the community helper vehicles that they learned about through stories and games in her classroom. Today, KIBO is a fire truck zooming through the street playing a siren sound that the children recorded on KIBO's Speaker module. Abby shares her experience in the online discussion with her ECT peers and this sparks a conversation about how to incorporate literacy by creating street signs, and how to plan for other interdisciplinary activities sparked by KIBO robotics in their classrooms.

Owen is a teacher in charge of the maker space in an urban school district, and is also an ECT student. Although he is very familiar with 3D printers and programming languages such as Python, and robotics systems such as Arduino, he doesn't know how to bring technology to early childhood. None of these can work with young students and the district is asking him to host kindergarden children in his maker space. Thus, Owen chose to join the ECT program. One of Owen's assignments for ECT is to program KIBO to perform a dance, and to share the code with his peers as part of the *Dances from Around the World* practice unit. He enjoys this activity so much that he brings it to his maker space. Kindergarten students visit Owen once a week as part of a specialist rotation. Owen worked with the teachers at his school and chose to incorporate this KIBO maker space activity on world culture through arts and dance. Students program their KIBO robots to enact cultural dances that they have selected from around the world, and decorate them to show off traditional dance costumes. As a culmination of the project, students show off their dancing robots to their fifth grade reading buddies. After posting videos and reflections about his experience in the online discussion for class, other students in Owen's ECT cohort start a thriving conversation about how to use community showcase events to give children an authentic audience for their coding work.

During the ECT in-person summer residency at Tufts University, early childhood teachers Jen, David, and Maria work together to design and teach a lesson at the Eliot-Pearson Children's School on sequencing. Using the storybook *The Very Hungry Caterpillar* by Eric Carle as inspiration, four-year-old students in the prekindergarten room create their favorite foods out of craft materials and lay them in a line on the big class carpet. During circle time, the three teachers introduce KIBO. They model how children can work in a group of three people with one robot. Jen built a short program for KIBO which Maria scans and David builds a decoration for KIBO's platform. The kids take time to try out each role as they program KIBO to pass by their food and "eat" it, in a retelling of Eric Carle's story that they call, *The Very Hungry KIBO*. As KIBO passes by food like bananas, spaghetti, and ice cream, children in the class call out the name of the foods they made. The children love dancing alongside their KIBO and pretending to eat the imaginary food. Back in the ECT seminar room, ECT instructor and Program Manager Angie Kalthoff invites Jen, David, and Maria to share their teaching experience. They explain how they used what they learned in ECT to plan the curriculum according to younger children's needs, and how they used the carpet in the room to help guide the children's play. Jen shared, "This is the highlight of ECT for me, sharing and getting ideas from all of you folks!" All the ECT students spend a few minutes sharing ideas for the three teachers about how to extend the activity during their next visit before moving onto a different group's share time.

As evidenced by the diversity of experiences described earlier, KIBO provides a playground for learning how to code. However, both teachers and children are not only developing technical skills and computational thinking, but they are also engaging in the six positive behaviors (six Cs), proposed by the PTD framework and reviewed in Chapter 10: collaboration, communication, community building, content creation, creativity, and choices of conduct (Bers, 2012).

KIBO and Positive Technological Development

KIBO involves children in making their own robots and programming their behaviors (i.e., creating content). The engineering design process required for building and the computational thinking involved in programming foster *competence* in computer literacy and technological fluency.

The classroom practice of keeping design journals during the creation process makes transparent to the children (as well as teachers and parents) their own thinking, their own learning trajectories, and the project's evolution over time. The formal steps of the engineering design process—posing a problem, doing research, planning, developing a prototype, testing, redesigning, and sharing solutions—gives students a tool for systematically addressing a problem (see Figure 12.9).

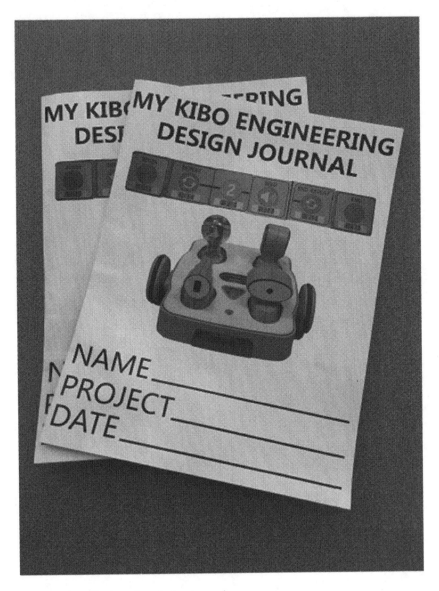

Figure 12.9 Engineering design journals.

KIBO promotes creativity, as opposed to efficiency, in problem-solving; the approach is informed by the original meaning of the word *engineering,* which derives from the Latin *ingenium,* meaning, "innate quality, mental power, clever invention." Through the process of solving technical problems in creative ways, children develop confidence in their learning potential.

Most educational robotic programs for older children, such as the National Robotics Challenge and FIRST (For Inspiration and Recognition of Science and Technology), are set up as competitions in which robots have to accomplish a given task, usually with the goal of outperforming other robots. However, research has shown that females tend not to respond well to teaching strategies that stress competition; further, such strategies also might not always be appropriate in the early childhood setting (Bers, 2008). With KIBO, and as shown in Mrs. Dolan's class and the ECT examples, the learning environment, instead of focusing on competition, can promote sharing and caring about each other.

The PTD framework speaks to the importance of providing opportunities for communication. While most of the work with KIBOs happens in teams, we also encourage structured ways for young children to communicate not only on a one-on-one basis with peers and teachers but also to the whole group. During technology circles, the teacher invites children to show their projects and asks questions such as, "What worked as expected and what didn't?" "What are you trying to accomplish?" "What do you need to know in order to make it happen?" The teacher then uses children's projects and questions to highlight powerful ideas.

Learning with KIBO is "hard fun" and a lot of work. Following the PTD framework, there is always an open house to invite friends and family to see and play with the KIBO projects. Similar to what happened in Mrs. Dolan's kindergarten class, most adults can't believe the sophisticated projects that young children can create until they get to see them. The public displays make learning visible to others, but also to the children themselves.

The last C proposed by the PTD framework, choices of conduct, reminds teachers about providing opportunities for children to experiment with "what if" questions and the potential consequences. However, choices of conduct are not only made by children; teachers also make them. For example, if the KIBO sensors are sorted by type and placed in bins in the center of the room (instead of given to each child or group as a presorted robotic kit), children learn to take what they need without depleting the bins of the "most wanted" pieces. They also learn how to negotiate. The PTD approach guides us in helping young children to develop an inner compass to direct their actions in a just and responsible way, and not only to become experts at KIBO robotics.

From Buenos Aires to Singapore

Most of the examples above show how individual classrooms or schools, museums or libraries, are using KIBO robots in different ways. However, different countries have made top-down decisions to integrate KIBO into the early childhood classroom in different ways.

For example, in 2018, the Ministry of Education for the city of Buenos Aires, Argentina, led by Minister Soledad Acuña, decided to implement robotics starting in the initial level, PreK and K, in accordance with new guidelines from the country's National Ministry of Education that required programming and robotics for all levels of education. Through professional development and the arrival of KIBO kits for the approximately 400 schools in the capital city of Buenos Aires, the first steps toward introducing computational thinking in early childhood were taken.

Valeria Larrart, who works as a digital pedagogical coach at the Ministry of Education in Buenos Aires, shares, "in early childhood, Argentine public schools have not paid enough attention to the inclusion of technology as a teaching resource. Now, with this new initiative, we are not only briging robotics but also computational thinking."

In her role as digital pedagogical coach, Valeria supports the integration of new technologies, such as KIBO, into the curriculum. "Different schools take on different approaches," she explains, "but they all used creative approaches to integrate coding into other areas of study, and our job is to help them." For example, at the Jardín de Infantes Nucleado E Juana Manso, led by María Marta Dallas, KIBO was included in the classrooms through integrated curricula in every discipline. At School N5, teacher Analía Mascioni, invited her kindergarten classroom to program KIBO to do a review of the year, by stopping at different stations representing some of their favorite projects. A KIBO with a GoPro attached to it was programmed to navigate through these stations and capture its own view and perspective. In School N17, kindergarten teacher Paola Ferreri included the use of KIBO in her unit about the environment and how to take care of it. For the final project, using art and craft materials, they created a scene representing different environments that were contaminated with paper and plastic, such as the ocean and the mountains, and programmed KIBO, and her friend "KIBA," to do a cleanup campaign to save the planet's natural resources. As the KIBO robots navigated and "cleaned up" the environment, children read texts that they'd created to talk about the importance of taking care of our planet. These examples, taken from public kindergartners in the city of Buenos Aires, involved the integration of curricular areas and the support of digital pedagogical coaches to help teachers to use KIBO in unique creative ways.

In another part of the world, with a different approach to why and how technology needs to be brought into early childhood, Singapore is introducing KIBO, amongst other technologies, into all early childhood classrooms. Singapore, along with many other nations, is well aware of the growing need for engineering and computer education in schools. As part of Singapore's journey to become a key player in the automated economy, Steve Leonard, then executive deputy chairman of Singapore's Infocomm Development Authority (IDA)[1] said, "As Singapore becomes a Smart Nation, our children will need to be comfortable creating with technology" (IDA Singapore, 2015). Thus, Singapore's government launched the "PlayMaker Programme" initiative to introduce younger children to technology (Digital News Asia, 2015). The goal of this program is to provide young children (aged 4–7) with digital tools to have fun, practice problem-solving, and build confidence and creativity in a developmentally appropriate way (Digital News Asia, 2015).

According to the director of digital literacy and participation at Singapore's Infocomm Media Development Authority (IMDA[2]), Singapore is trying to change the idea of what technology in preschool settings looks like, from a screen-based approach to a maker-centered approach (Chambers, 2015). This vision is consistent with my playground approach, and therefore I was invited to train a first cohort of early childhood teachers as part of the PlayMaker Programme and to conduct a research study following different centers in understanding learning outcomes with KIBO. One hundred and sixty preschool centers across Singapore were given a suite of age- and developmentally appropriate technological toys that engage children with robotics, programming, building, and engineering, including: Bee-Bot, Circuit Stickers, littleBits, and KIBO robotics. In addition, early childhood educators also received training and on-ground support on how to use and teach with each of these tools embedded into the center's curriculum.

Our study focused on research questions such as:

1. What programming concepts do preschool children master after being introduced to KIBO?

2. How engaged were children with the different aspects of the PTD framework while participating in the KIBO robotics curriculum?

3. What was this experience like for the participating teachers? What areas of this initiative did they feel were successful, and what areas need improvement?

Our exploration of the KIBO robot was situated within our DevTech curricular unit called *Dances from Around the World*. The *Dances from Around the World* unit is designed to engage children with STEAM content through an integration of music, dance, and culture using engineering and programming tools (DevTech Research Group, 2015). This unit was chosen specifically to appeal to the multicultural nature of the Singaporean community. Singapore has a bilingual education policy where all students in government schools are taught English as their primary language. In addition to English, students also learn another language called their "Mother Tongue," which might be Mandarin, Malay, or Tamil. Because the students in Singapore speak different languages and have different cultural backgrounds, the *Dances from Around the World* curriculum easily integrated into cultural appreciation and awareness units already typically taught in the preschool classes. The implementation of the *Dances from Around the World* curriculum was rooted in the PTD framework.

Over the course of approximately seven weeks, teachers introduced their students to new robotics or programming concepts. While most teachers were generally novices when it came to teaching with technology, this did not present an obstacle for their teaching. "Even though we don't know, we're still very interested in it. We just touch it and learn and see how it works," summarized a young teacher (Sullivan & Bers, 2017). Lessons took place for approximately one hour once a week, leading up to a final project. Concepts from basic sequencing through to conditional statements were covered. For the final project, students worked in pairs or small groups to design, build, and program a cultural dance from around the world. This activity drew on the accumulation of students' knowledge throughout the curriculum. By the culmination of the project, all groups had a functional KIBO robotics project that they demonstrated during the final presentations.

All groups used at least two motors and were successful at integrating art, craft, and recycled materials to represent the dance of their choosing. Many groups also used sensors and advanced programming concepts such as repeat loops and conditional statements (Sullivan & Bers, 2017).

Students and teachers were also successful at integrating the arts in other ways through music, dance, costumes, and performances. For example, some groups decorated their KIBOs to represent different ethnicities in Singapore and chose music from that ethnicity. Other groups had children dressed up in clothing to represent the same cultures that their robots were representing. They performed, danced, and sang along with the robots. Their classrooms became playgrounds. What facilitated this? The design of KIBO as a developmentally appropriate tool and the open-ended nature of the curriculum, as well as the good alignment between the PTD framework and the pedagogical approach of these Singaporean educational settings.

Adeline Yeo, former senior manager of Education/Sector Innovation for Singapore's IMDA, after visiting a Learning Festival organized by one of the operators who had implemented PlayMaker and KIBO in 33 preschool centers, shared how impressed she was to see the children and teachers' effort. She recounts one particular experience (see also Figure 12.10):

> The teachers tried different programs to have KIBO go 'round and 'round like a carousel. In the end, they removed the wheels and programmed it to turn left forever. Great problem solving and collaboration involved. We are turning teachers into engineers!

Recognizing the importance of training early childhood teachers after the pilot project ended, Singapore's IMDA partnered with the Association for Early Childhood Educators Singapore (AECES) to create courses and different opportunities to teach how to integrate technology into the curriculum in a developmentally appropriate way. Mr. Adrian Lim, Director of Digital Literacy and Participation in Singapore's IMDA, explained,

> It helps demystify coding and shows that everyone can learn to code. A number of preschools still continue to use Play-Maker with new cohorts of students and it is heartening to know that more educators are receptive and willing to learn how to integrate the use of technology into their curriculum.

In addition, starting in 2020, IMDA is setting up a PlayMaker library of technology-enabled toys to support the teaching and learning by early

Figure 12.10 KIBO carousel created by teachers at a Learning Festival in Singapore.

childhood educators and preschoolers, and is also introducing the concepts and benefits of computational thinking to parents and their young children through PlayMaker workshops in community locations across Singapore.

The vision that Singapore showed early on, and its emphasis on start-ing in early childhood, did not go unnoticed. Since the launch of the IMDA PlayMaker Programme in 2015, it has been winning awards and recogni-tion locally and around the world, such as the IMS Global Learning Impact Awards 2017 - BRONZE, the ASEAN ICT Innovation Award (Public Sector) 2017 - GOLD, the Singapore Public Sector Transformation Awards 2018 (ExCEL Innovation Project), and the Singapore Ministry of Communications and Information Innovation Award 2018 (Innovation Project) - GOLD. As a researcher, educator, and KIBO designer, I am proud to have contributed to all of this. However, none of it could have happened without the vision of a country that not only believes in the importance of educating young children, but is also willing to make the needed changes.

Notes

1. Steve Leonard was the executive deputy chairman of IDA Singapore from June 2013 to June 2016.
2. IMDA was restructured from IDA in September 2016.

References

American Academy of Pediatrics Council on Communications and Media. (2016). Media and young minds. *Pediatrics, 138*(5). 2016–2591.

Bers, M. (2008). *Blocks to robots: Learning with technology in the early childhood classroom.* New York, NY: Teachers College Press.

Bers, M. U. (2010). The tangible K robotics program: Applied computa-tional thinking for young children. *Early Childhood Research and Prac-tice, 12*(2). 1–20.

Bers, M. U. (2012). *Designing digital experiences for positive youth devel-opment: From playpen to playground.* Cary, NC: Oxford University Press.

Bers, M. U., Seddighin, S., & Sullivan, A. (2013). Ready for robotics: Bring-ing together the T and E of STEM in early childhood teacher education. *Journal of Technology and Teacher Education, 21*(3), 355–377.

Bredekamp, S. (1987). *Developmentally appropriate practice in early childhood programs serving children from birth through age 8*. Washington, DC: National Association for the Education of Young Children.

Chambers, J. (2015). Inside Singapore's plans for robots in pre-schools. *GovInsider*.

Copple, C., & Bredekamp, S. (2009). *Developmentally appropriate practice in early childhood programs serving children from birth through age 8*. Washington, DC: National Association for the Education of Young Children.

DevTech Research Group. (2015). *Dances from around the world robotics curriculum*. Retrieved from sites.tufts.edu/devtech/files/2018/03/KIBO-Curriculum_DancesAroundtheWorld.pdf

Digital News Asia. (2015). IDA launches $1.5m pilot to roll out tech toys for preschoolers. Retrieved from www.digitalnewsasia.com/digital-economy/ida-launches-pilot-to-roll-out-tech-toys-for-preschoolers

Froebel, F. (1826). *On the education of man (Die Menschenerziehung)*. Keilhau and Leipzig: Wienbrach.

Google Research. (2016, June). *Project Bloks: Designing a development platform for tangible programming for children* [Position paper]. Retrieved from https://projectbloks.withgoogle.com/static/Project_Bloks_position_paper_June_2016.pdf

Horn, M. S., Crouser, R. J., & Bers, M. U. (2012). Tangible interaction and learning: The case for a hybrid approach. *Personal and Ubiquitous Computing, 16*(4), 379–389.

Horn, M. S., & Jacob, R. J. (2007). Tangible programming in the classroom with tern. In *CHI'07 Extended Abstracts on Human Factors in Computing Systems* (pp. 1965–1970). ACM.

IDA Singapore. (2015). *IDA supports preschool centres with technology-enabled toys to build creativity and confidence in learning*. Retrieved from www.ida.gov.sg/About-Us/Newsroom/Media-Releases/2015/IDA-supports-preschool-centres-with-technology-enabled-toys-to-build-creativity-and-confidence-in-learning

Manches, A., & Price, S. (2011). Designing learning representations around physical manipulation: Hands and objects. In *Proceedings of the 10th International Conference on Interaction Design and Children* (pp. 81–89). ACM.

McNerney, T. S. (2004). From turtles to tangible programming bricks: Explorations in physical language design. *Personal and Ubiquitous Computing, 8*(5), 326–337.

Montessori, M., & Gutek, G. L. (2004). *The Montessori method: The origins of an educational innovation: Including an abridged and annotated edition of Maria Montessori's the Montessori method.* Lanham, MD: Rowman & Littlefield Publishers.

Perlman, R. (1976). *Using computer technology to provide a creative learning environment for preschool children.* MIT Logo Memo #24, Cambridge, MA.

Shonkoff, J. P., Duncan, G. J., Fisher, P. A., Magnuson, K., & Raver, C. (2011). Building the brain's "air traffic control" system: How early experiences shape the development of executive function. Working Paper No. 11.

Smith, A. C. (2007). Using magnets in physical blocks that behave as programming objects. In *Proceedings of the 1st International Conference on Tangible and Embedded Interaction* (pp. 147–150). ACM.

Sullivan, A., & Bers, M. U. (2015). Robotics in the early childhood classroom: Learning outcomes from an 8-week robotics curriculum in pre-kindergarten through second grade. *International Journal of Technology and Design Education. 26*(1), 3–20.

Sullivan, A., & Bers, M. U. (2017). Dancing robots: Integrating art, music, and robotics in Singapore's early childhood centers. *International Journal of Technology and Design Education.* Online First. doi: 10.1007/s10798-017-9397-0.

Sullivan, A., Elkin, M., & Bers, M. U. (2015). KIBO robot demo: Engaging young children in programming and engineering. In *Proceedings of the 14th International Conference on Interaction Design and Children (IDC '15).* ACM, Boston, MA.

Sullivan, A., Strawhacker, A., & Bers, M. U. (2017). Dancing, drawing, and dramatic robots: Integrating robotics and the arts to teach foundational STEAM concepts to young children. In M. S. Khine (Ed.), *Robotics in STEM education: Redesigning the learning experience* (pp. 231–260). New York, NY: Springer, Cham.

Suzuki, H., & Kato, H. (1995). Interaction-level support for collaborative learning: Algoblock- an open programming language. In J. L. Schnase & E. L. Cunnius (Eds.), *Proceedings on CSCL '95: The First International Conference on Computer Support for Collaborative Learning* (pp. 349–355). Erlbaum, Mahwah, NJ.

Wyeth, P., & Purchase, H. C. (2002). Tangible programming elements for young children. In *CHI'02 Extended Abstracts on Human Factors in Computing Systems* (pp. 774–775). ACM.

13

Design Principles

Programming Languages for Young Children

As a designer of playground experiences for coding, I need to understand the developmental characteristics of young children and the contexts in which they are likely to engage with programming.

Early childhood is a wonderful time in life. Four- to seven-year-old children are curious and eager to learn, but they get fatigued easily and have short attention spans. They learn better when engaged in doing things, and they like to talk. They are active and energetic, but they need frequent breaks and rest periods. While they tend to have developed gross motor skills, they are still working on fine motor skills, thus activities that engage small muscles can be difficult for them. They enjoy organized games and are concerned about following rules and fairness. They are imaginative and enjoy being involved in fantasy play. They tend to be competitive, self-assertive, and self-centered. They are learning how to cooperate with others and become team players. While they understand other people's feelings they might be unaware of how their own actions affect them. However, they are very sensitive to praise and recognition and their feelings are easily hurt.

Children at this age tend to be inconsistent in their level of maturity and might behave one way at home and a different way at school; they might regress when tired and have a low level of tolerance for frustration. Academically speaking, there is a noticeable range of abilities: while some children might read, write, and be at ease with addition and subtraction, others are still working at recognizing letters and numbers. Given these developmental characteristics, designing programming languages for young children can be challenging.

Using the playground as a guiding metaphor is useful. It invites us to focus on the kinds of experiences we want children to have with technology and the kinds of interactions we want them to have with each other through coding.

The way we design can engage, encourage, and promote certain experiences while hindering others. For example, while programming with KIBO allows the use of materials such as recyclables and arts and crafts, programming with ScratchJr presents the opportunity to draw with computer tools. Tools have unique design features that enable different types of experiences. Experiences are powerful because they have an emotional impact (Brown, 2009). They transform us. They immerse us. They influence our worldviews. They engage us in action. When thinking about designing programming languages for children we must think first about the kinds of experiences we want them to have. Within the playground approach, we are concerned with promoting positive youth development, and not only with improving problem-solving and mastering the art of coding.

In previous work (Bers, 2012), I presented several dimensions to guide the design of positive youth experiences in the digital landscape: developmental milestones, curriculum connections, technological infrastructure, mentoring model, diversity, program scale, communities of users, design process, access environment, and institutional context. The following paragraphs apply these to coding for young children.

Developmental Milestones

What are the developmental needs of young coders? What are their developmental challenges and milestones? What are the developmental conflicts that they are most likely to encounter? Children accomplish different developmental tasks at different ages. Erikson (1950) described how each stage of development presents its own unique challenges, which he called "crises." Successful development of the personality (or psychosocial development) depends on meeting and overcoming these crises. The Eriksonian psychosocial framework proposes that at each stage the developing child, or adult, is confronted with a conflict of opposing forces.

Erikson described eight stages from infancy to adulthood (Erikson, 1950). All stages are present at birth but only begin to unfold according to both a natural scheme and one's ecological and cultural upbringing. In each stage, the person confronts, and hopefully masters, new challenges. Each stage builds upon the successful completion of earlier stages.

However, mastery of a stage is not required to advance to the next stage. The outcome of one stage is not permanent and can be modified by later experiences. Stages tend to be associated with life experiences and therefore with age. Erikson's stage theory characterizes an individual advancing through the eight life stages as a function of negotiating his or her biological and sociocultural forces.

How does Erikson's psychosocial theory influence the design of a programming language for young children? Let's look at ScratchJr and KIBO, designed for children between 4 and 7 years old, a range that includes two different Eriksonian life stages. On the one hand, children aged 4 to 5 years old are likely to traverse through the developmental crisis "initiative vs. guilt." The resolution, according to Erikson, comes when children develop a sense of purpose. On the other hand, children aged 5 to 7 are engaged in "industry vs. inferiority" and solve it by gaining competence. The child must deal with the demands of learning new skills or risk feeling inferiority, failure, and incompetence. Programming languages need to reward and encourage purpose and competence. With this knowledge at hand, we designed both ScratchJr and KIBO so that children could be challenged but, at the same time, master computer programming by making their own projects to share with others. Recognizing the importance of child-initiated activities, both environments can be used with minimum instruction. Both offer opportunities for challenges, and reward persistence and motivation. Design features accommodate different learning styles and developmental abilities in the continuum pre-operational to concrete cognitive stage development proposed by Piaget and followers (Case, 1984; Feldman, 2004; Fischer, 1980; Piaget, 1951, 1952). They also engage children with different preferences in terms of sensory skills and self-regulatory mechanisms, and support this learning through a playful, child-directed style (Scarlett, Naudeau, Ponte, & Salonius-Pasternak, 2005; Vygotsky, 1976). Children are challenged to achieve at a level just beyond their current mastery and have opportunities to practice newly acquired skills.

Curriculum Connections

How does coding facilitate or hinder the teaching of age-appropriate concepts and skills? How does it introduce ideas that children will encounter later, as they continue their educational journey? Sometimes learning computer programming is a goal itself; but most often, it is a way to learn about other things. For example, coding engages sequential and logical thinking, and this kind of thinking is also involved in literacy and math. When designing programming languages, it is wise to align interface design not only with the powerful ideas of computer science, but also with traditional school subjects. This strengthens curricular connections across disciplines.

For example, in ScratchJr we designed a grid that can be overlaid on the stage to help children understand the XY coordinates. While young children are not learning about the Cartesian system yet, it was important to us to have our software provide an experience that will later facilitate the understanding of those concepts. In KIBO we implemented sensors that take input from the environment. Most early childhood settings engage children in the study of their own five senses, so curricular connections can easily be made.

Technological Infrastructure

The digital landscape offers many technological platforms upon which to design computer programming languages for young children. For example, ScratchJr is an app that runs on tablets and computers; and KIBO is a stand-alone robotic kit that doesn't require another platform. As designers, it is important to understand the pros and cons of each platform and how they might have an impact on the usability of the tool (Bers, 2018). For example, while from a technological viewpoint it might have made sense to develop ScratchJr to work on a server and be accessible online, we discarded that option because most early childhood settings did not have reliable access to the internet in their preschool and kindergarten classes. With KIBO we experimented with incorporating the ability for users to 3D print their own sensor casings. We later decided against this because most teachers reported that they do not have access to 3D printers and lack the time to spend learning this process.

Mentoring Model

When developing programming languages for young children, we must think about how those young children will encounter the tool. Most likely, an adult, either in the home or school setting, will make the introduction.

Once children first learn about it, how will they code on a recurring basis? Programming is a longitudinal activity. It is not something that we do once or in just "one hour of code." Those are wonderful introductory activities but, just like textual literacy doesn't develop in one hour, neither does computational literacy. Will children need an adult every time they want to code? Can they access the programming environment on their own? Thinking about the role that adults can play is important when designing for young children. What kind of expertise do adults need? Are the adults serving as coaches and mentors in the learning process, or are they playing the role of gatekeepers of the experience? Are they taking on a teaching role? What kind of training, if any, should they receive? In the case of ScratchJr, the app itself needs to be installed by an adult but, after that initial intervention, children can figure things out on their own by trial and error. Although, to learn more sophisticated commands, they do need the help of an adult.

Young children might or might not read, so we decided to make all the icons self-explanatory. Adults told us that they wanted instructions on the screen, so we chose to have words displayed when the user taps the icons. This design decision provides the needed scaffold for adults, without distracting the children. In the case of KIBO, an adult needs to show the child the first time how to scan the blocks. But, after that, there is only one button to press to make the robot move according to its program. Once the child learns how to scan and when to press the button, the child can use KIBO on his or her own.

Diversity

The term "diversity" usually makes us think about ethnic, racial, religious, and socioeconomic composition. However, in this context, the fundamental diversity question we want to ask is: what are the diverse experiences that children can have when coding? Can they have diversity in their approaches to making projects? Can they reach diversity of solutions? The richness of a programming language is in its potential to use it as a tool to create anything. Just like a paintbrush and a paint palette, or the language of a poem or story, a programming language must support children in expanding their imaginations (Bers, 2018). But, when giving a paint palette to young children, we do not overwhelm them with hundreds of colors, nor do we begin teaching language by introducing all of the vocabulary at once (Hassenfeld

& Bers, 2019). Similarly, when creating a programming language, we give them a manageable palette of programming commands. Both KIBO and ScratchJr have simple commands that, when combined, can produce powerful results. To the expert adult programmer, it might seem that some important ones, such as variables, are missing, but for a young child who is not familiar with the concept, that is not a problem. As children grow, they will be ready to move on to more sophisticated programming languages that have bigger and more complex programming palettes (for example, from ScratchJr to Scratch, or from KIBO to LEGO robotics).

Program Scale

What is the size of the population we expect to use the programming language? Is there a need for a minimum critical mass to sustain participants' engagement (this tends to be the case when building a social network or a virtual community around the technology)? Is the language open source and, therefore, can others improve on it? If so, is that process going to be managed? How? In the case of both ScratchJr and KIBO we decided that, for now, we are aiming for users worldwide, but we would not invite developers to join us in working on the tools since we do not have the support mechanisms in place for a successful open-source experience. With ScratchJr, we initiated a process of language localization not only for the app itself, which has already been translated into seven languages including English, but also for the associated curricular materials and book (Bers & Resnick, 2015), which have been translated to multiple languages. The ScratchJr team publishes a new version of the ScratchJr app every three to six months to add new language translations. Meanwhile, the KIBO robot is being used in 48 states across the U.S., and in public and private schools, as well as in home settings. Globally, KIBO (which is not as reliant on words and translations as ScratchJr is) has been used in 43 countries and the number is steadily growing.

Communities of Users

Most programming languages, as they become successful, start to build a community of users. Some of these communities are virtual and others meet face-to-face. Some are active at developing support mechanisms for their members, and creating online tutorials, blogs, and YouTube channels, and others are more passive. In the case of programming languages for young children, the fundamental question is: who are the users that need to be part of the community? Is it the children themselves? Are parents, teachers, or other adults involved? How many different communities need to be in place? How are they managed? Depending on how we answer that question, different strategies need to be put in place.

With both ScratchJr and KIBO, we have active mailing lists with thousands of users. While the ScratchJr mailing list sends information about news, app updates, and community events, the KIBO mailing list is a monthly newsletter that includes tips for learning KIBO's new modules, articles featuring teachers who are using KIBO in innovative ways, and curricular ideas. Furthermore, since both ScratchJr and KIBO are meant to be used by two communities at the same time (children and adults), we decided to launch a Family Day initiative that brings together children and their families to learn about coding and technology through collaborative activities.

Design Process

When designing any product, it is important to involve all potential users in the design process. In the case of programming languages for young children, parents, educators, and children all need to be recruited in this effort. This might complicate things, as these are three distinct groups of users with different goals. However, these groups need to have their voices heard. Young children can't participate in online surveys and focus groups as adults can. In order to express their opinions and preferences, children need to have early access to prototypes. In the same way that they learn by doing, we learn by watching them. This poses some obvious challenges that can be mostly solved with low-tech prototypes and Wizard of Oz-style simulations. In the field of human–computer interaction, the Wizard of Oz technique is a research experiment in which subjects interact with a computer system that they believe to be autonomous, but which is actually being operated, or partially operated, by an unseen human being.

Teachers need to envision how they can integrate the programming language into their daily teaching routine; early studies with prototypes need to be conducted in classrooms and other settings where the programming language will be used. It is not enough to conduct pilot studies in the safety of the research lab. This iterative design process, in which all stakeholders are involved, is time-consuming and expensive. For example, for both KIBO and ScratchJr we engaged in at least three years of research with early prototypes before releasing the products.

Access Environment

To use a programming language, we need access to it. Are young children able to have access on their own or do they need the help of teachers and parents? At school, the teacher might play the role of coordinator to have the needed technology available. But, at home, things are different. For example, ScratchJr runs on a tablet. Do young children have access to one independently or do they need to use their parents' device? Are they competing for this resource with other family members? Many families only give young children a limited amount of "free choice" screen time each day. This means that children's access to programming apps like ScratchJr must compete with video games and television shows. On the other hand, the KIBO bin is easy for young children to open and close on their own and prompts children to take charge of cleaning up and putting away their own materials. However, robotics kits like KIBO may still raise similar access questions to ScratchJr. For example, do parents keep KIBO in their child's bedroom or playroom where they have free access to it, just like their other toys? Or do they treat it like their tablets and other "expensive technologies" and store it on a shelf that requires an adult's help to access? These questions of storage and access can change the way children experience the coding playground.

Institutional Context

What kind of financial model will make possible the design and later sustainability of the programming language? This question needs to be asked at an early stage. When a new product enters the educational market, teachers need to be trained, the curriculum needs to be adjusted, new materials need to be bought, etc. These changes won't happen if there is no assurance that the new environment will be "alive" and supported for as long as it is needed. Designing a programming language for young children is a major endeavor and financial sustainability is essential not only to launch the program, but also to update it and fix bugs. It is important to be aware of this before embarking on a project that might be well-thought-out and of excellent quality, but cannot pay the bills. In the case of both ScratchJr and KIBO, we received generous funding from the National Science Foundation (NSF) to initiate the projects. Now, the Scratch Foundation provides the needed financial support to continue the work on ScratchJr, allowing us to keep it as a free app; while KinderLab Robotics, through a competitive NSF Small Business Innovation Research (SBIR) grant, angel funding, and revenues from sales, can commercialize KIBO worldwide.

While the dimensions presented in this chapter do not focus on specific technological features, they provide a wider lens to understand the richness of the context in which the technology will be used. However, although it is important to design developmentally appropriate tools for early education, it is also important to understand that the learning of coding and the development of computational thinking happen in the context of an overall curricular experience. The next chapter will focus on teaching strategies for making a coding playground.

References

Bers, M. U. (2012). *Designing digital experiences for positive youth development: From playpen to playground.* Cary, NC: Oxford University Press.

Bers, M. U. (2018, April 17–20). Coding, playgrounds and literacy in early childhood education: The development of KIBO robotics and ScratchJr. *Paper presented at the IEEE Global Engineering Education Conference (EDUCON)* (pp. 2100–2108). Santa Cruz de Tenerife, Canary Islands, Spain.

Bers, M. U. (2019). Coding as another language: a pedagogical approach for teaching computer science in early childhood. *Journal of Computers in Education, 6*(4), 499–528.

Bers, M. U., & Resnick, M. (2015). *The official ScratchJr book.* San Francisco, CA: No Starch Press.

Brown, T. (2009). *Change by design: How design thinking transforms organizations and inspires innovation.* New York, NY: Harper Collins.

Case, R. (1984). The process of stage transition: A neo-Piagetian view. In R. Sternberg (Ed.), *Mechanisms of cognitive development* (pp. 19–44). San Francisco, CA: Freeman.

Erikson, E. H. (1950). *Childhood and society.* New York, NY: Norton.

Feldman, D. H. (2004). Piaget's stages: The unfinished symphony of cognitive development. *New Ideas in Psychology, 22,* 175–231. doi:10.1016/j.newideapsych.2004.11.005.

Fischer, K. W. (1980). A theory of cognitive development: The control and construction of hierarchies of skills. *Psychological Review, 87*(6), 477–531.

Hassenfeld, Z. R., & Bers, M. U. (2019). When we teach programming languages as literacy. (Blog post).

Piaget, J. (1951). Egocentric thought and sociocentric thought. In J. Piaget (Ed.), *Sociological studies* (pp. 270–286). London: Routledge. (Original work published 1951).

Piaget, J. (1952). *The origins of intelligence in children* (Vol. 8, No. 5, pp. 18–1952). New York, NY: International Universities Press.

Scarlett, W. G., Naudeau, S., Ponte, I., & Salonius-Pasternak, D. (2005). *Children's play.* Thousand Oaks, CA: Sage.

Vygotsky, L. (1976). Play and its role in the mental development of the child. In J. Bruner, A. Jolly, & K. Sylva (Eds.), *Play: Its role in development and evolution* (pp. 537–559). New York, NY: Basic Books.

Teaching Strategies
Coding in the Early Curriculum

In my previous life, before coming to the U.S. for graduate school, I worked as a journalist. As such, I learned to ask five questions: what, why, where, when, and how. Now, as we are nearing the end of the book, I will address each of these questions. The "what" is the core of this manuscript: coding, and the associated powerful ideas from the domain of computer science. The "why" has been answered throughout this book, but especially in the chapters of Part I when we explored the cognitive, personal, social, and emotional dimensions of coding. The "where" and "when" receive different answers according to the particular context and setting in which young children code: home, school, an after-school program, the library, a maker space, etc. The chapters on ScratchJr and KIBO provided some examples. Finally, the "how" is the overall approach and my contribution to this growing field: a playground approach to coding grounded on the Positive Technological Development (PTD) theoretical framework.

As teachers, theoretical frameworks are useful for providing guiding principles for designing, implementing, and evaluating curricular experiences. This chapter shares teaching strategies that I have found helpful over the years when introducing young children to coding.

Teaching can be defined as creating the needed conditions for children to encounter and explore powerful ideas. Let's go back to Seymour Papert's book, *Mindstorms: Children, Computers and Powerful Ideas* (1980). He used to regret that readers of his book thought that the key concepts were children and computers. In his perspective, the book was about powerful ideas. Papert's concept of powerful ideas is one of the most complex concepts to understand within Papert's Constructionist approach to education and, probably, one of the most intellectually rewarding.

The potential of computers for education lies in their power to engage children in encountering powerful ideas. Thus, curriculum should be built around powerful ideas. In this book, Chapter 8 explores the powerful ideas of computer science that young children encounter while coding. Throughout this book, and specifically in Part III, we learned about these powerful ideas and how they engage children in computational thinking.

Over the years, a growing community of researchers and educators has used the term "powerful ideas" to refer to a set of intellectual tools worth learning, as decided by a community of experts in each of the fields of study (Bers, 2008). However, different people have used the term in diverse ways and amongst the powerful ideas community there are divergent opinions about the benefits and dangers of presenting a unified definition (Papert & Resnick, 1996).

Papert's Constructionism is about powerful ideas (Papert, 2000). He envisioned the computer as a carrier of new and old powerful ideas and as an agent for educational change. While school reform is a complex topic, Constructionism contributes to this dialogue by proposing the introduction of coding into the classroom as a way to restructure learning and to encounter powerful ideas.

The importance paid by Papert and colleagues to the world of ideas and thinking derives from the Piagetian legacy concerned with epistemology: understanding how we know what we know, how we construct knowledge, and how we think. Thinking is at the core of why we introduce coding in early childhood. Coding helps children to think in systematic and sequential ways.

This book shows how thinking can happen in a playful way. The statue The Thinker, by Auguste Rodin, which shows a male figure sitting on a rock with his chin resting on one hand as though deep in thought, is often used to represent thinking as a stationary and passive activity. However, research shows that thinking is embodied and happens as we engage in all kind of activities, including playing (Hutchins, 1995; Kiefer & Trumpp, 2012; Wilson & Foglia, 2011). When coding, children think about algorithms, modularity, control structures, representation, the design process, debugging, hardware, and software, but they also think about their own thinking.

Powerful ideas are intellectual tools. They evoke an emotional response. Children can make connections between powerful ideas and personal interests, passions and past experiences. Early childhood education has paid particular attention to promoting learning environments in which children can make connections. Emergent curricula build upon children's interests and are responsive to the ideas, excitement, and questions from the children themselves (Rinaldi, 1998). NAEYC (National Association for the Education of Young Children) guidelines for promoting integrated curricula are close in spirit to the Constructionist notion of powerful ideas. These guidelines call for powerful principles or concepts applied generally across disciplines (i.e., that support the development of new ideas and concepts) and emerging from and connecting to children's personal interests (Bredekamp & Rosegrant, 1995).

How Do We Think about a Playground Coding Curriculum?

Curricula facilitate the encounter with powerful ideas in a connected and developmentally appropriate way. It is helpful to think about the following considerations when the goal of the curriculum is to promote computational thinking through playful coding.

1. **Pacing:** it's important to consider the scope and sequence of activities designed to engage with the powerful ideas of computer science. The curriculum can be designed to happen over the course of one intensive week of coding, over the course of a few months with one or two sessions per week, or over the course of a year.

2. **Types of coding activities:** some are structured challenges, while others involve free exploration. While structured challenges convey powerful ideas in a modular format and ensure that every child participating in the experience will be exposed to the same materials, free exploration provides opportunities for playing with ideas and discovering things independently. Allocating time for free exploration helps build a solid foundation.

3. **Materials:** to code we need tools. Although computational thinking can be explored through low-tech materials such as printed icons of the different programming commands of a programming language, this is no substitution for the programming language itself. Accessibility to the materials is important. For example, when

working with robots, some teachers may choose to give a complete robotic kit to each group of students. Children may label the kit with their name(s) and use the same kit for the duration of the curriculum. Other teachers may choose to take apart the kits and have materials sorted by type and place all the materials in a central location for children to choose as needed. If working with tablets, it is important to remind children that they need to be charged. Some schools provide carts that roll the tablets into the classroom and therefore children and teachers do not need to worry about batteries running out. Other classrooms have their own equipment, and it is therefore the teacher's responsibility to have everything ready to use. Regardless of the technological platform, it is crucial to set expectations for how to use and treat materials. These issues are important not only in making the curriculum logistically easier to implement, but also because, as described in the Reggio Emilia tradition, the environment can act as the "third teacher" (Darragh, 2006).

4. **Classroom management:** teaching in an early childhood setting requires careful planning and ongoing adjustments when it comes to classroom management. This may play out differently during technology-rich activities because of the novelty of the materials themselves. It is important to provide a clear structure and set of expectations for using the materials and for the routines of each part of the lessons (e.g., technology circles, cleanup time, etc.).

5. **Group sizes:** as in any other kind of early childhood initiative, the experience can be whole group, small group, in pairs, or individual. Whether individual work is feasible depends on the availability of materials, which may be limited. However, an effort should be made to allow students to work in as small a group as is possible. Some classes structure technology time to fit into a "center time" in the schedule, in which students rotate through small stations around the room with different activities at each location. This format gives students more access to teachers when they have questions and lets teachers tailor instruction and feedback, as well as assess each student's progress more easily than during whole-group work. Working in small groups is not similar to doing individual work. Let's use a comparison from literacy. When learning how to write, children do not share their pens. Each child has a pen and can spend as much time as needed struggling with it. While

group work promotes conversation, multiple voices, and viewpoints, it's still important to make time for individual work.

6. **Addressing state and national frameworks:** at the time of writing this book, there are no national frameworks in the U.S. that address computational thinking and coding in the early years. Many initiatives are on their way (e.g., Code.org, Computing Leaders ACM, & CSTA, 2016; U.S. Department of Education & Office of Innovation and Improvement, 2016), and several countries have already made coding mandatory. However, some of the powerful ideas involved in computational thinking are foundational for other academic subjects, such as math, literacy, engineering, and science. Additionally, coding provides a powerful way to integrate disciplinary knowledge and skills. Thus, it is useful to make a deliberate planning effort to map how each of the powerful ideas from coding relates to traditional disciplinary content knowledge and skills mandated by federal and state frameworks.

7. **Assessments:** with the playground approach to coding, children certainly have fun; however, evaluating the learning process and the learning outcomes is important. There are many ways to do this: documenting student's projects and ways of talking about and sharing their projects; analyzing their design journals where they keep different iterations of the same project; completing worksheets aimed at testing specific knowledge; collecting work portfolios; and using assessment instruments such as the Solve-Its tasks, computational thinking assessments, and "Engineering licenses" developed by my DevTech research group (DevTech, 2015; Relkin & Bers, 2019; Strawhacker & Bers, 2015, 2019). These tools can serve to evaluate individual children's learning, while they are working in groups or individually.

Before bringing coding into the early classroom, teachers will find it helpful to think about the seven conditions presented above. A curriculum of powerful ideas from computer science can be conveyed with different pedagogical approaches. This book presents the playground approach to coding, which is grounded on the PTD framework (Bers, 2012) and the six Cs or positive behaviors that can be found both in the playground and the coding class: collaboration, communication, community building, content creation, creativity, and choices of conduct. Let's review them (see Figure 14.1).

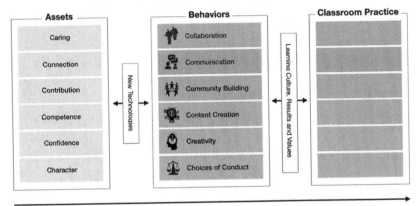

Figure 14.1 The PTD framework developed by Bers (2012). PTD proposes six positive behaviors (six Cs) that should be supported by educational programs that use new educational technologies. These are: collaboration, communication, community building, content creation, creativity, and choices of conduct. The third column, Classroom Practice, is left blank for educators to complete on their own, based on their own classroom cultures, practices, and rituals.

1. **Collaboration,** by engaging children in a learning environment that promotes working in teams, sharing resources, and *caring* about each other. Collaboration is defined here as getting or giving help with a project, programming together, lending or borrowing materials, or working together on a common task.

2. **Communication,** through mechanisms that promote a sense of *connection* between peers or with adults, such as technology circles. Technology circles present a good opportunity for problem-solving as a community. To cover all the important ideas without losing the children's attention, the discussions might be broken up and held throughout the day rather than all at once. It can also be helpful to make a "Technology Parking Lot" for the robots, tablets, or other technological materials while they are not in use, so that children can focus at the technology circles.

3. **Community building,** through scaffolded opportunities to form a learning community that promotes the *contribution* of ideas. Our long-term

educational goal is not only to foster computational thinking and technological fluency amongst the participating children and teachers, but also amongst the wider community. Open houses provide authentic opportunities for children to share and celebrate the learning process and tangible products with others who are also invested in their learning. During these open houses, family, friends, and community members visit the class for a demonstration of the children's final projects. Each child is given the opportunity not only to run their robot or project on a tablet or computer, but also to play the role of teacher as they explain how they built, programmed, and worked through problems.

4. **Content creation,** by making a project and programming it. The design process and the computational thinking involved in programming foster *competence* in computer literacy and technological fluency.

5. **Creativity,** by fostering opportunities for children to develop their own project ideas, as opposed to copying them from a booklet or following instructions, and by providing different materials for children to work with. As children approach solving technical problems in creative ways, they develop a sense of *confidence* in their learning potential.

6. **Choices of conduct,** which provide children with the opportunity to experiment with "what if" questions and potential consequences, and to provoke examination of values and exploration of *character traits*. Taking care of materials, respecting rules about technology use, and differentiation of roles are important to the growth of a responsible learning community. Teachers may assign children "expertise badges" that carry the responsibility of helping others on a topic for which the child is an expert and, at the same time, encourage the child to try on new roles and be flexible. The focus on learning to code is as important as helping children to develop an inner compass to guide their actions in a just and responsible way. Choices of conduct are not only made by children. Teachers also make important choices in the way they display and introduce the materials to the children.

Developmentally appropriate programming languages are crucial for introducing coding in early childhood education. Furthermore, in this book I show how these environments are best suited when designed with a "coding as literacy" approach, as opposed to a "coding as problem-solving" approach. This means that children can easily develop fluency with the language to become producers of their own computational projects to share with others. In the process of programming they solve many problems, but the educational goal is beyond problem-solving. The goal is personal expression and communication.

When young children are learning to read and write, we provide them with different kinds of books and different types of writing materials that are developmentally appropriate. Diversity enriches their literacy experience; likewise, this is true with coding tools. Being able to fluently use ScratchJr, KIBO, and any of the other programming languages described earlier enriches their computational thinking.

Educators who want to introduce coding into the early childhood classroom need these programming languages, but they also need a curriculum of the powerful ideas of computer science that is developmentally appropriate and a guiding framework that understands the whole child. Chapter 6 provided an example by exploring the CAL curriculum. I have proposed the PTD framework and its six positive behaviors as a framework that integrates cognitive, personal, social, emotional, and moral dimensions of early childhood. Armed with the programming languages, the curriculum, and the framework, the early childhood educator can venture into the fun of a coding playground.

References

Bers, M. (2008). *Blocks to robots: Learning with technology in the early childhood classroom.* New York, NY: Teachers College Press.

Bers, M. U. (2012). *Designing digital experiences for positive youth development: From playpen to playground.* Cary, NC: Oxford University Press.

Bredekamp, S., & Rosegrant, T. (Eds.). (1995). *Reaching potentials: Transforming early childhood curriculum and assessment* (Vol. 2). Washington, DC: NAEYC.

Code.org, Computing Leaders ACM, and CSTA. (2016). Announcing a new framework to define K-12 computer science education [Press release]. *Code.org.* Retrieved from https://code.org/framework-announcement.

Darragh, J. C. (2006). *The environment as the third teacher.* Retrieved from www.eric.ed.gov/PDFS/ED493517.pdf.

DevTech Research Group. (2015). *Sample engineer's license.* Retrieved from http://api.ning.com/files/HFuYSlzj6Lmy18EzB9-sGv4ftGAZpfkGS-fCe6lHFFQmv8PaelQB-4PB8kS6BunpzNhbtYhqnlmEWpFBwQJdfH7y-FrJrgUUrl/BlankEngineerLicense.jpg.

Hutchins, E. (1995). *Cognition in the wild.* Cambridge, MA: MIT Press.

Kiefer, M., & Trumpp, N. M. (2012). Embodiment theory and education: The foundations of cognition in perception and action. *Trends in Neuroscience and Education, 1*(1), 15–20.

Papert, S. (1980). *Mindstorms: Children, computers, and powerful ideas.* New York, NY: Basic Books, Inc.

Papert, S. (2000). What's the big idea? Toward a pedagogy of idea power. *IBM Systems Journal, 39*(3–4), 720–729.

Papert, S., & Resnick, M. (1996). Powerful Ideas. *Paper presented at Rescuing the Powerful Ideas, an NSF-sponsored Symposium at MIT,* Cambridge, MA.

Relkin, E., & Bers, M. U. (2019). Designing an assessment of computational thinking abilities for young children. In L. E. Cohen & S. Waite-Stupiansky (Eds.), *STEM for early childhood learners: How science, technology, engineering and mathematics strengthen learning* (pp. 85–98). New York, NY: Routledge.

Rinaldi, C. (1998). Projected curriculum constructed through documentation—Progettazione: An interview with Lella Gandini. In C. Edwards, L. Gandini, & G. Forman (Eds.), *The hundred languages of children: The Reggio Emilia approach—Advanced reflections* (2nd ed., pp. 113–125). Greenwich, CT: Ablex.

Strawhacker, A., & Bers, M. U. (2019). What they learn when they learn coding: Investigating cognitive domains and computer programming knowledge in young children. *Educational Technology Research and Development, 67*(3), 541–575. doi:10.1007/s11423-018-9622-x.

Strawhacker, A. L., & Bers, M. U. (2015). "I want my robot to look for food": Comparing children's programming comprehension using tangible, graphical, and hybrid user interfaces. *International Journal of Technology and Design Education, 25*(3), 293–319.

U.S. Department of Education, & Office of Innovation and Improvement. (2016). *STEM 2026: A vision for innovation in STEM education.* Washington, DC: Author.

Wilson, R. A., & Foglia, L. (2011). Embodied cognition. *Stanford Encyclopedia of Philosophy.*

Conclusion

It is 3 p.m. on a sunny Monday and I've just finished giving a talk for hundreds of early childhood teachers in the Boston area. As I am making my way out of the room, a shy woman approaches me. She wants to know if she should allow her 6-year-old to use ScratchJr on her own and how often. I smile at her. I have heard this question many times. I ask her, "Will you allow her to read a book? How often? Will you allow her to write a story? How many of them? Always?" She replies:

> It depends. It depends what book and it depends when she wants to write. I will not let her write a story while we are having a family dinner, and I certainly do not let her read some grown-up books I have at home. They can be scary for her.

In order to answer my question, this woman carefully considered the context. Similar logic applies to the use of technology: it depends.

Since the first edition of this book, the question of how, when, and where young children should encounter technology is only getting more complicated. As tablets and cell phones are increasingly taking over the social landscape of adults, they are playing an increasingly more prominent role in children's lives. At the writing of this book, I struggle with this issue. There is no replacement for face-to-face interaction and for manipulating the world around us through tangible objects. Furthermore, it worries me that screens are coming to occupy a vacuum left by the absence of adults and peers. Even when they are present, if they themselves are busy with their own devices, there is an absence. Of course, there are many ways to use screens, and some of them are positive. I hope that through this book I was able to show you some examples. However, the question is not whether children should be in front of screens or not. The question is what are they doing with those screens.

As shown in this book, coding, with or without screens, can become a new form of play and can engage in positive experiences. The Positive Technological Development (PTD) framework can guide our understanding of the developmental milestones and playful learning experiences that children can have while developing computational thinking and exploring powerful ideas from computer science. Coding is a playground. It offers many opportunities for learning and personal growth, exploration and creativity, mastery of new skills, and ways of thinking. We do not always take children to the playground. There are other places to visit and other skills to develop. But when we do go to the playground, we want it to be a developmentally appropriate space.

The playground approach to coding that I present here moves the conversation beyond the traditional view of coding as a technical skill. Coding is a literacy. As such, it invites new ways of thinking and carries the ability to produce an artifact detached from its creator, with its own meaning. There is a producer with an intention, with a passion, with a desire to communicate something. Coding, like writing, is a medium of human expression. Through this expressive process, we learn to think, feel, and communicate in new ways. This book takes a stance against problem-solving as the primary goal of teaching young children to code. Instead, I propose coding to support fluent personal expression.

In the coding playground, young children create their own projects to communicate ideas and express who they are. They become producers, and not merely consumers, of technological products. They need developmentally appropriate tools, like KIBO and ScratchJr. They engage in problem-solving and storytelling; they develop sequencing skills and algorithmic thinking. They journey through the design process from an early idea to a final product that can be shared with others. They learn how to manage frustration and find a solution, rather than giving up when things get challenging. They develop strategies for debugging their projects. They learn to collaborate with others and they grow proud of their hard work. In the coding playground, children have fun while learning new things. They can be themselves and playfully explore new concepts and ideas, as well as develop new skills. They can fail and start all over again.

In this coding playground, children encounter powerful ideas from computer science that are useful not only for future programmers and engineers, but for everyone. Coding is a way to achieve literacy in the twenty-first century, like reading and writing. It needs to start early. Today, those who can produce digital technologies, and not only consume them, will be in charge of their own destiny. Literacy is a medium of human power. Those who know how to read and write can assert their voices. Those who do not are disenfranchised. Will this be true for those who cannot code? For those who cannot think computationally?

It is our responsibility to introduce children to coding and computational thinking when they are young. We know that as a literacy, coding will open doors, many of them that we cannot anticipate now. But we also know that these young coders are still children. As such, they deserve the best that we can give them. It is not enough to copy models of computer science education developed for elementary or high school students. It is not good to give them programming languages created for older children, which are not developmentally appropriate for them.

As teachers, we need technologies and curricula specifically designed for young children that take into consideration their cognitive, social, and emotional needs. This is novel territory. Therefore, these children are our best collaborators, as they can guide us through the complexity of their thinking. As researchers, we need to explore the developmental stages of learning to code and the learning trajectories associated with computational thinking. We must understand what is truly happening when a 4-year-old programmes her robot to dance the Hokey Pokey, and a 5-year-old makes an animation. While there is a growing movement toward STEAM (Science, Technology, Engineering, Arts, and Mathematics) education and research methodologies from those disciplines, we also look at research on literacy to elucidate some of these learning processes. Coding can be studied not only as a problem-solving mechanism, but as a process that allows the creation of a shareable product of human expression.

As teachers all over the world begin to incorporate coding and computational thinking into early childhood education, may we have the clarity to understand how these can be integrated into preexisting early childhood educational practices. May we see the children in their totality, as individuals with their own voices and their own stories to tell, and not only as problem-solvers. May we encourage and support their playfulness as a way of learning and may we help them express themselves with both natural and artificial languages.